Salt Cod Cuisine

Salt Cod Cuisine
THE INTERNATIONAL TABLE

EDWARD A. JONES

Published by Boulder Publications
Portugal Cove-St. Philip's, Newfoundland and Labrador
www.boulderpublications.ca

© 2013 Boulder Publications

Editor: Stephanie Porter
Copy editor: Iona Bulgin
Design and layout: Alison Carr
Cover photograph: Ray Fennelly

Printed in China

Excerpts from this publication may be reproduced under licence from Access Copyright, or with the express written permission of Boulder Publications Ltd., or as permitted by law. All rights are otherwise reserved and no part of this publication may be reproduced, stored in a retrieval system, or transmitted in any form or by any means, electronic, mechanic, photocopying, scanning, recording, or otherwise, except as specifically authorized.

 We acknowledge the financial support of the Government of Newfoundland and Labrador through the Department of Tourism, Culture and Recreation.

 We acknowledge the financial support for our publishing program by the Government of Canada and the Department of Canadian Heritage through the Canada Book Fund.

Library and Archives Canada Cataloguing in Publication

Jones, Edward A., 1939-
    Salt cod cuisine : the international table / Edward A. Jones.

Includes bibliographical references and index.
ISBN 978-1-927099-05-6

    1. Cooking (Codfish). 2. Codfish--History. 3. Cookbooks. I. Title.

TX748.C63J66 2012   641.6'92   C2012-901273-4

There are places and species that have become inextricably linked in human history and in the human mind have taken on mythic proportions.... But there is no stronger definition, no stronger attachment or symbolism, than Newfoundland and Labrador with the Atlantic cod.

—George Rose, *Cod*

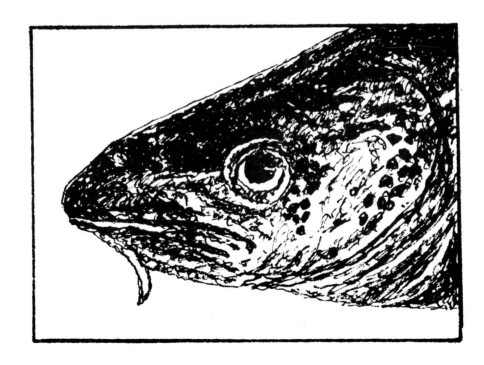

Contents

Acknowledgements 9
Introduction 11

PART I: THE STORY OF SALT COD 13
    Codlandia: Home of the Cod 15
    Catching Cod: The Fishery 25
    Making Fish: Fresh Cod into Salt Cod 39
    Salt Cod: Culture and Cuisine 59
    Cooking Salt Cod: At Home 77

PART 2: RECIPES 87

    Celebrating Outdoors 91

    Salads 105

    Tapas and Mezes 125

    Hors d'Oeuvres 139

    Soups and Chowders 161

    Stews and Ragouts 175

    Boiled Salt Cod Dinners 193

    Simmered Dishes 205

    Fried Dishes 221

    Baked Dishes 233

    Puddings 259

    Stovetop Variations 267

    Other Salt Cod Parts 277

    Stock and Sauces 295

Appendices 305

Endnotes 308

Bibliography 311

Photo Credits 313

Index of Recipes 314

About the Author 319

Acknowledgements

I am greatly indebted to Bob Hardy of Hardy Fish Company and to Gordon Slade of the Shorefast Foundation and the Battle Harbour Historic Trust for generously giving their time, enthusiasm, knowledge, and skills. They contributed much help and advice.

For the salt cod, I am grateful to Francis Chafe, Wilf Curran, Pete Decker, Bob Hardy, Henry Lake, Jason Kearley, Gordon Slade, Larry Small, Ed Thistle, Desmond Whelan, and Taylor's Fish, Fruit, and Vegetable Market.

Many thanks for the variety of visuals from J.P. Andrieux, The Rooms Provincial Archives, Phillip Cairns, Boyd W. Chubbs, Roy Dwyer, Ray Fennelly, Department of Geography (Memorial University of Newfoundland), Shirley George, Bob Hardy, Keith Hardy, Pam Hall, Jason Kearley, Maritime History Archives (Memorial University of Newfoundland), *Them Days* Archives, Gordon Slade, Valerie Sooley, and Gerry Squires.

This work was shaped by the research of many people who documented in articles and books the history of salt cod and by the many chefs and editors of cookbooks who collectively published thousands of recipes for salt cod dishes. To these people I give a sincere thank you. Recipes, by their very nature, are passed from person to person. Every effort has been made to trace and credit the source and/or inspiration for the recipes in this book.

For recipes, discussions, cookbooks, encouragement, manuscript advice, general support, and help in countless ways, I want to thank, among the many not included above: Annamarie Beckel, Randy Bell, Eleanor Bennett, Margaret Best, Chris Brookes, Annie Brown, Joan Bursey, Alan Byrne, Pat Byrne, Bob Chan, Lionel Clarke, Sharon Coady, Zita

Cobb, Mary Compagne, Charlie Conway, Garry Cranford, Wilf Curran, Helen Daw, Jared Donaway, Kitty Drake, Judy Dwyer, Everett Fancey, Mark Ferguson, Loretta Forsyth, Cliff George, Glenn Gillard, Jeff Gilhooly, Herb Hopkins, Jan Hopkins, Tom Jacobs, Stephen Jones, Gordon King, Aiden Maloney, Lorraine Moores, Joanne Morris, Shirley Noble, Jenny Norman, Chris O'Neill-Yates, Margie Nurse, Gord Ralph, Rose Samson, Rosanne Shaw, Lorrie Small, Reg Taylor, Ruth Taylor, Charlie Tucker, Steve Vardy, and Phil Walsh.

This book owes a great deal to my incredibly good fortune in finding the right project manager and editor, Stephanie Porter; copy editor, Iona Bulgin; designer, Alison Carr; and publisher, Gavin Will, of Boulder Publications.

I acknowledge the financial support of the J.R. Smallwood Foundation for Newfoundland and Labrador Studies, Memorial University of Newfoundland, and the Department of Fisheries and Aquaculture, Government of Newfoundland and Labrador, which greatly helped with research, travel, permissions, validation, ingredients, materials, testing, and photography.

I owe a special acknowledgement and thank you to Florence Donaway, who was knowledgeable on a thousand questions, challenged many decisions, and always seemed to intuitively *know*. Florence is a part of *Salt Cod Cuisine: The International Table*. I dedicate this book to her.

Unless otherwise noted, all line drawings in this book are by Boyd W. Chubbs and were created especially for *Salt Cod Cuisine*.

Introduction

Salt cod is the heart and soul of Newfoundland and Labrador. Central to the province's history, salt cod gave birth to Newfoundland's settlement and development and remains part of its identity, culture, economy, and cuisine.

First sought out by the Vikings, Newfoundland and Labrador's cod stocks were eagerly pursued by the Basques and then by the British, Portuguese, Spanish, and French. These fishers processed fresh cod into salt cod and traded it for spices, wine, salt, oils, sugar, molasses, and manufactured goods. As Newfoundland developed as a colony, it also exported salt cod. Trade networks emerged; salt cod travelled well and could keep for long periods of time.

International trading routes brought salt cod to tables as far away as Greece, Italy, the Caribbean, and Brazil, where it was introduced to local ingredients, people, and traditions. The recipes in *Salt Cod Cuisine: The International Table* link the cultures of 30 countries, just as earlier trading patterns did.

Once salted as a practical measure and often perceived as poor man's food, today salt cod is treasured for its rich flavour and the firm meaty texture of its lean white flesh and as a concentrated source of protein. Known as *fiel amigo* ("faithful friend") to the Portuguese, this cross-cultural comfort food is also known as *bacalhau* in Portugal, *bacalao* in Spain, *salt cod* and *saltfish* in Canada, *morue* in France, and *saltfish* in the Caribbean.

This collection of recipes is a celebration of salt cod. Dishes range from the traditional to the new; salt cod is becoming part of the repertoire of avant-garde chefs on both sides of the Atlantic. This book is not only a testimony to the role of Newfoundland and Labrador in the cod fishery but an opportunity for you to participate in it, by cooking a dish from this collection or even salting your own cod. In doing so, you will continue a living legacy.

It is with a sincere appreciation of and admiration for the salt cod dishes themselves and for the flow of the culinary influences of salt cod that I offer *Salt Cod Cuisine: The International Table*.

Cod Lines, a 2011 work in clay by Newfoundland and Labrador ceramicist Florence Donaway.

PART I

The Story of Salt Cod

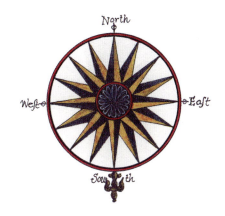

CODLANDIA[1]

Home of the Cod

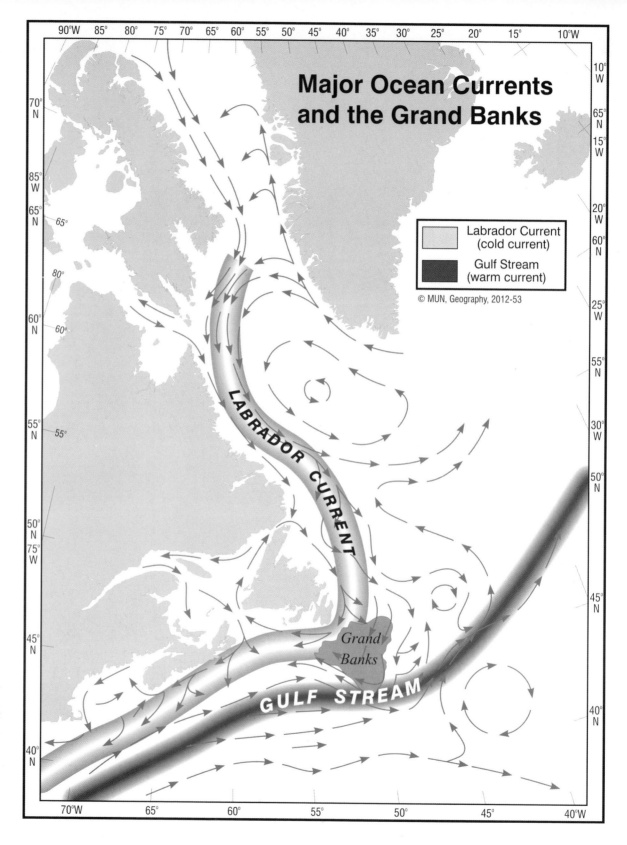

Major ocean currents and the Grand Banks off Newfoundland. (Charlie Conway, Department of Geography, Memorial University of Newfoundland)

Home of Atlantic Cod

The geography and ecosystems of both sides of the North Atlantic supported cod stocks, gave them a home, and allowed them to flourish. In the Northeast Atlantic, cod are found in the Celtic Sea, Irish Sea, East Channel, North Sea, Northeast Arctic, in the waters around the Faroe Islands and Iceland, and off the west coast of Scotland and the east coast of Greenland. In the Northwest Atlantic, cod are distributed along the west coast of Greenland, the Labrador coast, and the coast of Newfoundland. They are also found farther offshore, on the Flemish Cap, Grand Banks, St. Pierre Bank, Nova Scotian Shelf, in the Gulf of St. Lawrence and the Gulf of Maine, and as far south as Cape Hatteras.

It is on the Grand Banks, southeast of Newfoundland on the North American continental shelf, that cod had their best home. The Grand Banks, with their "unique combination of location, form, and depth,"[2] intercept and direct the cold Labrador Current and the warm waters of the Gulf Stream. Nutrients are brought to these relatively shallow underwater plateaus by the movement and the mixing of these waters. As a result, "[h]istorical catch rates of Atlantic cod in these waters were likely higher than in any fishery the world has ever known."[3]

The bountiful stocks of cod on the Grand Banks and in Newfoundland's coastal waters gave birth to the Newfoundland salt cod industry at the end of the fifteenth century. They were the foundation of the economy and the impetus for many international trading patterns.

The Vikings and the Basques

The history of cod fishing in Newfoundland is the stuff of legends. It begins with the Vikings, who settled Iceland, moved on to Greenland, and then pushed on to new discoveries. While identities of some of these places are not certain, it is known that the remains of a Viking camp were found in L'Anse aux Meadows on Newfoundland's Great Northern Peninsula by Helge and Anne Stine Ingstad in 1961. Historians have since dated Norse settlement in Newfoundland to about A.D. 1000.

As recorded in the Icelandic sagas, Vikings travelled great distances on several expeditions between 985 and 1011. They could do so because they had learned to preserve the cod they caught as they went by drying it in the wind.

At about the same time, Basque whalers started building better ships, inspired by those of the visiting Vikings, with hulls of overlapping planks. With that, they could sail greater distances more safely: "With their sturdy, new, long-distance ships equipped with enormous storage holds, the Basques were no longer limited to the whale's winter grounds in their native Bay of Biscay. They loaded their rowboats onto ships … By 875 [they] … made the 1,500-mile journey [2,400 kilometres] to the … Faroe Islands."[4]

In those northern waters, the Basques discovered Atlantic cod, a commodity which proved more profitable than whale. Applying their knowledge of using salt to cure whale meat, they began to salt cod. By combining salt with the almost fat-free, white flesh of cod, the Basques initiated a perfect marriage. They found a market for salt cod among those used to eating other kinds of salt fish. It was a matter of quality: "[T]he Basques had a salt fish to sell that, after a day or more of soaking in fresh water, was

The *Gaia*, a replica of a Viking ship, sailed into St. John's harbour in 1991. (Capt. H.W. Stone Collection, Maritime History Archives, Memorial University of Newfoundland)

whiter, leaner, and better, according to many, than the dark, oily, Mediterranean species that had been used before."[5]

Efficient and successful fishers, the Basques dominated the salt cod market. In the early fifteenth century, other countries also fished for cod but none brought back as many as the Basques. How far had the Basques gone across the sea in pursuit of cod? Did they reach North America before 1497? The ruins of a Basques whaling station dating back to 1530 were discovered in 1976 on the coast of Labrador. Were there others? Just as fishers today are secretive about good fishing areas, so were the Basques.

Early Icelandic and Greenlandic Trade

By the late medieval period, cod was already a valued resource. By the thirteenth century, it was a sought-after international product, beginning "with the regulation of Icelandic and Greenlandish trade by the Norwegian kings. Initially this regulation limited access to the cod fisheries to dependents of the Norwegian crown, but by the end of the fourteenth century, when the kingdoms of Denmark and Norway were united, trading licenses were granted to the Hanseatic cities of Germany …"[6] This represented a weakening of Dano-Norwegian control, and the English began sailing to Iceland and Greenland to catch or buy cod.

By the early 1400s, the English had established direct trade relations with Greenland for dried cod, commonly called stockfish. Because of competition for cod from Iceland and Greenland, English ships were targeted and seized by the Danish authorities with increasing frequency. Ultimately, the English were forced to seek fisheries further away and were ready, after Cabot's 1497 voyage, to explore and fish the Northwest Atlantic.

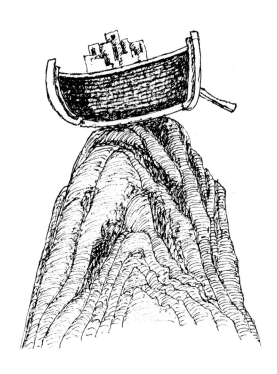

Fifteenth Century and Cabot's Voyage

By the early fifteenth century, English ships from Bristol had "an established trade route that sent them to Portugal in the spring for salt, then to Iceland for cod, back to Portugal where the fish were sold and where cargoes of oil, wine, and salt were purchased for sale in England."[7] Later, with the establishment of the North American fisheries, the market broadened and enabled the English to bring cod and herring to Italy in exchange for spices and other goods from the eastern Mediterranean.

Italian explorer John Cabot (as he was known when he settled in Bristol, England; he is also referred to as Giovanni Caboto, Ioani, Johan, Zuan, and Zoanne) sailed from Bristol in the *Matthew* in the spring of 1497. On June 24, 1497, Cabot and his crew officially discovered Newfoundland for the king of England. After his voyage, this now-famous description was recorded: "The sea is full of fish which are taken not only with the net but also with a basket in which a stone is put so that the basket may plunge into water."[8]

The race was on for the fishing nations of Europe, in particular Portugal, England, France, and Spanish Biscay (Basques), to harvest the rich cod stocks off Newfoundland. Salt cod from Newfoundland became a key currency for international trading routes across the Atlantic. Others included sugar, molasses, slaves, and rum.

Sixteenth Century

The English did a brisk business bartering cod, which they had access to in both the Atlantic Ocean and the North Sea, for a commodity Greece produced in abundance: raisins. This is perhaps why salt cod is still a significant part of people's diet in the Peloponnesos, where raisins are produced. The two are often cooked together.[9]

Newfoundland's sixteenth-century trading patterns were even more elaborate, such as this example of triangular trade: "Merchants (from England) sent crews, ships, provisions, fishing equipment, and fishery salt to the Grand Banks; trading ships carried salt fish (from the Grand Banks) to southern Europe; there, the fish was profitably traded for wines, salt, iron, and linens (which were brought back to England)."[10]

Seventeenth Century

Newfoundland was central to an international network that dominated the salt cod trade of the seventeenth century: "Mediterranean and Iberian ports imported Newfoundland cod. These southern markets exported wine and fruit to English and Dutch ports. England, in its turn, exported labor and supplies to Newfoundland …"[11] All the elements of such a trade were seasonal, and "[t]heir respective commercial cycles meshed perfectly: raisins reached market in August; the vintage was shipped in September, October, and November; and olive oil was traded in the winter. Commercial efficiency dictated that the sack ships carrying Malaga and other Spanish wines to Britain were, in the main, ships that had arrived from Newfoundland with fish."[12]

Eighteenth Century

By the 1760s, many Newfoundland coves and fishing grounds were home to planters, and the production of cod was shifting quickly from migrant fishing ships to the settlements. A rapidly expanding fleet of trade freighters, or sack ships, took dried cod to markets in Europe and the Caribbean in exchange for trade goods. Cargoes of salt cod were taken from Newfoundland in late summer each year by sack ships to the rich markets of Spain and Portugal; salt, wine, olive oil, and fruit were taken from there to England to pay for products needed in the fishery and to provide a livelihood for the fishers and a profit for fish merchants and companies.

Transatlantic trade continued during the eighteenth and early nineteenth centuries, carrying slaves, cash crops, and manufactured goods. British North American colonies exported salt cod to feed slaves and planters in the West Indies and received sugar and molasses from the Caribbean and various manufactured goods from Great Britain and other European countries. All trading partners got what they wanted.

Nineteenth Century

Newfoundland and Labrador salt cod began to reach markets in countries ready to trade locally produced goods for cod: "The European countries produced salt, fruit, nuts, wine, and other goods, Brazil offered cotton and coffee, while the West Indies exported sugar, molasses, and rum to Newfoundland and Labrador for cod."[14] Not every market received salt cod of the same quality. Newfoundland fishers produced a wide variety of grades of their product, which allowed them access to multiple markets: "Merchantable fish sold well in Europe, while Brazil bought Madeira cod, and the West Indies preferred the lowest and most inexpensive grade of saltfish. Spain, northern Italy, and Greece also accepted Labrador No. 1 and No. 2."[15]

Newfoundland encountered significant competition, as several countries imported and exported salt cod in trade patterns touching all sides of the Atlantic:

> Norway sold its product in Spain and, later, Portugal and Brazil; France provided for its home market, its Caribbean and north African possessions, Greece, and during the latter part of the century especially, exported to Italy and Spain; Iceland eventually became a major exporter to eastern Spain; Nova Scotia and the United States supplied much of the Caribbean demand, while Quebec sold to Italy and southern Brazil; and the Faroese and Shetland fisheries were heavily dependent on the Spanish markets.... Newfoundland exported to Portugal, Spain, Italy, Greece, northern Brazil and the Caribbean. In addition, some Newfoundland fish was also sold to Nova Scotia, the United States and Great Britain.[16]

A Barrel of Flour for a Quintal of Fish

According to George M. Story, folksongs like "A Great Big Sea Hove in Long Beach" were "a formula for the simple hard life ... the grim words born in a time of depression, made palatable, endurable by the jaunty tune and refrain."[13] Two stanzas, in particular, highlight the reality of low fish prices:

Oh, fish is low and flour is high,
Right fal-or-al taddle diddle I-do;
Oh, fish is low and flour is high,
So Georgie Snooks he can't have I.
To me right fol-didy fol-dee.

But he will have me in the fall,
Right fal-or-al taddle diddle I-do;
If he don't I'll hoist my sail,
And say goodbye to old Canaille
To me right fol-didy fol-dee.

Once, before singing this song, Aiden Maloney, the first President of the Canadian Salt Fish Corporation, explained that a century ago the fishers knew that all would be well if they could get a barrel of flour (196 pounds/89 kilograms) for a quintal of salt cod (112 pounds/50 kilograms). If not, the balance was not right and rough times lay ahead.

Twentieth Century

Newfoundland continued to export and trade salt cod with the Caribbean, Brazil, Spain, Portugal, and the Mediterranean in the early 1900s. As competition increased, Newfoundland merchants and trading companies took drastic steps to keep up, lowering prices, settling for lower quality products, and marginalizing fishers. Meanwhile, Norway, Iceland, and other countries reorganized, emphasized quality and constant supply, and marketed vigorously.

At this time, Sir William Coaker emerged on the Newfoundland fisheries scene. Coaker fought to retain trade and find new markets for Newfoundland salt cod, while attempting to establish fisheries regulations dealing with quality control, minimum pricing for fish exports, and fair prices for fishers. In 1908 Coaker formed the Fishermen's Protective Union. Although he became Minister of Marine and Fisheries in Newfoundland in 1919, his work could not overcome the merchants' push for cheap cod. Newfoundland salt cod began to decline in quality and importance.

Vestiges of this broad background of five centuries of international trading, settlement, and colonization still remain. Their influences can be seen throughout the recipes in this book.

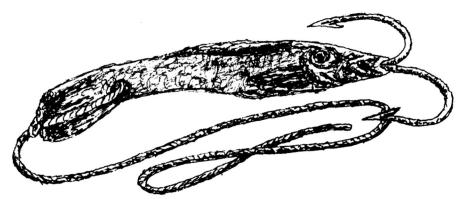

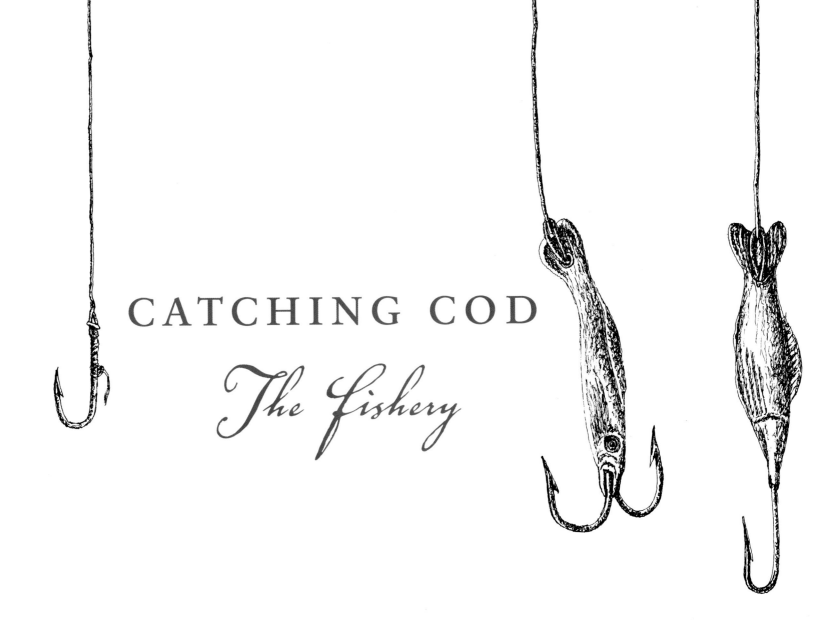

CATCHING COD
The Fishery

Boyd W. Chubbs's drawing based on a photograph by Ben Hansen.

In nautical terminology, a "mainstay" is the rope from the mainmast head forward that steadies the mast in that direction. For Newfoundland and Labrador's economy throughout the nineteenth century and for much of the twentieth century, the salt cod fishery was its mainstay, with three branches: an inshore fishery off the island's coast, a summer Labrador fishery, and an offshore bank fishery.

Inshore Fishery

The inshore fishery is the oldest of the three fisheries, with roots in the English migratory fishery. Starting in the 1500s, Newfoundland became a seasonal residence for many fishers seeking cod—an ideal commodity, as it was a good source of protein that preserved well and transported easily. Shiploads of fishers arrived from Europe each spring and spent a few months catching cod. Most returned home in the fall.

The migratory fishery continued for 300 years, with the English, French, and, to a lesser extent, Spanish and Portuguese dominating at different times. Gradually, some fishers choose to remain on the island of Newfoundland year-round to safeguard fishing gear and secure access to prime fishing grounds for the next season. Most settled in relatively sheltered coastal areas near good fishing grounds and a supply of wood, establishing the island's population distribution. Rough seasonal fishing camps gave way to permanent settlements; larger mercantile communities at St. John's, Trinity, Placentia, and elsewhere became more densely populated commercial centres. The migratory fishery turned into a resident fishery.

For residents, the inshore fishery was a family-based industry. Fishers left their coastal homes early each morning to row or sail to nearby fishing grounds, returning later with their catch. Most family members helped with the curing process, which involved cleaning, salting, washing, and drying. The fish were traded to merchants for supplies and credit. This cycle of work intensified and became more profitable during the wars in the early nineteenth century—the Anglo-American War (1812-1814) and the Napoleonic Wars (1803-1815). As warring nations withdrew from the salt cod trade, Newfoundland gained almost complete control over this industry. Prices rose and residents increased their

Cod Jiggin' (1998), watercolour painting by Gerry Squires.

catch rate. The Napoleonic Wars brought economic prosperity to Newfoundland and an increase in its permanent population.

When Napoleon "met his Waterloo," and the war and wartime prosperity ended, the price of cod dropped. For fishers to maintain their incomes they had to adopt more efficient methods of fishing for cod, which were becoming scarce in some areas. To their use of conventional jiggers, handlines, and trawls, they added cod seines, gillnets, bultows, and cod traps. The cod trap, which could easily catch several tonnes of cod in one haul, quickly became the dominant gear for inshore fishing. As fisheries scientist George Rose estimates, "[a]bout 5000 traps were in use each year throughout the 1930s and 1940s. The cod trap would seal the fate of the aged handline fishery."[17]

Labrador Fishery: Livyers, Stationers, and Floaters

English merchants had a strong presence on the shores of Labrador by the late eighteenth century. Company employees built and maintained homes, establishing themselves and their families as year-round residents. They became known as livyers, a title shared with those who married native Labrador Innu and Inuit women.

At about the same time, stationers came to fish off Labrador. Arriving primarily from the bays on the east coast of Newfoundland, stationers lived in coves and sheltered inlets that turned into small-scale fishing stations along the Labrador coast. They came north from Newfoundland in the early summer and stayed until the early fall. They set up living quarters on shore, fished from small boats, and salted and cured their catch on shore shortly after it was caught. Stationers were often outfitted by merchants from their home communities.

As cod stocks diminished in some Newfoundland bays, and countries such as France, England, and Spain reentered the salt cod trade, an increasing number of fishers and buyers turned to the Labrador fishery. Known as floaters, these fishers lived on board their

---

Jigger: Unbaited, weighted hook(s) used with a line to catch cod by giving a sharp, upward jerk.[18] Usually a pair of large hooks was fixed back to back with lead run upon the shanks in the shape of a capelin. Today, stainless steel Norwegian jiggers are available.

Handline: One or more baited hooks on a line, with a heavy lead weight keeping the bait near the bottom. Fishers often tended a handline on each side of a boat.

Trawl: A long line to which many short lines with baited hooks are attached at regular intervals. In some places, float trawls were set at depths of 3 to 5 fathoms (18 to 30 feet or 5.5 to 10 metres) during the capelin season by fishers who generally used jiggers and handlines. Trawls were set with a small anchor at each end and marked by buoys.

Cod seine: A large vertical net placed in position around a school of fish, the "foots" drawn together to form a bag and hauled at sea or in shallow water near the shore.[19]

Gillnet: A net set vertically in the water so that fish swimming into it are entangled by their gills. The bottom of the net is sunk by weights on the lower (lead) line, the top (float) line is maintained with flotation devices, and the ends are marked with buoys. The net may be set at different depths by adjusting the flotation or the weights. Nets are hauled into the boat to remove the fish and then reset.

Bultow: Of French origin, a long, buoyed fishing line (similar to a trawl) with closely placed and baited hooks attached at intervals. Bultows are placed in different directions from the fishing boat, let down, and secured with suitable moorings.[20]

Cod trap: A box-shaped net used in inshore waters with a net leader stretching from the shore to the entrance through which cod enter the box and are trapped.[21] The floor of the mesh cod trap rests on the bottom; its sides are suspended by many small floats and large buoys at the corners, sides, and back, all moored by heavy anchors or grapnels.

schooners and sailed up and down the Labrador coast. They packed their cod in salt and brought it back to Newfoundland at the end of each season to be dried. The floater fishery resembled the early migratory fishery, but the home ports in this case were in Newfoundland.

The first decade of the twentieth century was the high point of the floater fishery. By the 1920s, it had started to decline. Not only did this fishery encounter the same problems with competition and different fishing methods as the Newfoundland inshore fishery did but it also faced the added challenges of a short Labrador fishing season (June to September/October) and high start-up and operating costs. When the price of cod

Battle Harbour Commemorates the Labrador Fishery

Battle Harbour, once known as the capital of Labrador, is on an island 9 miles (15 kilometres) off the southeast coast of Labrador, between Battle Island and Great Caribou Island. The harbour was an anchorage for fishing vessels plying the Labrador coast.

The mercantile fishing premises at Battle Harbour were established by John Slade & Company of Poole, England, between 1750 and 1775. In 1871, the Slades sold their Battle Harbour premises to Baine Johnston & Company, Newfoundland, who operated the site until 1955, when it was sold to Earle Freighting Service, Ltd. of Carbonear. The Earles continued to operate Battle Harbour until the decline of the inshore fishery in the early 1990s. At that time it was donated to the Battle Harbour Historic Trust.

The buildings and structures of the Battle Harbour premises, often referred to as rooms, were erected by English and Newfoundland-based merchants. It was used for the processing of cod, salmon, seals, and herring, as well as the production of barrels, the packaging and shipping of fish products, the storing of nets, ropes, and sails, and the mending of nets. It was also the source of flour, salt meat, molasses, and fishing supplies for the fishing crews. Battle Harbour's flake, or fish-drying platform, was the biggest in Labrador, and its wharf and waterfront premises were the hub of the community.

Since 1997 Battle Harbour has been restored as a nineteenth-century fishing port and settlement featuring the province's last salt cod mercantile premises. Historic photographs and some 500 site-specific artifacts on display commemorate the Labrador fishery. A plaque by artist Boyd W. Chubbs honouring the fishery and the generations who participated in it was unveiled in Battle Harbour

Visitors from the Old New York Yacht Club at the restored Battle Harbour premises, 2006. (Photo by Keith Hardy)

on August 14, 1997. Already declared a National Historic Site in 1996, Battle Harbour and its entire cultural landscape (heritage buildings and open spaces) was named a National Historic District in 1997 by the Historic Sites and Monuments Board of Canada.

dropped in the early 1950s, the floater fishery became even less profitable. The number of participants in the fishery decreased yearly, and by the time of the 1992 cod moratorium the enterprise had disappeared.

Offshore Bank Fishery

The offshore bank fishery, also called the international fishery, required fishers to work far from their homes for weeks at a time. During the early decades of the twentieth century, fishers from Newfoundland and other countries (especially Portugal) sailed to the Grand Banks, typically in wooden schooners. Once on the Banks, they rowed dories and small open boats to nearby fishing grounds early each morning to catch cod with handlines, trawl lines, and jiggers. They returned to the larger vessels several times a day to unload their catch, which they gutted, split, and salted while at sea. Vessels made up to four trips to the Banks each season, from March to October, and remained there for weeks before returning home. Such trips generally coincided with the availability of bait such as herring, capelin, and squid.

Spreading fish in Battle Harbour, c.1900. (Ayre & Sons postcard, *Them Days* Archives)

The Decline of the Cod Fishery

Jigging and handlining are two of the oldest methods for catching cod off Newfoundland. To these were added trawls, cod seines, gillnets, bultows, cod traps, and, eventually, mechanical means of baiting hooks, purse and pair seiners, and otter, side, and stern trawls. This new fishing gear and more efficient fishing nets allowed cod to be harvested over larger areas and at greater depths.

In the early 1900s, inshore fishers increasingly used diesel-powered longliners instead of small open boats; at the same time, the bank fishery used trawlers or draggers to replace schooners. Larger, faster, and more seaworthy boats allowed fishers to get to productive fishing grounds with greater ease and to remain at sea for longer periods of

Built in 1937, the Portuguese schooner *Creoula* took part in the cod fishery from 1938 to 1973. (Capt. H.W. Stone Collection, Maritime History Archives, Memorial University of Newfoundland)

time. The use of fish finders, more powerful winches, and factory trawlers resulted in ever-increasing catches of cod. As well,

> Advances in sonar, radar, and other fish-finding technologies from the 1960s onwards made the fisheries even more efficient. Echo sounders, Loran C navigational aids, and other devices allowed fishers to locate and harvest the most productive fishing grounds with greater ease than ever before. Even as stocks dwindled, these technologies allowed fishers to track and harvest whatever concentrations of cod remained in inshore and offshore waters.[22]

The Portuguese White Fleet and the Bank Fishery[23]

Immediately after Portuguese explorer Corte Real brought home reports of large quantities of cod in Newfoundland waters in the early 1500s, Portuguese companies formed to send vessels across the Atlantic. These early vessels fished in sheltered harbours close to the Bonavista Peninsula, but in the early 1620s they were forced through conflicts with the British to fish offshore on the Grand Banks.

As J.P. Andrieux notes in *The Grand Banks: A Pictorial History*, "The Portuguese fishers would cross the Atlantic in sturdy fishing vessels on the spring east wind to fish on the Grand Banks some 2,000 miles away. They fished with hook and lines, filled their holds with cod, and raced back home before the fierce northern winter caught them."[24] On the Grand Banks, the Portuguese fishers left their ships and fished, one man to a dory, and "[e]ach dory stayed out until it was deep in the water with cod or until a recall flag was hoisted."[25] After a day's fishing, the cod had to be split, cleaned, and stowed in salt in the cargo hold. When the vessels' holds were filled, or when late September arrived, the boats headed back to Portugal. For centuries these schooners were prominent among Europeans fishing off Newfoundland. The handlining fleet was joined by Portuguese trawlers in the 1930s.

Portugal remained neutral during World War II, and, in order to safely continue its fishing activities, vessels were painted white and clearly displayed the name of the boat and country of registry. These Portuguese vessels became known as the White Fleet, "an affectionate and nostalgic expression that has remained forever."[26]

During the 1950s and 1960s, the White Fleet was joined by trawlers from other countries. Cod had to be caught in deeper and deeper water, and the methods used by the deteriorating three- and four-masted schooners of the White Fleet were no longer sustainable. By the early 1970s, low catch rates, the loss of several schooners, and political turmoil in Portugal (the social uprising of the Carnation Revolution inspired White Fleet fishers to demand higher wages and different methods of payment) had taken their toll. On July 24, 1974, "[t]he last remaining member of the White Fleet, the *Novos Mares*, with her dories neatly stacked on her deck, sailed through the Narrows on her way back home."[27]

Heavily laden dories of the Portuguese White Fleet, c.1940-1950. (Courtesy of Flanker Press. Originally appeared in *The Grand Banks: A Pictorial History*, J.P. Andrieux)

France, Portugal, Spain, and Italy engaged in the deep-sea fishery on the Grand Banks in the first half of the twentieth century using what new technology they had. In the early spring of 1954, two Soviet side trawlers appeared and, with that, Eastern Bloc countries began fishing on the Grand Banks. Trawlers came from East Germany, Poland, Bulgaria, and Romania. A Soviet fleet grew from those two vessels in 1954 to 160 by 1960.[28] Dutch, Greek, Israeli, Moroccan, Faroese, and Norwegian fishing vessels also had a presence on the Grand Banks.

Cod catches peaked in the 1960s, declining dramatically in the 1970s. As fishing technology became more efficient and widespread, the industry became less sustainable. In an effort to prevent a total collapse of the cod fishery, quota regulations were introduced in 1974, and in 1977 Canada extended its jurisdiction to 200 nautical miles in an attempt to curtail the activities of foreign fishing vessels. With extra attempts at monitoring and conservation efforts, stocks improved slightly. However, it was not enough. After decades of overfishing, the cod fishery collapsed in the 1990s.

The Northern Cod Crisis, a report for the Political and Social Affairs Division of the Government of Canada, offered several reasons for the sharp decline:

> … quotas set above sustainable levels as a result of questionable stock assessment methods or the need to accommodate social concerns; poorly understood environmental factors, including unusually cold water temperatures; and overfishing by foreign vessels. Seals, an inadequate enforcement regime, misreporting, wasteful fishing practices, harvesting fish that were too small or immature, ghost fishing by abandoned gillnets, and catch pressures on capelin (a major food for cod) may have also contributed to the decline. As well, there has been much controversy regarding the environmental effects of groundfish trawlers on the ecosystem …[29]

Or, as J.P. Andrieux concludes, "technology of the twentieth century went much faster than the possibility of countries to react quickly enough to extending their limits and take other conservation measures. The predictions of the Newfoundland fishers of the 1920s had stated that if the trawlers were not forbidden from fishing, it would spell the end of the fishery."[30]

The Trawler at Sea (1998), watercolour painting by Gerry Squires.

The Cod Moratorium and Beyond

On July 2, 1992, the Canadian government announced a two-year moratorium on the Northern cod fishery. It affected the Northern cod stock in NAFO divisions 2J3KL, which extend from Hopedale in southern Labrador to the northern part of the Grand Banks. The moratorium put about 30,000 people in Newfoundland and Labrador out of work and ended a 500-year-old industry. The moratorium marked its 20-year anniversary in 2012, leaving only limited recreational, commercial, and sentinel fisheries in 2J3KL.

Recreational Cod Fishery

The Canadian Department of Fisheries and Oceans has permitted a few weeks of recreational cod fishing in areas 2J3KL during most years since the moratorium. Although there are strict daily catch limits, this "food fishery" has given Newfoundlanders and Labradorians a chance to do what many grew up doing—jig a cod for dinner. While much of this cod is eaten fresh or fresh frozen, a strong tradition holds for those who want to salt their own cod.

The recreational cod fishery in Trinity Bay, NL, 2011. (Photo by Shirley George)

Commercial Cod Fishery

In some areas outside 2J3KL, a commercial cod fishery with limited total allowable catches exists: a fixed gear commercial fishery in NAFO area 3Pn4R and a full commercial fishery in 3Ps. At times since the moratorium commercial fish harvesters in 2J3KL are permitted to catch a limited amount of cod within the 12 miles of Canada's inshore zone. Information from the sentinel fishery is used to help determine these limited amounts.

A fishing boat returning from the recreational fishery, Notre Dame Bay, NL, 2011. (Photo by Valerie Sooley)

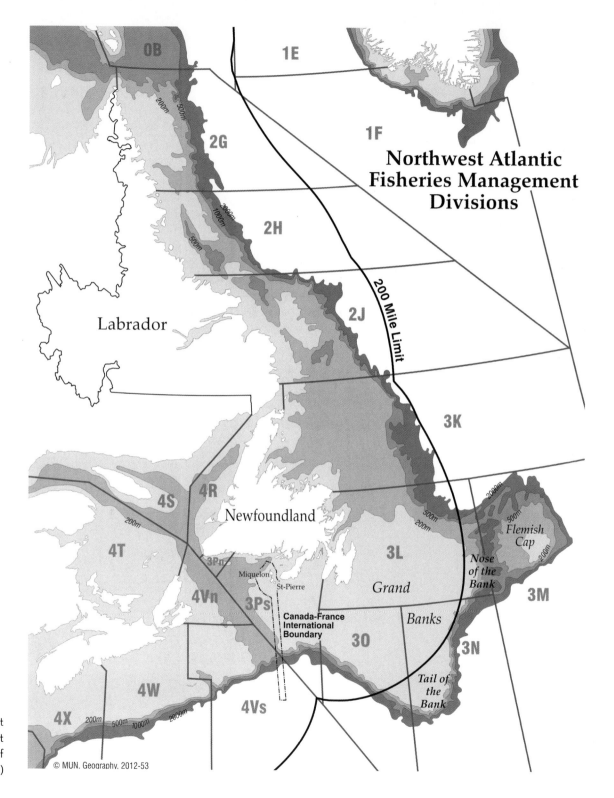

Northwest Atlantic Fisheries Management Divisions. (Charlie Conway, Department of Geography, Memorial University of Newfoundland)

Sentinel Fishery

The Fisheries Resource Conservation Council of the Department of Fisheries and Oceans implemented a sentinel fishery in 1994. As part of the program, fishers from communities within the boundaries of identified coastal areas monitor the evolution of cod stocks. Fish harvesters were selected and trained in scientific sampling methods and equipment, computer use, and resource assessment basics.[31]

The Sentinel Fishery (1998), watercolour painting by Gerry Squires.

Cod Pot Fishery: An Alternative Harvesting Method

Cod pot fishery trials started in Newfoundland and Labrador during the mid-1990s. Using a modified version of technology already in use in Alaska, prototypes developed by Philip Walsh, Centre for Sustainable Aquatic Resources, were tested in Placentia, Trinity, and Notre Dame bays. In 2010, fishers caught the 3,125-tonne quota of Northern cod in baited pots from the waters around Fogo Island.

Baited cod pots control selectivity and quality during fish harvesting. Live cod can be protected in ideal conditions until needed, and bled immediately. Small juvenile cod can escape or be released. Harvesters have more control over the composition of their catch, and conservation principles can be more effectively followed.

Re-membering HOOK and LINE, by Pam Hall, from Towards an Encyclopedia of Local Knowledge, a collaborative art and knowledge project with 80 collaborators in Bonne Bay and the Great Northern Peninsula, Newfoundland and Labrador. (Courtesy of Pam Hall)

MAKING FISH
Fresh Cod into Salt Cod

Salt storage boxes used in the first half of the twentieth century, St. Shotts, NL, 2009. (Photo by Jason Kearley)

Salt: A Natural Preservative

Salt begins in the sea. Chloride and sodium ions—the components of salt—move around in a solution of ionized minerals and compounds such as magnesium, calcium, and potassium. For salt to form from this solution, evaporation must occur. Mark Bitterman, who specializes in culinary salt, describes the process:

> Theoretically, if you filled a hundred-foot-tall cylinder with ocean water and let it evaporate, you would end up with a three-foot-thick layer of crystallized sodium chloride sandwiched between two thinner layers of other crystallized salts and trace minerals—mostly magnesium and potassium salts (which precipitate last) on the top and calcium salts (which precipitate first) on the bottom.... (This is why nearly pure sodium chloride can be mined from rock: it is taken from the massive middle layer formed by the evaporation of ancient seas.)[32]

The two classifications of salt, rock (mined) salt and solar or evaporated salt, differ in when and how the evaporation took place. Rock salts, mined from underground salt deposits, are the remains of a dried-up salt lake or an isolated arm of an ancient ocean. Evaporated salt is obtained naturally by the solar evaporation of seawater or industrially by mechanical methods such as vacuum pan evaporation:

> ... a brine (produced by pumping water into underground salt deposits to dissolve the salt buried in the rock) is pumped back up to the surface. The water is processed with chemicals such as carbon dioxide and sodium hydroxide to precipitate out unwanted calcium and magnesium salts and any other minerals. The refined brine is then boiled off in series vacuum evaporators until salt crystals form.[33]

These salt crystals have various particle shapes and sizes. Artisan salt makers can adjust the process of evaporation to get the desired mineral content or to modify any salt after it has been crystallized or mined. Such techniques include "cold or hot smoking with hardwoods or other botanicals; baking in an oven or firing in a kiln to impregnate with flavors and/or develop texture; melting salt into a liquid form to crystallize anew as it solidifies; saturating salt with a flavorful liquid such as wine or essential oils; and blending salt with flavorful and aromatic ingredients."[34]

Chefs experiment with artisan salts in the salting of cod. Joseba Jimenez de Jimenez, a chef from San Sebastian, Spain, is passionate about both salt and cod:

> I use 63 different salts … depending on what I'm going to do with it. Each salt tastes different. Red sea salt from Molokai is high in terra-cotta and has a sweet, earthy flavor. I use it in cold preparations like carpaccio of salt cod with extra-virgin olive oil and truffles. Or I use Salies de Bern semisweet river salt, which is very light and very dense at the same time for my green sauce salt cod.[35]

Off-loading salt from a wooden freighter, the *Eastern Venture*, at Battle Harbour, Labrador, c.1980. (Photo by Bob Hardy)

The purity of salt depends on the evaporation and precipitation processes. Commercial grades of salt used for salting cod contain about 94 to 99 per cent sodium chloride. To achieve the best quality of salt cod one must use "the salt having the greatest amount of sodium chloride and the least amount of calcium and magnesium impurities."[36]

Impurities often found in salt, including calcium sulfate, magnesium sulfate, lime, and iron, can affect the preservation process and the appearance, texture, and taste of cod. Calcium and magnesium chlorides and sulfates, even in small amounts, reduce the rate of salt penetration into the flesh of the cod. Magnesium chloride and other impurities readily absorb moisture from the air, even after the salt cod has been dried. This creates ideal conditions for the growth of bacteria and moulds such as "pink" and "dun."

Regulations were introduced in Newfoundland and Labrador in 2009 to ensure that the salt used to cure cod is not a source of contamination. As well, the Canadian Food Inspection Agency requires salt to be certified as food grade. Extreme care and cleanliness are needed at all times, no matter what salt is used to process cod.

Preserving Cod with Salt

When cod are salted, osmosis takes place: the naturally occurring solution within each cell passes out through the semi-permeable membrane surrounding the cell, and the prepared salt solution passes in. Eventually a balance is reached. Salting slows down the internal breakdown of tissue, as "[t]he removal of water appears to limit bacterial growth and enzyme activity, thus preserving the fish. Additionally, the high salt content prevents growth of the normal spoilage microflora on the fish."[37]

The sooner salt is applied to fresh cod the better the preservation will be. When salting cod at home, begin before spoilage starts. Cover the entire surface of the cod with sufficient salt for the cure desired. Use a broad-grained salt for heavy salting, as "fine-grained salt dissolves quickly in the fish muscle fluids causing a too rapid withdrawal of moisture from the surface tissue," and, consequently, "a rapid protein denaturation and coagulation occurs, preventing further penetration of the salt into the fish," resulting in "salt burn."[38]

Women making fish, Grand Bank (postcard c.1940). During busy periods of the cod trap fishery, women were generally responsible for working the flakes; many became renowned for their skill in producing good-quality cod. (Provincial Archives Photography Collection, The Rooms Provincial Archives Division, A 18-173)

Stages

Before the cod moratorium, stages perched on pilings or on wharves crowded the shoreline in hundreds of Newfoundland and Labrador communities. Morning and evening, boats heavily laden with cod tied up to these stages to unload their catch. The interior of many stages had two spaces: one for cleaning the cod (sometimes done outside the stage door), the other for salting and curing. The section where the cod were gutted, headed, split, and washed was designed for speedy work, efficiency of movement, and access to a supply of clean water. The salting space—cool, dry, and always governed by cleanliness and good drainage—contained bins or pounds.

In addition to being a place for work, stages were focal points of the community and were described by some writers as "cathedral" or spiritual in significance, with a life of their own:

> You heard the talk of tired men
> Late at night
> When the sky was black,
> Moving in their own shadows,
> Listening to them when they did not talk, ...
> —Larry Small, "The Foundering Stage"[39]

Practically all of the working stages and stores are gone. A few remain, "[l]ike punch drunk boxers they shake in every gale and totter in every sea. So far they have refused to go down, doggedly exemplifying the determination and stubbornness of their builders."[40]

The 12,000 Stages Society, formed in 2009 at Cape Charles, Labrador, is devoted to celebrating the culture of the cod. The 12,000 of the title is an estimate of the number of stages associated with the fishing industry when it was at its peak in Newfoundland and Labrador.

Albert Dwyer's stage, Tilting, Fogo Island, NL, 2011. (Photo by Roy Dwyer)

Making Fish

"Making fish"—the traditional name for processing fresh cod into salt cod—was labour-intensive and often involved many members of the fisher's family. The work is outlined below as three phases: (i) bleeding, cutting, gutting and heading, splitting, and cleaning; (ii) salting; and (iii) washing and drying. More than simply interesting and culturally informative, these descriptions contain advice for salting cod at home. Some of the traditional ideas are not applicable today but may provide inspiration for improvisation.

Bleeding, Cutting, Gutting and Heading, Splitting, and Cleaning

Four men splitting fish, 1908. (International Grenfell Association Photograph Collection, The Rooms Provincial Archives Division, VA 118-30.3)

The centrepiece of the stage was "the 'splitting table,' where in a counter clockwise rotation, the fish were tabled, their throats cut and a slit made down the middle. They were then gutted and beheaded before being passed across to the splitter, who with quick deft strokes removed the sound bone and dropped the fish into a tub which, when full, was dragged to the salting area."[41]

Cutting the throat. (Photo by Bob Hardy)

Bleeding

Nothing is more important to the production of salt cod than a supply of top-quality fresh cod that has been bled properly and handled carefully. Immediate bleeding reduces the chance of blood clotting and gives the flesh a whiter appearance than that of a cod that is not bled right away. Traditionally, cod could not be bled until the inshore boats returned home or the dories returned to the main ship in the bank fishery. Immediate bleeding could not be done with a glut of cod caught in a cod trap.

To bleed cod immediately after catching, cut the throat forward of the heart, cut the gills, or simply break the gills with your finger. Allow the cod to bleed for a minimum of one to two minutes before removing the gut. Bleeding is more effective if the cod is placed in a tub of water; this helps prevent bruising of the flesh and keeps the cod from flapping on the bottom of the boat. It is also important to keep the cod cool and away from the sun. Heat can cause texture breakdown, which results in soft cod with an unpleasant smell.

Cutting

To properly cut a cod, cut the throat through to the backbone, making sure to cut off the stomach, which will enable easy gut removal. Hold the cod on the splitting table with its abdomen facing you, and cut the belly straight to the vent. If it is not cut through, it is more difficult to split. Do not cut to one side or beyond the vent as this could cause "slivers," which affect the quality of the product.

Gutting and Heading

After the cod has been cut, hold it open and take out the liver. Hold the intestines near the vent area and, in one movement, remove all of the inner organs. To remove the head, hold the cod firmly with one hand, with its neck on the edge of the splitting table. With the other hand, hold the head in such a way that a quick push exerted by both hands forces it from the body, the table edge acting as a lever and cutting edge.

For large cod, the best method for removing the head is to "jowl" it: "Cut just behind the gills up each side of the collar bone towards the back of the fish. This reduces damage to the flesh and breakage along the collar bones. Do not rip the head, but gently push the body away from the head. The table edge should be thin and bevelled at the heading station."[42] All gut material and liver should be removed before the cod is split.

Splitting

Splitting is probably the most difficult task in making fish. If you are right-handed, hold the cod with your left hand against a small stick (or cleat) nailed to the table, which helps keep the cod in place. The splitting knife should enter, on the side of the soundbone furthest away from you, at the point where the head came from the body. From there, make a cut at the depth of the bone, right back to the tail, slicing the cod so that it falls open flat all the way. Hold it by the soundbone and make a cut into the part of the backbone (about the third joint behind the vent) that remains in the tail. Move the tip of the knife back up the cod to "rise the bone." Remove the bone completely.

The Dried Codfish Industry, a monograph written for the Newfoundland government in 1935, offers a succinct description of splitting:

> In splitting, the point where the backbone is cut should be just far enough back to avoid leaving a blood spot, and the knife must not be allowed to slip deep into the flesh, forming a crevice where conditions become ideal for the activities of decomposition…. The final appearance of the fish should show the fish split evenly along the backbone from head to tail, with the backbone cut, not broken, about half way down, with no round tail and no ragged edges, no sliver and no gashes.[43]

Many fishers maintain that one sign of a well-split cod is if the place where the soundbone is cut gives the appearance of a figure eight. This can occur when the splitter

Three generations of the Troake family filleting cod in Twillingate, NL, during the recreational cod fishery, 2011. From left: Jack Troake, Hardy Troake, and Dillon Troake. (Photo by Valerie Sooley)

points the knife toward the tail and cuts through two joints of bone at once in a sloping direction.

At this point, the black skin on the nape is visible. Whether it is left on or removed is a matter of aesthetics. If it is to be removed, it is best done at this point.

Cleaning

Careful washing of the split cod before it is salted is as necessary today as it was in 1935:

> Every fisherman knows that, after gutting, beheading, trimming, and splitting a fish, and before salting, the fish is washed to remove traces of blood, guts, and dirty matter. Every fisherman knows, too, that this process takes up a fair amount of time … Actually the care shown and time taken at this stage in cleansing the fish thoroughly of all traces of dirty matter will decide the final amount of bacterial decomposition, and, … the successful control of this factor is half the battle to successful preservation.…
>
> It is now well known that bruising and crushing of the fish increases the rate of autolytic decomposition. There is absolutely no doubt that rough handling of fish increases the rate of decomposition and makes it all the more difficult to get a successful cure. Fish should be carried about, not thrown about …[44]

Cleaning a split cod with a soft brush. (Photo by Bob Hardy)

Lots of clean, cool seawater (seawater is better than fresh water) is essential for washing the split cod. Running water, or many changes of water, helps remove any debris and pieces of offal that have washed off other fish.

Use a soft nylon brush or a small scrubbing brush to wash the back of the cod carefully and to remove any slime along the back fins. Use a cloth, a sponge, or an extremely soft brush to clean the flesh side of the cod. Do not allow the cod to remain in water too long or the flesh will soften. A top-quality split cod is immaculate and ready for immediate salting.

Salting

Methods of Curing

Traditionally, cod was preserved for storage, shipment, and market distribution through salting and drying. But not all cod underwent the same amount of salting and the same intensity of drying. Different types of cure, with different amounts of salt, were often dictated by local conditions and resulted in light or heavy salted cod.

Light salted cod did not remain long in salt and had to be immediately dried after salting to lower the water content. Heavy salted cod were kept a relatively long period in salt. More water was removed by the use of salt and less by drying than in the case of the light salted cure. Heavy salting was originally used for Labrador fish because drying times were restricted. Different quantities of salt (between light and heavy) were used for cod caught in the Strait of Belle Isle and those caught by banking schooners.

The ideal preservation method would result in a product capable of taking up almost as much water as has been removed. Although this perfect reversibility could never be attained, light salted, shore-cured cod had a greater degree of reversibility than more heavily salted cod.

Traditional salting required considering many variables, including cod size and thickness, weather conditions, local traditions, catch location, distance from the place of salting, the market, the method of distribution to the market, and the environmental conditions expected prior to consumption or use of the product. Undoubtedly, only a few of these factors need to be considered when salting your own cod.

A well-split cod on salt. (Photo by Bob Hardy)

Kench Curing

In kench curing, the salting of cod in piles, salt and split cod are placed in alternating layers. For a heavy salted cure, select a clean location and cover it with a clean piece of plastic. Use a pallet with good drainage or other board for the base, and cover the salting area with a layer of coarse fishery salt approximately 0.25 inches (0.5 centimetres) thick. Arrange the cod on the flat, nape to tail, face up, without twisting or overlapping the flesh. Cover with a layer of salt. Do not let the napes or tails stick out or overhang. Sprinkle more salt on thick than on thin cod, with more salt over the thickest part of each cod. Add a second layer of cod, then a layer of salt. Layer cod and salt until the pile is completed, with the last layer completely covered with salt and the entire kench being no more than 4 feet (1.2 metres) high. Guidelines for amounts of salt and time are given in Appendix 1.

Generally, heavy salted cod requires about 21 days for a sufficient amount of water to leave the cells of the cod and for adequate salt penetration. At this point, the cod is "struck." Striking happens faster at higher rather than lower temperatures. Heavy salted kench-cured cod is referred to as "salt bulk fish."

The amount of salt used and the length of time the cod are in salt differentiate the types of kench-cured cod:

Kench curing of salt cod. (Photo by Bob Hardy)

> A light salted fish is very different from a heavy salted fish, having its own characteristic colour, flavour and odour. Light salted cod, which is dry salted in a kench, is prepared for salting in the same manner as heavy salted fish; however, the salting procedure is different. The salt is spread evenly over the fish with 12-15 lbs. (~5-7 kg) of salt used per 100 lbs. (~45 kg) of split fish. It is extremely important that the correct amount of salt be used. Too much salt will result in a product which resembles heavy salted fish. Slack salting will result in uncharacteristic colour and spoilage. Depending on temperature, the fish must remain in salt for 5-9 days. Light salted codfish are not preserved totally by the salt; therefore, they must be dried quickly after removal from the kench.[45]

Pickle Salting

In pickle salting, like kench salting, dry salt is used, but the cod is placed in perfectly tight containers so that the pickle does not drain away. Traditionally, puncheons, butts, puncheon tubs, or barrels were used; more recently, heavy plastic tubs or boxes.

As with kench salting, the cod had to be carefully laid open with its flesh side up in orderly tiers. More specifically, as Mark Ferguson writes in "Making Fish: Salt-Cod Processing on the East Coast of Newfoundland":

> Salting, at the most superficial level, involved throwing handfuls of salt on fish, but there was much more to it than that. Each and every fish required salt and the amount used depended upon the fish's size and thickness and its placement in the container (bottom, middle, or top); as well, different parts of a fish received more or less salt…. an experienced salter made many decisions from instant to instant, assessing each fish from various standpoints, and then cast, usually by hand, more or less salt depending on the fish's condition.[46]

Small-scale pickle salting. (Photo by Roy Dwyer)

The water extracted from the cod during pickle salting collects in a container and within a short period of time covers the entire pile. Keep the cod in this brine until it has struck through and absorbed enough salt throughout the depth of the flesh to stop normal bacterial spoilage. This process must be very carefully watched; the final product is not as durable as that from kench salting. Adding more salt to the container from time to time can make a more durable, heavy salted product.

Heavy salted pickled cod requires approximately 40 pounds (18 kilograms) of salt per 100 pounds (45 kilograms) of split cod.[47] As the cod forms its own pickle, the top layer must be immersed. It would normally stay in this pickle for 21 days or longer as the striking time is temperature dependent. Light salted pickling requires approximately 10 pounds (4 kilograms) of salt per 100 pounds (45 kilograms) of split cod. Keep the top layer of cod immersed in the pickle with the use of a weight. Depending on temperature and other conditions, the cod sits in the pickle for four to six days and is then washed and dried.

Corning

To corn split cod or fresh cod fillets (usually with skin on), lightly cover them in salt for 20 minutes to three hours. Use a watertight container as for pickling, or salt as in the kench method. Since corning is primarily for home use, the amount of salt and the length of time vary with taste. When it is ready, remove the corned cod, rinse quickly, and refrigerate until used. The taste should be between that of a fresh and a salt cod.

Brine Salting

In this wet salting method the cod is soaked in a homemade brine, usually 18-25 per cent sodium chloride, w/w ("by weight"). That means the mass of the salt (sodium and chloride) is 18-25 per cent of the total mass of the solution. The salt content of the cod can be regulated by the length of time it is left in the brine and the temperature of the brine. Usually cod is brined for two to four days.

Some Newfoundlanders and Labradorians maintain that the brine is right when a potato can be floated in it—and for a saltier solution, when a potato with a nail inserted in it floats. In *De Agricultura*, a practical guide to rural life from the second century B.C., Roman writer Cato suggested testing brine for sufficient salinity for use in pickling by seeing if an anchovy or an egg would float. This egg test is still used in many parts of the Mediterranean.

Potatoes floating in brine solution. (Photo by Valerie Sooley)

Washing and Drying

Flakes at A.H. Murray fish merchants, St. John's, NL, c.1935-38. (Stanley Truman Brooks, Newfoundland Tourist Development Board fonds, The Rooms Provincial Archives Division, VA 15B-61.4)

Man spreading fish to dry on a flake, Battle Harbour, Labrador, 1921. (The Rooms Provincial Archives Division, VA 116-30.3/E.P. Hayden)

Salt cod drying in Twillingate, NL, 2011. (Photo by Valerie Sooley)

Salt cod drying in the sun in Aveiro, Portugal. (Photo by J.P. Andrieux)

SALT COD CUISINE: THE INTERNATIONAL TABLE

Fish drying on lines in a back garden, in Carbonear, NL, 2011. (Photo by Bob Hardy)

In this phase the salted cod is brought as close to perfection as possible. The time-honoured method is to dry off or evaporate the water—to "make the fish"—using the sun, the wind, and the general drying properties of the atmosphere.

Before drying, the cod must be washed, followed by a short period of piling to press out the pickle and water still on and in the cod. Then comes the extensive drying stage, which involves spreading and piling the cod several times.

To begin, wash the cod in tubs, preferably with salt water. (I often use the landwash area along a stretch of beach.) Use clean salt water and change it frequently. Make sure each cod is as clean as possible, without soaking it too much. The washing removes the pickle and some salt as well as any blood that might have been missed earlier.

Pile the washed cod face down on a pallet and allow it to drain. This procedure, referred to as the waterhorse or drainage stage, reduces the moisture content of the cod and gives it a smoother surface due to the pressure of the pile, which can be from three to five layers high. Waterhorsing could last from a few hours to 24 hours.

In this "making" process, traditionally the cod were spread, back down, onto flakes constructed of longers (long tapering poles, usually a conifer with bark left on) laid over horizontal supports, held up by posts and shores and covered with a matting of sticks and dry spruce boughs (without needles). The flakes were often 10-12 feet (3-4 metres) high to ensure good air circulation. The *Newfoundland Fisheries Development Committee Report* from 1953 defined a good drying day as:

> … having a temperature of 40°F. [4.5°C] or higher, with a breeze of 10 miles per hour or over and a spread of 4° between wet- and dry-bulb temperatures (indicating a suitable relative humidity for drying); a doubtful day as one on which showers occurred or which had a borderline relative humidity (indicating poor drying conditions); and a poor day as one which had fog, rain or drizzle or on which the relative humidity approached saturation.[48]

When there was insufficient flake space, cod was spread on any available rocks or beach to dry. Hand flakes, sometimes made of small frames that could be carried to any free spot, were approximately 4 feet by 6 feet (1.2 metres by 1.8 metres), covered by round pickets and often moved during the day to face the sun.

Cod becomes more resilient to contact and heat as it dries. When it becomes drier and stiffer, the backs of the cod are occasionally turned up to the sun. Cod should be turned face down during the night so their skins form a protective layer from the elements. In the evening, the cod are piled into small stacks, which increase in size as the cod dries. The cod on the first tier are laid with their backs down, the rest with backs up; they alternate head to tail at each tier. The pile tapers up to a single cod as it rises; this last cod is generally a larger one and forms the top overlapping shingle. If the weather is good, the cod are spread again the next day.

After a week or so, with four or five days of good drying (with a day or two of sweating), the cod are placed into very large stacks or, more usually, into round piles to work and flatten. This working in round piles helps season and toughen the cod. They are round-piled the first time for approximately a week; then they are spread for a day and round-piled again. Each piling presses out more water.

After drying, the salt cod was traditionally packed in large rectangular piles in the fish store before being shipped to the merchant. For small-scale home salting, cured salt cod may be stored in a cool dry place in an outdoor shed or in a freezer, or it may be watered and then frozen.

Culling and Grading

Everyone in the community, including the fish makers themselves, knew top-quality cod when they saw it and tasted it. There was great satisfaction in producing near-perfect cod—the golden amber hue of a well-dried, clean, thick, perfectly split cod, with "a little flour" (a dusting of salt) on its face. Good market prices brought further satisfaction.

> The culler starts his solitary judgements
> Of a summer's catch
>
> ...
>
> But in the market-place,
> With a keen eye and
> A gentle hand
> He must, without deliberation,
> Pass judgements,
> (A crucible for jurisprudence)
> On fish that will please
> The Portuguese, the Spanish, the Italians and the Greeks.
> —Larry Small, "The Culler"[49]

Dried cod were either brought to the merchant by the fishers or collected from them by the larger export businesses or buyers, who selected cod to meet the requirements of their international customers. In Tilting, Fogo Island, the scene was described like this:

> When this fish, cured by sun and wind was ready to ship, Bryan's wharves and those of the Trading Company were the busiest places in Tilting. There on fine autumn days, the fishermen arrived by boat or arrived pushing trollies, wheelbarrows or drays to await their turn to yaffle their fish onto the 'culling board.' In this exchange, there was no negotiation and while grooves on the board determined the size, the culler was the sole arbitrator of quality and, with the deft hands of a card dealer, threw fish into assorted piles on the wharf.[50]

Prior to 1932, shore-cured cod were graded into three categories based on a visual examination: merchantable, Madeira, or cullage. Merchantable cod, which included large and small cod of the best quality, were well cured with an even surface, free of blood spots at nape and soundbone, perfectly split, with no salt visible on the face. The worst-quality cod were cullage (inferior or spoiled)—broken, slimy, appearing to have too much salt, or damp or insufficiently dried. All cullage, because it would not sell in other markets, was shipped to West Indian markets. Madeira cod were large and small cod that had, on the whole, a darker colour than merchantable cod.

After being collected from the fishers and prior to export, the cod were culled into categories, largely arbitrary, suitable to the markets of a particular exporter. Thus the thick cod necessary for the Spanish market could be divided into two or more grades. Hard-dried cod went to the Brazilian market. Sometimes one exporter's second grade might rival another exporter's first grade. Appendix 2 contains the historical grades of salt cod.

Three men weighing salt fish, Battle Harbour, Labrador, 1909. (The Rooms Provincial Archives Division, VA 103-6.3)

Industry Grading Standards

Canada

Industry grading standards for salt cod are Choice or Select, Standard, and Commercial or Cullage; these are also known as Grades A, B, and C. Salt cod is also categorized as extra large, large, medium, small, and extra small as determined by a weight classification system.

Norway

Norway is the largest supplier of salt cod today and its product appears around the world. Specialized graders categorize salt cod into different classes: Imperial or Superior, Universal, Popular, and Mixed. The price of salt cod is contingent on its size (length and weight); smell, colour, and stiffness of the surface; presence/absence of production errors; and water content of the flesh. Most salt cod is dried to obtain a low moisture and high salt content, a process that leads to a stable product that can be stored for several months.

Loading salt cod on the schooner MV *Bacalac Transport*, owned by Capt. Morrissey Johnson, at Battle Harbour, Labrador, 1989. (Photo by Bob Hardy)

SALT COD

Culture and Cuisine

The recipes in this book originate from 30 countries or regions. Canada (Newfoundland and Labrador), France, Portugal, Spain, Greece, Italy, the Caribbean, and Brazil are the most prominent, with six or more recipes from each region. A closer examination of the salt cod culture and cuisine of these selected regions follows; the salt cod food practices explored have developed from the interaction of settlement patterns and their history, the salt cod trade, environment, climate, economy, religion, sociology, urbanization, and innovation.[51]

Just as festivals with songs, plays, arts and crafts, music, and dance are emblematic of the people who produce them, so too are salt cod dishes. The presentation of salt cod is part of the heritage and cultural cuisine of many countries; it is part of the foodways of a culture and a subject of study in folklore.

Salt Cod Cuisine contains recipes from around the world:

NORTH ATLANTIC	MEDITERRANEAN	CARIBBEAN	SOUTH AMERICA
Belgium	Greece	Anguilla	Brazil
Denmark	Italy	Antigua	
England	Malta	Bermuda	
France		Cuba	
Germany		Dominican Republic	
Iceland		Guadeloupe	
Netherlands		Haiti	
Norway		Jamaica	
Portugal		Martinique	
Scotland		Puerto Rico	
Spain		St. Kitts/Nevis	
Canada (Newfoundland and Labrador)		St. Lucia	
		St. Vincent and the Grenadines	
		Trinidad	

Newfoundland & Labrador

History and Settlement

Salt cod food patterns in Newfoundland and Labrador, Canada, have evolved from the traditions of the English, Irish, Scottish, and French settlers who adapted their cooking to a climate suitable for growing a limited variety of vegetables and fruits.

Until the eighteenth century, most food was imported. From England and America came breadstuffs; Ireland, salt pork; and America and the West Indies, rum and molasses. Lists of supplies imported by Newfoundland during 1677 and 1742 show a limited base of provisions—flour, dried peas, and oil, for example—that would not spoil during travel. By the mid-nineteenth century the variety of imports, including food and drink from America, had expanded.[52] The list of local ingredients increased as settlers began farming and became more self-sufficient.

Ingredients

Salt pork, salt cod, and ship's biscuit were part of the bulk provisions from Brittany, Normandy, and the Basque region. These ingredients, along with onions, potatoes, and carrots, formed the basis of many salt cod meals and have remained a tradition in Newfoundland and Labrador. Salt Cod Fish Cakes with savoury, Fish and Brewis with salt pork and hard bread, and Salt Cod Chowder are favourites. Turnips, turnip greens, dandelions, and potatoes are traditional vegetables of choice and have been joined by spinach, leeks, and other vegetables.

The most regularly served of all salt cod dishes in Newfoundland and Labrador is the Boiled Salt Cod dinner, also known as fish and potatoes. This is usually served with one of four sauces: drawn butter; scrunchions; garlic, onions, and olive oil; or mustard.

Cultural Significance

Newfoundlanders and Labradorians use salt cod, as indeed they use many other foods, to draw people together into a social, religious, or cultural family or community. Fish and brewis, often considered the quintessential Newfoundland meal, remains the focus of social occasions for many, whether it is a dish at a Christmas party or served at a community church or as a service club fundraiser. In some Newfoundland and Labrador communities, parishioners often included whole salt cod with harvest vegetables as part of their offerings to the church or the clergy on Thanksgiving Sunday.

Cod "parts" such as heads, tongues, cheeks, sounds, and roe are part of Newfoundland and Labrador's salt cod cuisine. Making use of all that was available was a matter of necessity and some tradition still holds for these salt cod parts; a love of salt cod heads and tongues has carried on through generations.

Newfoundland and Labrador has many easy one-dish salt cod meals (casserole, pie, and hash) involving rice, rolled oats, or potatoes. Hash made from leftover salt cod from a boiled salt cod dinner is eaten either at home or in the country while picking berries or trouting. Buttered homemade bread, toasted on an open fire and smothered in salt cod hash with white sauce, is worth every effort.

Within the past 30 years, hotels and restaurants in Newfoundland have begun to serve salt cod. The Albatross Hotel in Gander was one of the first to list salt cod on its menu. The owner, Harry Steele, comes from Musgrave Harbour, a traditional fishing community and the source of his salt cod. New salt cod dishes, such as Kippered Salt Cod Benedict,[53] have joined traditional salt cod fare on Newfoundland and Labrador menus.

Fatback pork.

Newfoundland savoury. (Photos by Valerie Sooley)

Portugal

Fiel Amigo—Faithful Friend

Bacalhau is part of Portugal's identity. As *New York Times* reporter Elaine Sciolino explains, "Bacalhau ... is to Christmas Eve in Portugal what turkey is to Thanksgiving in [North] America. Treasured since the 16th century, when Portuguese fishermen first brought it back from Newfoundland, it bore the name fiel amigo—faithful friend. Its correct preparation is a source of pride, a sign of respect for family values."[54]

The early popularity of bacalhau owed much to the Catholic Church, which forbade the eating of meat on many days, including Fridays, Lent, and many festive occasions. Bacalhau, which usually came from Norway (*Baclhauda Noruega*) or Newfoundland (*Bacalhauda Terra Nova*), became a staple of Portuguese cuisine and has remained so.

Ingredients

The region's geography, topography, and erratic climate have had a strong influence on all things Portuguese. Today, each region of the country adheres to its own manner of cooking, even choosing different names for the same basic dishes. Portuguese salt cod recipes are not as complex as they seem—the flavourings are simple, subtle, and natural. The strength of the cooking comes from the combination of ingredients, which is never spiced to alter basically simple tastes.

A statue of Gasper Corte-Real is located in front of the Confederation Building in St. John's, Newfoundland. Its plaque contains this inscription:

> Gasper Corte-Real Portuguese navigator—He reached Terra Nova in the 15th century—At the beginning of the Era of Great Discoveries.
>
> From the Portuguese Fisheries Organization as an expression of gratitude on behalf of the Portuguese Grand Banks fishermen for the friendly hospitality always extended to them by the people of Terra Nova, May, 1965.

A cuisine of the countryside and the sea, Portuguese salt cod dishes make the most of produce in season. Many have been passed down through the centuries by word of mouth. For this reason, the recipes belong to the people in a very personal way, and each region has its own set of traditions that are not often known by others. Ingredients such as olive oil, garlic, and parsley, however, are common to all regions and are used in many Portuguese bacalhau dishes. All 11 regions of Portugal are represented in the recipes in this collection.

Salt cod market in Portugal. (Photo by J.P. Andrieux)

Spain

Ingredients

Spanish salt cod cuisine reflects local ingredients and a bond between produce and people. Spanish cooking is easily identified by the presence of local olive oil and, less commonly, garlic. Saffron, the dried stamens of the *Crocus sativus*, is also vital to the Spanish table, revered and used as in no other cuisine. Saffron is the spice that gives *paella* its unforgettable colour and taste. Like salt, it brings out the flavour of the foods it seasons, adding its own scent and unmistakable yellow hue. Seventy per cent of the world's saffron grows in the fields of La Mancha,[55] a high plateau just south of Madrid.

The Basques welcome salt cod in any season and on any table. Salt Cod with Red Pepper Sauce (Bacalao à la Vizcaina) is noteworthy because of its few ingredients—salt cod, dried peppers, and onions. The same can be said for Salt Cod with Pil Pil Sauce (Bacalao al Pil Pil), a distinctly Basque method of frying salt cod with garlic and oil until the gelatin of the fish is released and forms a jelly.

Saffron strands. (Photo by Jason Kearley)

Tapas

Throughout Spain, people from many walks of life congregate in lively tapas bars to have a drink (sherry, beer, cider, or wine), sample little bites, and talk. Bacalao is used in several types of tapas; salt cod salads and salt cod stews can also be served as tapas. The Spanish tapas tradition is as much social as gastronomic. Like good songs tapas roam from one region to another naturally, but they are never quite the same from one town to the next. Tapas exemplify the creativity, skill, ingenuity, and zeal of the people who create them.

Stews and Salads

Although each area of Spain has its own particular salt cod stew, there is a nationwide formula of three basic ingredients: salt cod, pulses (dry beans, broad beans, and chickpeas), and local vegetables. Spinach and Chickpeas with Salt Cod Dumplings is one example: salt cod is mixed with dumplings and then simmered in a classic Spanish Lenten potage of chickpeas and spinach.

El mojo sauce or dressing is found practically everywhere in the Canary Islands and accompanies many salt cod stews and boiled salt cod meals. It is made with oil, vinegar, garlic, salt, and spices, which vary with the mojo: paprika, red mojo; piquant peppers, el mojo picon; and coriander, green mojo.

The cod in Spanish salt cod salads can be raw, semi-cooked, cooked, or marinated with a variety of sauces. Salad of Salt Cod with Oranges (Ensalada de Bacalao con Naranja) combines both a light vinaigrette dressing with the greens and a heavier mayonnaise dressing with the salt cod, brightly garnished with orange slices and parsley. Red onions, Spanish onions, green olives, black olives, greens, raisins, tomatoes, peppers, and Seville oranges ensure extremely colourful salads for everyday meals and festive occasions.

France

Regional Specialties

France, roughly hexagonal in shape, is bordered by the Lowlands, the Rhine, the Alps, the Mediterranean, the Pyrenees, the Atlantic, and the English Channel. The country has a long, varied history and an extraordinary range of different geographies and climates that support the production of a great diversity of local ingredients, many of which are used in salt cod dishes. Many regional specialties have become popular throughout France, others are enjoyed mainly in their areas of origin. France includes Burgundians and Provençals, German-speaking Alsatians, Celtic-speaking Bretons, Basques, and Catalonians.

French Mediterranean salt cod recipes use the fruit, vegetables, and herbs that grow well locally. There, the sun and the sea inspire the salt cod cuisine and the fertile soils produce richly coloured vegetables and fruits, aromatic herbs, olives, and olive oil. Bouillabaisse and Salt Cod and Leeks (La Quinquebine Camarguaise) are two classic French recipes under these influences.

Brandade is proof that salt cod dishes vary by region and many regional specialties have become popular throughout France. Brandade, a purée of salt cod, olive oil, and milk, is a specialty of Languedoc and Provence and does not include garlic. In Marseille and Toulon, crushed garlic gives a regional flavour to the dish.

Ingredients

French salt cod dishes are richly flavoured with herbs and spices, but they are not spicy. A classic bouquet garni, a necessary staple for the French kitchen, consists of a sprig of thyme, a bay leaf, parsley stems, and a leek leaf tied in a bundle with kitchen twine, or in a sachet if using dried thyme and bay leaves. Other distinctive additions include orange zest, lemon, wine, wine vinegar, Pernod, cognac, anchovies, or black olives.

Butter and the rich cream sauces of Burgundy sometimes take precedence over olive oil, herbs, and tomato-based ingredients. In Salt Cod with Black Butter (Morue au Beurre Noir), the easiest of dishes to prepare, butter is melted over a low heat until the milk solids turn dark brown and when lemon juice or vinegar is added black butter is ready for use.

Bouquet garni. (Photo by Valerie Sooley)

Ingredients

The landscape and climate of Greece are ideal for growing olives and lemons, both fundamental to the Greek preparation of salt cod. Leeks, onions, spinach, and generous portions of garlic are also widely used. Parsley, both cultivated and wild, is often the herb of choice.

Skordalia holds the heart of Greece. Nippy with the tang of crushed garlic, and more a paste than a sauce, this national comfort food is lavishly spread over fried fish, vegetables, or bread. Salt Cod Patties with Garlic Sauce (Bakaliaros Kefte Skordalia) and Batter-Fried Salt Cod with Skordalia (Bakaliaros Tighanitos me Skordalia) are fried salt cod dishes, both commonly served on the Greek Orthodox Church celebration of the Annunciation on March 25.

Fish roe is a characteristic food for Lent. *Botargo*, the roe of the red or grey mullet, *caviar*, that of the sturgeon, and *tarama*, the salted and aged roe of the cod or carp are all relished, especially during the season of religious fasts. Tarama is a basic ingredient of taramosalata, a favourite Greek meze traditionally eaten during Lent. Meze is a collective name (similar to the tapas of Spain) for a variety of small dishes, typically served with wines or anise-flavoured liqueurs such as ouzo or homemade tsipouro.

Grilling, roasting, baking, frying, and stewing are favourite Greek cooking methods. A large percentage of recipes from Greece are in the Fried Salt Cod section.

The art of Greek cooking of salt cod lies in keeping it simple by incorporating and celebrating the taste of ingredients in season and effective combinations of herbs and spices. Rarely is a plate of salt cod served without olives. The olive tree ("the tree that feeds the children," according to Sophocles) is integral to the traditions and culture of the Greek people. "I ate bread and olives with him," say the Greeks to denote good friendship.

Athena, the Greek goddess of peace and wisdom, won in a contest with Poseidon the honour of giving her name to the city, Athens. Her gift of the olive tree was deemed more valuable than Poseidon's gift of salt water.

Historical Factors

Although most of Italy's baccala now comes from Norway, the tradition of baccala has its roots in trade with the English and Portuguese. The markets, even in the first half of the nineteenth century, consisted of various city-states, many of which had connections with Newfoundland salt cod. In fact, the Italian city of Leghorn developed a preference for Labrador-cured salt cod.

Due to Italy's late unification (in 1861) and the historical autonomy of the regions of the Italian Peninsula, many food traditions and customs are strongly regional yet can be identified as Italian. Italy is known for pasta, pizza, lasagna, focaccia, espresso, gelato, granita, polenta, risotto, and more. Baccala does not obviously fit into this list, although it is popular and widely available. Salt cod does combine with well-known Italian dishes: Pan-Simmered Salt Cod with Fried Polenta and Whipped Creamy Salt Cod with Soft Polenta, for example. In Veneto, Salt Cod au Gratin with Anchovy Sauce (Baccala alla Vicentina), slowly cooked with onion, anchovies, and milk, is a beloved regional dish.

Breads are part of Italian salt cod soups. Grilled Salt Cod (Baccala alla Brace), a good example of regional Italian cuisine, is from the Puglia region (the "heel" of the Italian boot) and its simplicity represents the essence of home-based cuisine. Salt Cod with Sour Cherries, a recipe from a landmark publication in Italian cuisine (*Talismanodella Felicita*, originally published in 1928), is also renowned for its simplicity and superb blending of flavours. Traditionally, many baccala dishes were eaten on Fridays, when meat was forbidden for religious reasons, and today many are prepared for Christmas Eve dinners.

Ingredients

Salted anchovy fillets. (Photo by Valerie Sooley)

The environment and the climate, especially in southern Italy, ensure a supply of seasonal vegetables and an abundance of herbs. More than half of Italian salt cod salads use cooked salt cod with a citrus vinaigrette; the others use raw salt cod with either a marinade of olive oil, garlic, and basil, or a combination of thyme, marjoram, oregano, and oven-roasted tomatoes. All Italian recipes for salt cod in this collection use olive oil, one of the great products of the country.

Anchovies are abundant in the Mediterranean and are regularly caught off the coast of Sicily and used to give extra bite to many Italian salt cod dishes. In Venice, and elsewhere in Italy, small bars serve dishes of sardines in salt, marinated eggplants, anchovies, and Beaten Dried Cod (Baccala Mantecato), a creamy salt cod mixture served on grilled polenta or simple crostini.

Caribbean

National Dishes and Special Occasions

A number of Caribbean countries honour the importance of salt cod by including it in their national cuisine. Green Fig and Saltfish Pie in St. Lucia, Saltfish and Ackee in Jamaica, and Spicy Plantains and Breadfruit in St. Kitts and Nevis are examples. The first two recipes are included in this collection.

Annual salt cod cooking contests attest to the continued popularity of salt cod dishes. Two recipes from the Dominican Republic were winners in a 2009 national contest sponsored by Norge, the Norwegian marketing council for seafood and fish: Norwegian Salt Cod over Stew of Grapes (Bacalao Noruego Sobre Estofado de Uvas) and Salt Cod Fillets in Plantain Crust with Green Sauce (Lomo de Bacalao en Costra de Platano en Salsa Verde).

Salt cod figures prominently in the food eaten during many religious holidays, celebrations, and festivals in the Caribbean. A traditional dish served by Haitians for dinner on Good Friday is salt cod in sauce, accompanied by root vegetables, salad, white beans, and white rice. In St. Lucia, cod cakes are specialties for the Good Friday meal.

It is a tradition for some families in Bermuda, where traders often stopped en route to the Caribbean, to make cod cakes on Good Friday. This may be the only place in the world where cod cakes are eaten in a British-style sweet hot cross bun with a cod cake topped with a Bermudian twist of mayonnaise.

Ingredients

The Caribbean boasts ideal conditions for a large variety of fruits and vegetables, many of which combine with salt cod in popular dishes: ackee, avocado, bell pepper, breadfruit, cassava, coconut, okra, plantain, pumpkin, and yam. Scotch bonnet peppers, closely related to habanera peppers, are, for many, the defining flavour of Caribbean cooking, as in Salt Cod on Onions and Cucumber Slices from Guadeloupe. In Trinidad and Tobago, the chili pepper of choice is a congo chili, a pod-type pepper.

Soups, chowders, and stews often start with basic seasonings: green onions, coriander, parsley, chives, peppers, and chilies. Caribbean cooking makes full use of the proliferation of herbs and spices, often growing wild, in this tropical region. Curry and dumplings, two Caribbean favourites, combine in Curried Salt Cod and Dumplings from Antigua in which the dumplings are filled with curried salt cod. In other recipes, fried dumplings or "dumplins," known as "bakes" in Trinidad and Jamaica, are often served with salt cod. The use of curry reflects the East Indian influence in the Caribbean.

The directions for many of the recipes suggest the simple seasoning of salt cod, fruits, and vegetables with fresh citrus juices. Lemons and limes were brought from Spain by early explorers.

Caribbean salt cod recipes use a variety of oils: coconut, corn, palm, and vegetable oils. However, the French, Spanish, and Portuguese influences account for a fairly widespread use of olive oil as well.

A Triangle of Cuisines

For centuries Brazil was a colony of Portugal, during which time Brazilians learned much about the Portuguese tradition of eating dried salt cod. Early trading patterns also reinforced this tradition. The Portuguese sailed to the fishing banks off Newfoundland and packed the cod they caught and split in salt. They returned to Portugal to dry the cod, which was shipped to the Caribbean and Brazil.

Brazil's salt cod dishes were influenced by the cooking styles of the Amerindian (indigenous peoples of the Americas), the conquering Portuguese, and the African slaves the Portuguese brought to work in the sugar cane fields. This triangle of cuisines converged and blended, later encountering the cooking styles of immigrant homesteaders from Europe, Africa, the Middle East, and Asia.

The Amerindian diet was based on corn and cassava, supplemented with legumes and food obtained through hunting and fishing. Salt cod was a welcome addition. Hot peppers and potatoes were also available. The European influence accounted for the use of olive oil, wine, and wheat. Other foods associated with the Portuguese and Spanish conquerors of South America were tubers, bulbs, leafy vegetables, orchard fruits, legumes, and a variety of aromatic plants. Saffron and capers were used as condiments. The African diet contributed millet, sorghum, wild rice, legumes, fruits, vegetables, and palm oil.

Cassava root. (Photo by Valerie Sooley)

Ingredients

The recipes for moqueca (stew) are recognizably Brazilian with the heartiness of thick coconut milk and the authentic flavour of dende (palm) oil: Brazilian Fish Stew (Moqueca de Peixe) and Salt Cod with Coconut Milk (Bacalhau com Leite de Coco) are good examples.

Brazilians love *salgadinhos* (small salted things), eaten as snacks or as a prelude to a more substantial meal. Popular salgadinhos, Salt Cod Fritters are often served at parties and receptions, with drinks at bars, and at street vendor stalls. Brazilian-influenced appetizers make good use of herbs (parsley, bay leaf, mint, and coriander) and spices (paprika and piri piri).

Coconut half. (Photo by Jason Kearley)

Regional Influences

Brazil is a land of exciting contrasts. It is home to the Pantanal, the world's largest wetlands, the Amazon River and tropical rain forest, world famous beaches, and the Iguacu Falls. With such size and diversity, it is not surprising that Brazil has a collection of regional cuisines. Each of Brazil's five geographic regions (with a total of 26 states) offers distinctly different cuisines, some of which are featured in this book.

COOKING SALT COD

At Home

Salt cod, a luxury item where the tradition still holds, has a variety of names:

Basque country	bakailao
Brazil	bacalhau
Canada	salt cod
Caribbean	buljol/saltfish
Catalonia	bacalla
Finland	salt torska
France	morue
Iceland	saltfiskur
Italy	baccala
Malta	bakkaljaw
Portugal	bacalhau
Scandinavia	klippfisk/clipfish
Spain	bacalao

Yet let me tell you, Sir, what I love best
Its a *Poore John* thats cleane, and neatly drest:
There's not a meat found in the Land, or Seas,
Can Stomacks better please, or lesse displease.
—Robert Hayman, 1628[56]

An appreciation of and eventual love for salt cod did not come easily to me. As a child in the 1940s I watched my father wrap salt cod in brown paper and roast it in glowing wood embers in the kitchen stove. On those Sunday mornings, I picked over my breakfast rather carefully. It was later, while eating cod cakes and fish and brewis as an adolescent, that I developed a taste for salt cod. That density, texture, and flavour now draw me to salt cod with increasing enthusiasm.

Salt curing changes the texture and taste of cod. The firm texture and rich flavour of salt cod lends itself to a wide variety of dishes and successful combinations with a global array of ingredients. Whether coupled with Spanish chorizo and fresh tomatoes or served as zippy Jamaican Stamp and Go fritters, salt cod inspires cooks around the world. It goes with butter and cream as well as olive oil, lemon, herbs, tomatoes, garlic, or combinations of them all; it lends itself to soups, chowders, and stews; it can be broiled, boiled, roasted, deep-fried, sautéed, baked, or steamed. It can be served any time of the day.

Various cuts of salt cod. (Photo by Valerie Sooley)

SALT COD CUISINE: THE INTERNATIONAL TABLE

Cuts of Salt Cod

Many cooks traditionally preferred large fillets of salt cod, containing bones and skin, which are removed either after the fish is soaked or cooked, or not at all. Some argue that the skin and bones enhance the taste of the salt cod.

Different cuts of salt cod can vary in flavour. Fillets or pieces of cod can be bought separately at the fish market or made by cutting a full split salt cod. Depending on its size, a cod can be cut to the preferred size, or that required in a recipe, by slicing across its width. Alternatively, the cod can be cut down the backbone (or to one side of the backbone) to the tail and the lengths cut across. Sometimes thin belly pieces are sold separately, as are the vens.[57]

Boned and skinned salt cod fillets are also available, packed in wooden boxes or on plastic-wrapped food trays. Some recipes in this book call for these prepared fillets or steaks. Salt cod can also be flaked or shredded (known as *megas* in Portugal) before being watered. These strips or pieces are usually sold in 1-pound (454-gram) packages; however, you may flake or shred the cod yourself.

Watering Salt Cod

For most salt cod recipes, the cod needs to be watered. Advance planning is required to remove a sufficient amount of salt before mealtime. There are exceptions: some salads require raw salt cod, others marinated cod, and others cod that is merely rinsed. Steps for watering salt cod are outlined below; however, it is important to note:

> There is no general agreement on how to resuscitate stockfish or saltfish. No two pieces of cured cod are of the exact same thickness, dryness, or saltiness, and furthermore, different people prefer different tastes, often depending on the type of dish being made.... Most cooks agree that the only way to know when a cured fish

---

The terms *watered* or *watering* are used in the recipes in this book. Chefs and others writing about salt cod employ a variety of terms:

bathed
desalinated
desalted
fluffed up
flushed
freshened
leached
plumped
reconstituted
rehydrated
resuscitated
revitalized
soaked
softened
sweetened
tempered

is ready for cooking is to break off a piece and taste it. The more it has been dried, the longer it must be soaked.[58]

To water salt cod:
1. Rinse off any surface salt.
2. Place the salt cod in a glass, crockery, or earthenware dish; an enamel or stainless steel pot; or a plastic bucket or washbasin. If more than 3 pounds of salt cod are being watered, use more than one bowl.
3. Cover with cold water to at least 2 inches (5 centimetres) over the top of the fish or up to twice the thickness of the fish. The larger the soaking area, the more water that is needed to absorb the salt and hasten the process. If the salt cod is to be cooked, experiment by adding milk, white wine vinegar, lemon, or herbs to the water for the final soak.
4. Soak the salt cod for approximately 10-12 hours, or longer if the pieces are big, thick, and heavily salted. Degrees of saltiness vary from batch to batch; use your own judgment. Sometimes the packaging bag or box contains recommendations.
5. Water salt cod in a place that is neither too cold nor too warm. Preferably, small amounts can be watered in the refrigerator, where the desalting will take longer and the water will have to be changed more often. If the salt cod is soaked in a warm place, the water can become syrupy and acquire an unpleasant odour. Rehydrated cod can be delicate; use great care when soaking or it will flake around the edges.
6. After a certain period of soaking, the liquid is saturated with salt; you will need to change the water at least once. Frequent changes of water hasten the watering process.
7. Near the end of the soaking period, taste a small piece from the inside of the fish: it should be a little salty but sweet, with a chewy consistency and a mildly fishy aroma. If it is too salty, change the water and continue to soak. There is a fine line between removing too much and not enough salt. If the fish is over-soaked, flavour is lost. Only through tasting and experience can you tell when the fish is ready.

You may also want to look for frozen, ready-to-cook bacalhau—cod that has been salted and dried, then soaked, prepared like traditional bacalhau, and frozen—which accounts for an increasing percentage of the market. Watered salt cod that has been vacuum packed and frozen is also available in some markets.

I am often asked if it is better to water the salt cod skin side up or down. My polling indicates a slight preference for skin side up. It probably does not matter. However, one acquaintance recommends skin side down for the first watering and, with a change of water, skin side up. This ensures remembering if the water has been changed. Chefe Silva, author of *Bacalhau a Portuguesa*, however, advocates that bacalhau be soaked with the skin facing down.

Cooking Tips

Unlike land-based animals, cod do not support their own weight as they move—the water does that. As their muscles are not required to exert such large forces, they are generally weaker. The proteins in cod muscles, unlike those in mammals, are not arranged in long fibres running right through the muscle but are organized into short bundles joined by delicate membranes. These "muscle fibers are arranged in sheets a fraction of an inch thick" and "[t]here are about 50 muscle sheets or 'flakes' along the length of a cod."[59]

As Peter Barnham explains in *The Science of Cooking*, the lack of tough connective tissue in cod muscles affects its cooking time: cod does not need to be cooked for long periods to tenderize. Cooked cod falls apart as the tissue between the muscle fibres is destroyed by heating.[60]

Adding Flavour

Salt cod cooks fairly quickly. Any seasonings or flavour must be added to the cooking liquid before the cod. For example, a bouquet garni should be simmered in water before adding the salt cod. The same principle applies to sautéing ingredients (such as onion and garlic) before adding salt cod to the frying pan or grill plate; if the salt cod is marinated for 20 minutes, it will have absorbed the flavour of the marinade before the cooking process.

Methods of Cooking

Cooking salt cod is easy; overcooking is probably easier. The following methods are used in this book to prepare salt cod and are listed in the order of increasing likelihood of overcooking.

Steaming

Steamed salt cod is cooked entirely in an atmosphere of steam, normally using a special fish kettle. Water is boiled at the bottom of the steamer, while the cod sits on a perforated platform or basket above the water. In steaming, the temperature never rises above 212°F (100°C), so there is no risk of burning, and the cod is kept moist. Sprigs of herbs may be placed under and over the salt cod in the steamer basket.

Poaching

Salt cod is poached partially in water and partially in steam in a pan with a tight-fitting cover. Usually it is placed on a bed of vegetables or greens and water or stock is added to cover the vegetables. The liquid is kept simmering. The pan is either heated in the oven or on the stovetop.

Salt cod is poached before being made into brandade. (Photo by Valerie Sooley)

Simmering

It is easy to be misled by the expression *boiling fish*. It is hardly ever appropriate to boil salt cod; *simmer* can almost always be substituted for *boil* in directions for cooking salt cod. To simmer is to cook a food slowly and steadily in a sauce or other liquid over a gentle heat, just below boiling point, so the surface of the liquid bubbles occasionally. In general, simmer salt cod for 10-20 minutes, depending on the thickness, until it flakes easily with a fork.

Sautéing

Sautéing in oil enables the outside of the cod to get hot enough for chemical reactions to occur and develop flavour. However, care must be taken to ensure that it does not develop a burnt taste. Dredging the salt cod in flour or other coating reduces the risk of burning. Using olive oil instead of butter (which burns at a lower temperature than saturated oils) also reduces this risk.

Deep-Frying

Deep-frying often suffers from poor implementation. The basic idea is to coat watered pieces of salt cod with a thick, almost solid batter, which will cook quickly in hot oil and seal in the moisture. The cod then steams in its own juices, as the outside becomes crisp and brown.

If the oil is not hot enough, some is absorbed by the food, resulting in greasy cod. As well, the outside does not become crisp or it takes too long to do so, forming a thick, hard, and greasy crust. A break in the batter allows hot oil to penetrate into the cod and steam from the cod's juices to escape, giving overcooked, dried-out cod.

For successful deep-frying, the pan should be no more than one-third full with cold oil; the level increases when ingredients are added and the oil bubbles up and spits. The

Deep-fried salt cod puffs. (Photo by Valerie Sooley)

proper oil is essential for good results and safe cooking. Individual recipes often recommend particular oils; in general, it is best to select oil with a high smoke point and preferably one that is light in colour, such as safflower, sunflower, canola, or corn oil. Cut the pieces of salt cod evenly so they cook at the same rate. Add the salt cod to the oil in modest batches so the temperature is not lowered too much.

To achieve a thick batter, use equal weights of liquid and flour. The liquid can be milk, water, or beer, depending on taste. To ensure that the batter sets easily, use beaten egg in the batter. Leave the batter to thicken for an hour or so, as the starch in the flour absorbs the liquid. The salt cod should then be completely immersed in the batter, removed, and left on a dry, lightly floured surface for a few minutes to allow the batter to set further before putting it into the hot oil.

Baking

Baking involves cooking the salt cod, often accompanied by vegetables, in a deep pan at a moderate oven temperature of 350°F (180°C). The steam that rises from the cod and vegetables remains above and around the cod as it cooks, helping to reduce the overall loss of water from the cod. Salt cod can also be securely wrapped in parchment paper and baked.

Oven Roasting

The salt cod is generally put directly on a shallow pan or on a rack over a shallow pan before exposing it to a 450°F (230°C) oven. When cooked properly, the cod skin will crisp up, providing a good combination of textures from the crisp outer layer to the moist and tender flesh inside. As the risk of overcooking is great, this method needs plenty of practice.

Roasted/baked salt cod with potatoes. (Photo by Valerie Sooley)

Open Fire Roasting

Many variations of this method of cooking salt cod are found in the Celebrating Salt Cod Outdoors section and include roasting in the glowing embers of an outdoor fire, roasting in a wood-burning stove, grilling over coals, toasting with tongs in an open flame, and plank grilling.

Grilling

Grilling is a fast way to cook salt cod; it requires much practice to master. In a well-grilled piece of cod, the high heat at the surface activates the chemical reactions that generate flavour, while the speed of cooking prevents the middle from becoming hot enough to damage the delicate texture of the cod. Ideally the grill will be powerful and the salt cod cooked for just a few minutes. If the grill is less powerful or if the cod is left for more than a minute or two, the denaturing of the muscle proteins and the removal of moisture will lead to a dry and sometimes tough product.

Plank-grilled salt cod on a barbecue. (Photo by Jason Kearley)

Notes on Recipes

Pinch and Dash

Several of the recipes in this book use such measures as pinch or dash. These are less precise measures than gram or teaspoon, but they do have advantages. Pinches will obviously vary from hand to hand but this very inexactness requires close attention to the character of each ingredient and adjusting recipes accordingly. Ingredients vary in weight, volume, and consistency, and the amount of salt in a teaspoon varies from salt to salt.

Most recipes suggest adding salt, pepper, and hot pepper sauce to taste, requiring users to get to know their preferences and their food by touching, smelling, and tasting it.

Weight, Volume, and Temperature

The recipes in this book use ounces (oz) and pounds (lb) as primary weight measures, and teaspoons (tsp), tablespoons (tbsp), cups (cup), and quarts (qt) as primary measures of volume. All recipes also include metric equivalents since in Canada weight is measured in grams (g) and kilograms (kg), and volume in millilitres (ml) and litres (L). Temperatures are given first in Fahrenheit (°F) and then Celsius (°C).

"In days gone by the handiest measuring utensil in the kitchen was the palm of the hand, and often, if you borrowed a recipe, the list of ingredients would include 'a dash of this' and 'a smidgen of that' or 'enough to taste,' and somehow the amounts and the methods were always foolproof."[61]

PART 2

Recipes

Whole salt cod.

CELEBRATING OUTDOORS ... 91
- Roasted over the Embers
- Grilled

SALADS ... 105
- Uncooked
- Marinated
- Scalded
- Simmered
- Grilled

TAPAS AND MEZES ... 125

HORS D'OEUVRES ... 139
- Brandade, Spreads, Dips
- Croquettes, Cakes, Patties, Puffs
- Dumplings

SOUPS AND CHOWDERS ... 161

STEWS AND RAGOUTS ... 175

BOILED SALT COD DINNERS ... 193

SIMMERED DISHES ... 205

FRIED DISHES ... 221
- Sautéed
- Battered
- Deep-Fried

BAKED DISHES ... 233
- Soufflés
- Au Gratin Style
- Baked in Other Sauces
- Vol-au-Vents, Pies, Tartlets
- Oven Roasted

PUDDINGS ... 259
- Salt Cod Puddings
- Salt Cod Loaf
- Burial of the Cod

STOVETOP VARIATIONS ... 267
- Hash
- Fish and Brewis
- Scrambled

OTHER SALT COD PARTS ... 277
- Heads
- Tongues, Cheeks
- Sounds
- Roe, Liver
- Vens, Bellies, Tails

STOCK AND SAUCES ... 295

Boiling the kettle over an open fire.

CELEBRATING OUTDOORS

Roasting in the glowing embers of an outdoor wood fire or in a wood-burning stove, toasting with tongs in an open flame, and grilling over coals, on a plank, or on a barbecue are all ideal methods of cooking salt cod outdoors.

    The recipes in this section are perfect for a gathering in the back garden, a day at the beach, a reunion, or a come-home celebration. They could be the centrepieces for a festival in celebration of the salt cod or a cook-off. All use few ingredients, are easy to prepare, and allow experimentation. If you have time, I suggest reading this entire section first—ideas from one recipe may help in the preparation of another.

ROASTED OVER THE EMBERS

Martinmas Cod (Bacalhau de S. Martinho)	*Portugal*
Roasted Scrod on a Wood Fire	*Newfoundland and Labrador*
Fishermen's Roasted Cod (Bacalhau Assado dos Pescadores da Tocha)	*Portugal*
Salt Cod over Embers (Bacalhau no Borralho)	*Portugal*

GRILLED

Salt Cod Grilled over Coals (Bacalhau Assado na Brasa)	*Portugal*
Grilled Salt Cod with Milk and Olive Oil	*Newfoundland and Labrador*
Grilled Salt Cod with Olive Oil and White Wine Vinegar	*Portugal*
Grilled Salt Cod in Coriander Dressing (Bacalhau Grelhado com Coentros)	*Portugal*
Grilled Salt Cod (Baccala alla Brace)	*Puglia, Italy*
Grilled Salt Cod with Punched Potatoes (Bacalhau Assado com Batatas a Murro)	*Portugal*
Salt Cod Burgers	*Newfoundland and Labrador*
Planked Salt Cod with an Open Fire	*Newfoundland and Labrador*
Plank-Grilled Salt Cod on the Barbecue	*Newfoundland and Labrador*

roasted over the embers

Martinmas Cod (Bacalhau de S. Martinho)

Portugal

This dish is for those who like chestnuts, new wine, good deeds, and salt cod. The good deeds are associated with St. Martin, a Roman soldier who was buried in Tours, France, on November 11, A.D. 387. St. Martin is celebrated with agricultural fairs, feasts, festivals, and the tasting of new regional wines throughout parts of Europe. In Madeira, Portugal, Bacalhau de S. Martinho is sometimes served for supper on November 11 (Martinmas), accompanied by new wine and bread. Cooked chestnuts flavoured with aniseed and figs stuffed with walnuts are eaten after the meal.

Aguardente de cana is a Brazilian alcohol, similar to rum, made from sugar cane.

2 salt cod steaks

4 garlic cloves, crushed

Olive oil

White vinegar

Alcohol for toasting (*aguardente de cana* if possible), or the glowing embers of an outdoor wood fire

1. Wash steaks several times in running water. Soak in water for 30 minutes or simmer for a few minutes to remove more salt. Rub dry.
2. Rub garlic on both sides of the steaks.
3. Lift steaks with long toasting tongs or a fork. Light alcohol or an outdoor wood fire; toast steaks on both sides.
4. Break steaks by hand into a bowl; season with olive oil and vinegar.

Adapted from Maria de Lourdes Modesto, *Traditional Portuguese Cooking*

SERVES 4

Whole chestnuts.

CELEBRATING OUTDOORS

Roasted Scrod on a Wood Fire

Newfoundland and Labrador

Scrod are small cod split, corned, and partly dried. They are of little market value because of their size and are mainly prepared for use at home in the early part of summer. Scrod, rounders, and larger pieces of salt cod can be roasted in an open wood fire or in a wood stove. They can also be wrapped in brown paper, as in this recipe, and put in the fire of a wood-burning kitchen stove—a traditional way of cooking salt cod in Newfoundland and Labrador.

Fire-roasted salt cod with hot tea, homemade bread, and fresh butter is perfect for any meal or a mug-up in the woods.

> What could one ask for more than to build a fire by a stream amongst the rocks, suspend the tin kettle on a stick over the blaze, and roast dried caplin, or a rounder?
>
> —*DNE*, s.v. "rounder"

1. Use watered salt cod (page 80) or, in the case of scrod, watered in cold water for 5-6 hours. Drain and wipe dry.
2. Wrap cod in 3 or 4 layers of brown paper; fold edges firmly.
3. Wait for the embers to burn down. Place the package on the fire or in the stove and pull some embers around and over it.
4. Remove cod from the fire when the paper is completely charred. Peel off the paper to reveal the golden brown and moist contents.
5. Rinse cod in hot water, or give it a quick dip in the "stream amongst the rocks."
6. Serve cod in any manner desired.

Scrod.

Cod steak wrapped in brown paper.

Paper being peeled off roasted cod.

SALT COD CUISINE: THE INTERNATIONAL TABLE

Fishermen's Roasted Cod (Bacalhau Assado dos Pescadores da Tocha)

Portugal

It is best to prepare the sauce at home before going to the beach. Combine the ingredients in a container to bring with you. The salt cod is roasted over the glowing embers of an open fire, while the potatoes cook, covered with hot rocks and sand. Get ready for a culinary experience of the finest order.

4 x 7 oz (200 g) salt cod steaks

8 medium potatoes, preferably new russets

Coarse salt

1 red onion, thinly sliced, for garnish

SAUCE

1 1/2 cups (375 ml) olive oil

3 garlic cloves, finely chopped

1 tsp (5 ml) sweet paprika

Freshly ground black pepper

1. Use watered salt cod (page 80). Drain and dry.
2. Prepare a wood fire on a sandy and pebbly beach and let it burn until the sand is hot. Wait until the fire burns down, then moisten potatoes, dip them into coarse salt, and slightly bury them in the sand at the bottom of the fire. Rekindle the fire. Let it burn for approximately 30 minutes.
3. Spread the burning embers. Use a wire rack or long toasting tongs to roast the pieces of cod directly over the embers.
4. Heat sauce slowly in a small saucepan by the fire.
5. Remove potatoes carefully and break them open. Serve with cod and sauce. Garnish with slices of onion.

Adapted from Chefe Silva, *Bacalhau a Portuguesa*

SERVES 4

Roasted potatoes with coarse salt.

CELEBRATING OUTDOORS

Salt Cod over Embers (Bacalhau no Borralho)

Portugal

Slices of bacon, cabbage leaves, and parchment paper protect salt cod cooked in the final glowing embers of an outdoor wood fire. The bacon slices could be either smoked or fresh and the leaves green cabbage, Savoy cabbage, kale, or collards. Thin slices of salt pork instead of bacon would also offer good protection and flavour.

4 thick salt cod steaks

4 bacon slices

4 or 8 cabbage leaves, depending on size

1 cup (250 ml) olive oil

6-8 potatoes, boiled, unpeeled

1 lb (450 g) turnip greens or spinach, boiled or steamed

Crusty bread

1 red onion, thinly sliced, for garnish

1. Use watered salt cod (page 80). Drain.
2. Wrap steaks with slices of bacon and then with cabbage leaves. Tie with kitchen twine. Wrap with parchment paper.
3. Cover cod packages completely with the glowing embers. Remove when cod begins to sizzle.
4. Remove paper, cabbage leaves, and bacon; place steaks in serving dish and pour olive oil over top.
5. Serve with potatoes, greens, and chunks of crusty bread. Garnish with slices of onion.

Adapted from Maria de Lourdes Modesto,
Traditional Portuguese Cooking

SERVES 4

Salt Cod Grilled over Coals (Bacalhau Assado na Brasa)

Portugal

I first made this dish, using a camp stove, in 1991. It was an early morning breakfast for a party of four by the side of Shoal Harbour River, Newfoundland—and exactly what we needed after a night of revelry and before a 9 a.m. workshop.

4 skinless salt cod steaks

2 1/2 cups (625 ml) milk

4 potatoes

Salt and freshly ground black pepper

4 onions, divided

1 bay leaf

2 sprigs fresh parsley, divided

3 garlic cloves, chopped

1 cup (250 ml) olive oil

20 black olives, for garnish

1. Use watered salt cod (page 80). Put cod in milk, bring to a boil, and simmer 2 minutes. Discard milk and wash cod thoroughly in cold water. Set aside.
2. Boil potatoes in their jackets in salted water. Set aside.
3. Heat a saucepan of water containing salt and pepper, 1 onion (halved), 1 bay leaf, and 1 sprig of parsley. Keep warm.
4. Slice remaining onions. Heat olive oil in another saucepan; add sliced onions, garlic, and remaining parsley. Cook gently.
5. Grill steaks over charcoal, taking care not to burn them.
6. Place grilled steaks in the saucepan containing the hot water and simmer 3 minutes. Drain. Transfer to the saucepan containing olive oil and simmer 10 minutes, turning once.
7. Peel and slice potatoes and spread on 4 plates. Place cod on top of potatoes and cover with the onion sauce used to simmer the steaks. Garnish with olives.

Adapted from Maria de Lourdes Modesto, *Traditional Portuguese Cooking*

SERVES 4

CELEBRATING OUTDOORS

Grilled Salt Cod with Milk and Olive Oil

Newfoundland and Labrador

4 x 6 oz (170 g) salt cod steaks, skin on

Vegetable or olive oil

Milk

4 garlic cloves, chopped

Fine bread crumbs

1/4 cup (60 ml) olive oil

6 medium potatoes, peeled

1. Use watered salt cod (page 80). Drain. Marinate with equal amounts of oil and milk for 5-6 hours in a cool place.
2. Coat steaks with bread crumbs. Slowly grill over coals.
3. Boil potatoes; halve.
4. Heat 1/4 cup (60 ml) olive oil. Add garlic and let brown just a little.
5. Serve grilled steaks and boiled potatoes drizzled with the browned garlic and olive oil.

SERVES 4

Grilled Salt Cod with Olive Oil and White Wine Vinegar

Portugal

Salt cod is grilled in practically all regions of Portugal. The grilling is basic, but the dressings differ slightly. In this recipe from the Alentejo region, the dressing is a simple combination of olive oil and white wine vinegar; in the next recipe, fresh coriander is added.

The watered salt cod is grilled on a grill plate on the barbecue. Use thick pieces of salt cod if possible, as the flakes are bigger and more succulent.

4 x 6 oz (170 g) thick pieces salt cod, skin on

Extra-virgin olive oil

White wine vinegar

1. Use watered salt cod (page 80). Drain and pat dry.
2. Lightly brush cod with olive oil and put it flesh side down on the grill plate for 4 minutes. Turn; continue to cook for 4-5 minutes.
3. Place on 4 serving plates; drizzle with olive oil and vinegar to taste.

Adapted from Mitchell Tonks, *The Fishmonger's Cookbook*

SERVES 4

Grilled Salt Cod in Coriander Dressing (Bacalhau Grelhado com Coentros)

Portugal

4 x 6 oz (170 g) salt cod steaks

1/2 cup (125 ml) fresh coriander, chopped

DRESSING

1/2 cup (125 ml) olive oil

3 tbsp (45 ml) white wine vinegar

2 garlic cloves, chopped

1/2 tsp (2.5 ml) white sugar

1/2 tsp (2.5 ml) sambal oelek or other chili paste

Freshly ground black pepper

1. Use watered salt cod (page 80). Drain and pat dry.
2. Whisk together dressing ingredients.
3. Grill steaks over hot coals. Turn often and baste with half the dressing.
4. Take steaks from the grill. Remove bones and shred coarsely.
5. Place cod in a serving bowl. Sprinkle coriander and spoon remaining dressing over cod. Toss to blend.

Adapted from Carla Azevedo, *Uma Casa Portuguesa*

SERVES 4

Grilled Salt Cod (Baccala alla Brace)

Puglia, Italy

In 1953, a group of people came together in Milan with the bold idea to preserve the culinary heritage of their country. They founded Accademia Italiana della Cucina (Italian Academy of Cuisine), an organization of over 7,600 members. Over the decades, academy members swept across the countryside, visiting villages in every province to record the classic recipes, techniques, and ingredients of regional cooking. *La Cucina* contains more than 2,000 of these recipes, of which about 20, including Baccala alla Brace, are for salt cod.

2 lb (900 g) salt cod

MARINADE

5 tbsp (75 ml) extra-virgin olive oil

2 tbsp (30 ml) white wine vinegar

2 tbsp (30 ml) fresh parsley, chopped

Salt and freshly ground black pepper

1. Use watered salt cod (page 80). Divide cod into 8 pieces; remove skin.
2. Combine marinade ingredients.
3. Add cod; marinate 2-3 hours.
4. Grill over the coals, turning cod from time to time, and brush with marinade. Serve hot.

Adapted from Accademia Italiana della Cucina, *La Cucina*

SERVES 4

Grilled Salt Cod with Punched Potatoes (Bacalhau Assado com Batatas a Murro)

Portugal

Punch the potatoes with your hand when they are about half cooked. The potatoes will be slightly broken—not pulverized—and seasoned with coarse salt. Be careful when breaking the potatoes that the hot coarse salt does not burn your hands and wrists.

4 x 6 oz (170 g) salt cod pieces

4 baking potatoes of similar size

Coarse salt

1 cup (250 ml) olive oil

3 garlic cloves, thinly sliced

Freshly ground black pepper

VARIATION

- Use rosemary to season the punched potatoes.

1. Use watered salt cod (page 80). Drain well.
2. Wash potatoes, blot dry, and roll in coarse salt. Bake on the barbecue or charcoal grill at 400°F (200°C) until about half cooked.
3. Give potatoes a blow with the hand to squash them a little, until their skins split open in the middle. Sprinkle more salt on them and return to the grill until fully baked.
4. Grill cod about 10 minutes per 1 inch (2.5 cm) thickness, or until cod browns and a knife inserted in the centre is warm to the touch.
5. Heat olive oil in a small frying pan over low heat until it shimmers. Add pepper and garlic; cook until garlic is golden and oil infused with garlic flavour.
6. Flake cod and place in olive oil.
7. Serve cod with punched potatoes in their skins. Add pepper to taste; drizzle potatoes with remaining garlic oil.

SERVES 4

Punched potatoes with coarse salt.

Salt Cod Burger

SALT COD CUISINE: THE INTERNATIONAL TABLE

CELEBRATING OUTDOORS

Salt Cod Burgers

Newfoundland and Labrador

These salt cod patties are barbecued outdoors or pan-fried or grilled to a golden brown indoors. Be creative in the use of condiments. Spread the bottom half of the bun with mayonnaise, or a mixture of garlic mayonnaise and sweet pickle relish, or use partridgeberry mayonnaise (page 302). On the top half of the burger, try sweet red pepper jam or red currant jelly. When I last made these burgers, I used whatever happened to be in the refrigerator: garlic mayonnaise, peach chutney, and smoky peach chipotle sauce. I had hoped to find quince jelly or rhubarb chutney.

This recipe can be shaped into full-sized burgers or mini burgers for hors d'oeuvres.

12 oz (340 g) salt cod

3 tbsp (45 ml) olive oil, more if pan-frying

3/4 cup (185 ml) all-purpose flour

1 large egg

1/2 tsp (2.5 ml) dried savoury

2 tbsp (30 ml) fresh parsley, finely chopped

1 garlic clove, finely grated

3 tbsp (45 ml) shallots, finely chopped

1 egg white

TO SERVE

4–6 burger buns or 8–10 mini buns

1/2 cup (125 ml) mayonnaise (page 302)

1/4 cup (60 ml) sweet pickle relish

2 medium tomatoes, thinly sliced

Lettuce, a few leaves

Sweet red pepper jam

1. Use watered salt cod (page 80). Simmer gently, covered, until cod is tender, about 15 minutes. Reserve 1/4 cup (60 ml) cooking water. Drain cod; remove any skin and bones. Finely shred cod.
2. Mix olive oil, flour, egg, savoury, parsley, garlic, shallots, and some reserved cooking liquid in a bowl until smooth. Stir in cooked cod. Add extra water if batter is too thick.
3. Beat egg white to soft peaks and fold into cod mixture. Shape into the desired number of patties.
4. Grill for about 4-5 minutes per side, until lightly browned.
5. Mix mayonnaise and relish in a small bowl. Prepare buns and condiments.
6. Spread the bottom part of the buns with the mayonnaise mixture. Layer on lettuce, tomato, and patties. Dollop patties with a small amount of red pepper jam; crown with the tops of the buns.

VARIATION

- Serve your favourite cod cake recipe (pages 146-158) as salt cod burgers.

SERVES 4

Planked Salt Cod with an Open Fire

Newfoundland and Labrador

In Newfoundland and Labrador, salmon is the fish of choice to be smoked; however, trout, herring, and mackerel are also smoked. A smoked fish tradition in Newfoundland dates back to the Beothuk, who inhabited the island at the time of its discovery by Europeans in 1497. The Beothuk were hunters, gatherers, and fishers who moved seasonally in order to harvest coastal and inland resources.

I first saw this type of plank model used in Sop's Arm, Newfoundland. More basic techniques are detailed in the next recipe. Improvise as necessary.

This drawing represents a fishing boat, a symbol of Beothuk mythology, as drawn by Shanawdithit, the last of the Beothuks, who died in 1829.

PREPARE THE PLANK

- Screw pieces of board (cedar, maple, etc.) onto 2 pieces of strapping that extend 4 inches (10 cm) on each side of the board (see photo next page). The plank in the photo is 15 inches (38 cm) wide and 21 inches (53 cm) high.
- The strapping is used as cleats against which to place adjustable shores at least 36 inches (90 cm) long to hold the plank near the fire.
- Before using, soak the plank for 30 minutes to help prevent burning.

PREPARE THE SALT COD

- Use any pieces of watered salt cod (page 80) with the skin on. Whole fillets are preferable.
- Use corned cod or traditionally salted and dried cod.
- Marinate cod, if desired.

SECURE THE SALT COD TO THE PLANK

- Space the cod (skin side down) on the plank.
- Drive finishing nails at 2-inch (5 cm) intervals around each piece of cod and lace very small stainless steel wire around the nails and over the cod.

BUILD THE FIRE

- Beach rocks by the ocean offer a secure place to build a fire.
- Stand the plank with the cod on it upright or possibly tilted forward or backward, depending on the heat. Use the prevailing wind to help the heat radiate toward the plank and cause the flames to flick by.

CELEBRATING OUTDOORS

Back of plank.   Front of plank.   Salt cod on the plank.   Lighting the fire.   Salt cod on plank by fire.

COOK THE SALT COD

- Baste cod periodically with your favourite herbs, spices, and/or sauce, if desired.
- Carefully remove cod to a plate when it flakes easily with a fork.

SERVE THE SALT COD

- Serve the salt cod alone or with any of the accompaniments used in this section: oil and vinegar, roasted punched potatoes, onions, black olives, coriander, parsley, or turnip greens.
- With the beach as your table, enjoy.

Salt cod on beach rock table.

SALT COD CUISINE: THE INTERNATIONAL TABLE

Plank-Grilled Salt Cod on the Barbecue

Newfoundland and Labrador

Here's a quick guide to planking salt cod. Untreated cedar is the most popular wood for the plank; alder, oak, maple, or cherry are also suitable.

PRE-SOAK THE PLANK

- Submerge the plank in warm water for at least 4-6 hours (overnight is ideal).
- Add white wine, apple cider, beer, or fresh herbs to the soaking water to infuse different flavours.

PREPARE THE PLANK

- Dry the plank a little on the top; lightly coat the top surface with olive oil or a flavoured oil.
- Rub the plank with salt, pepper, and garlic.
- Preheat the barbecue grill on high for 5 minutes with the lid closed. Adjust the grill to medium heat; preheat plank for 5 minutes. It will begin to crackle and smoke.

PREPARE THE SALT COD

- Choose salt cod steaks of about equal size and thickness, one per person.
- Use watered steaks (page 80), preferably with the skin on. Drain and pat dry. The steaks can be marinated, if desired.

COOK THE SALT COD

- Place steaks, skin side down, on the plank.
- Keep grill cover closed as much as possible to maintain temperature and maximize smoking. Planked food does not have to be turned during cooking.
- Baste steaks with your favourite spices, herbs, or prepared sauce after 6-8 minutes.
- Close lid and continue to cook until the cod flakes easily with a fork. Carefully remove from the hot plank to a platter and serve.

Caution: Keep a spray bottle filled with water nearby so that flames can be extinguished if the plank starts to burn. Use just enough water to extinguish the flames; you do not want the plank to stop smouldering. Make sure the plank is completely extinguished before discarding it.

Plank-Grilled Salt Cod on the Barbecue

SALADS

These salads are arranged by method used to prepare the salt cod. Some recipes require that the salt cod be used uncooked, others marinated, scalded, simmered, or grilled. All dishes are extremely colourful with combinations of fruits and vegetables: oranges, black and green olives, avocados, lemons, limes, onions, leeks, chives, salad greens, cucumbers, carrots, tomatoes, green peas, chickpeas, green beans, and red, yellow, and green peppers. Other additions include anchovies, eggs, pine nuts, hazelnuts, almonds, and raisins. There are salads for a variety of festive tables and ample choice for Christmas Eve.

UNCOOKED

Saltfish Salad	*Anguilla*
Shredded Raw Cod (Bacalhau Cru Desfiado)	*Portugal*
Raw Cod with Onions and Sauce (Bacalhau Rapido)	*Portugal*
Salt Cod Carpaccio with Oven-Roasted Tomatoes and Herbs	*Italy*
Shredded Salt Cod with Tomatoes and Olives (Esqueixada de Bacalao)	*Spain*

MARINATED

Catalan Salt Cod and Sweet Pepper Salad (Esqueixada)	*Spain*
Salt Cod Carpaccio with Lemon Juice and Olive Oil	*Italy*
Shredded Salt Cod Salad (Chiquetaille de Morue)	*Haiti*

SCALDED

Salt Cod Salad (Buljol)	*Trinidad*
Salt Cod on Onions and Cucumber Slices	*Guadeloupe*

SIMMERED

Salt Cod and Cauliflower Salad (Insalata Fredda di Baccala e Cavolfiore)	*Italy*
Warm Salt Cod Salad with Oranges	*Spain*
Salt Cod Salad with Small New Potatoes	*Portugal*
Salt Cod with Olive Salad (Baccala con Olive)	*Italy*
Salad of Salt Cod with Oranges (Ensalada de Bacalao con Naranja)	*Basque Country*
Orange, Red Onion, Black Olive, and Salt Cod Salad	*Spain*
Salt Cod, Red Pepper, and Potato Salad	*Spain*
Salt Cod Salad with Olives and Avocado (Serenata de Bacalao)	*Puerto Rico*
Salt Cod Salad with Aioli	*France*

GRILLED

Salt Cod Salad with Beans	*Spain*

uncooked

Saltfish Salad

Anguilla

In this classic Anguillan version practically all traces of salt are removed through watering, pressing, and drying the cod. It is sometimes served as a traditional breakfast.

- 1/2 lb (225 g) salt cod
- 1 green bell pepper, chopped
- 1 red bell pepper, chopped
- 1/4 hot chili pepper, finely chopped
- 2 medium onions, finely chopped
- 3 tbsp (45 ml) olive oil
- 2 tbsp (30 ml) freshly squeezed lemon juice
- 3 tomatoes, cut in wedges
- 4 hard-boiled eggs, quartered
- 1 medium avocado, sliced, for garnish
- Lettuce, shredded, for garnish

1. Water salt cod in fresh water for two 2-hour intervals, squeezing out water each time. Remove any skin and bones, flake cod, water once more for 20 minutes; drain and squeeze dry.
2. Place cod in a bowl and mix in red and green peppers, chili pepper, and onions.
3. Stir in oil and lemon juice; toss to combine.
4. Mound cod mixture in the centre of a slightly chilled serving dish. Alternate tomato wedges and eggs around the outside of the dish.
5. Garnish with avocado slices and shredded lettuce.

SERVES 4

Saltfish Salad

SALADS

Shredded Raw Cod (Bacalhau Cru Desfiado)

Portugal

1 lb (450 g) salt cod

4 tbsp (60 ml) olive oil

3 tbsp (45 ml) white vinegar

1 small onion, finely chopped

1 garlic clove, finely chopped

Freshly ground black pepper

1. Remove any skin and bones from cod and shred into thin strips.
2. Put cod in a bowl of cold water. Wash by hand, shaking and squeezing the cod. Repeat in two more changes of cold water.
3. Place cod in a salad bowl; pour oil and vinegar over it. Sprinkle with onion, garlic, and pepper.

SERVES 4

Raw Cod with Onions and Sauce (Bacalhau Rapido)

Portugal

1 lb (450 g) salt cod

4-6 potatoes, boiled, sliced

2 small onions, thinly sliced

2 hard-boiled eggs

2 tbsp (30 ml) olive oil

1/2 lemon, juiced

1 sprig fresh parsley, chopped

1 tsp (5 ml) white sugar

Olives, for garnish

Lettuce, for garnish

1. Remove skin and bones from the salt cod; shred. Wash pieces in 2-3 changes of water until completely white. Squeeze, drain, and dry cod.
2. Spread shredded cod on a serving dish and cover with boiled potatoes and onions. Sprinkle 1 chopped egg on top of the mixture.
3. Whisk together olive oil, lemon juice, parsley, and sugar. Pour over cod, potatoes, and onions.
4. Serve with a garnish of olives, lettuce, and slices of the remaining egg.

SERVES 4

Salt Cod Carpaccio with Oven-Roasted Tomatoes and Herbs

Italy

Carpaccio refers to a dish of raw meat or fish, very thinly sliced. There are many versions of baccala carpaccio. Salt cod slices with seasonal vegetables, olives, and bell peppers served with confit tomatoes are popular. If you prefer, steam the salt cod for a few minutes.

1 lb (450 g) salt cod steaks

10 plum tomatoes, cut in half or in small chunks

1/4 cup (60 ml) extra-virgin olive oil

Salt and freshly ground black pepper

1 bunch fresh oregano or marjoram, leaves only

1 bunch fresh parsley, leaves only

1 bunch fresh thyme, leaves only

DRESSING

3 tbsp (45 ml) extra-virgin olive oil, plus more for drizzling

1 tbsp (15 ml) freshly squeezed lemon juice

Salt and freshly ground black pepper

1/4 cup (60 ml) balsamic vinegar

1. Use watered salt cod (page 80). Drain and pat dry. Refrigerate. Slice or break cod into very thin slices or pieces; set aside.
2. Preheat oven to 250°F (120°C).
3. Place tomato halves, flesh side up, on a rack sitting on a baking sheet. Mix oil, salt, and pepper; coat tomato halves with this mixture. Oven-roast for 2-3 hours until tomatoes dehydrate but are still tender.
4. Combine oregano, parsley, thyme, and tomatoes in a large salad bowl. Toss with lemon juice, olive oil, and salt and pepper to taste.
5. Divide salt cod onto 4 chilled salad plates. Top each serving with herbs and tomatoes. Drizzle with olive oil and balsamic vinegar.

SERVES 4

SALADS

Shredded Salt Cod with Tomatoes and Olives (Esqueixada de Bacalao)

Spain

In its simplest form, this traditional recipe from Catalonia is a salad of salt cod, tomatoes, black olives, and olive oil.

1/2 lb (225 g) salt cod

4 ripe plum tomatoes, skinned, grated, strained

3 tbsp (45 ml) extra-virgin olive oil, divided

16 black olives, pitted

2 green onions, thinly sliced

1 tbsp (15 ml) fresh chives, finely chopped, for garnish

1. Use watered salt cod (page 80). Drain cod and pat dry. Remove any skin and bones. Shred into small pieces; set aside.
2. Mix 1 tbsp (15 ml) olive oil with grated tomato pulp. Set aside.
3. Layer cod on 4 salad plates. Spoon a layer of tomato pulp on top. Arrange olives on each plate; sprinkle with onions.
4. Drizzle with remaining olive oil to ensure cod is well covered. Garnish with chives.

Adapted from Simone Ortega and Ines Ortega, *The Book of Tapas*

SERVES 4

VARIATIONS

- Chop tomatoes into small pieces instead of grating them. Tomatoes of different textures may also be added. Grated rather than chopped tomatoes integrate better into the cod.
- Serve with black olive oil: Cut 1/2 green bell pepper and 1/2 red bell pepper into thin julienne strips. Mix peppers and cod together. Dress with olive oil. Divide mixture onto 4 salad plates. Spoon grated tomatoes on top and layer with green onions. Purée 12 kalamata olives with olive oil in a blender. Spoon black olive oil around the edge of each plate. Garnish with chives.

Shredded Salt Cod with Tomatoes and Olives

SALT COD CUISINE: THE INTERNATIONAL TABLE

Catalan Salt Cod and Sweet Pepper Salad (Esqueixada)

Spain

Esqueixada comes from the Catalan verb "to shred." Shredded cod is pickled by vinaigrette rather than being cooked. It should be translucent and mild.

1/2 lb (225 g) salt cod, thick pieces

1/2 small onion, thinly sliced

3 tbsp (45 ml) olive oil

1 tbsp (15 ml) red wine vinegar

Freshly ground black pepper

2 red bell peppers, thinly sliced

2 ripe tomatoes

12-18 small ripe olives, for garnish

4 hard-boiled eggs, for garnish (optional)

Fresh oregano leaves, chopped, for garnish (optional)

1. Use watered salt cod (page 80). Drain. Remove any skin and bones. Dry cod well with paper towels.
2. Shred cod finely and place in a salad bowl. Add onion.
3. Combine oil and vinegar; pour over cod. Sprinkle with black pepper, toss, and refrigerate 3 hours to marinate.
4. Pour boiling water over red peppers and soak for 10 minutes to soften a little. Drain and dry peppers.
5. Quarter and skin tomatoes, carefully removing seeds and membrane. Slice flesh.
6. Stir cod, peppers, and tomatoes together gently.
7. Arrange on 4 salad plates and garnish with olives, quartered hard-boiled eggs, and chopped oregano.

Adapted from Pepita Aris, *Recipes from a Spanish Village*

SERVES 4

VARIATION

- Add 1 tbsp (15 ml) lemon juice to the marinade; substitute 3 green onions sliced thinly on the diagonal for the onion. Garnish with 2 tbsp (30 ml) chopped fresh parsley instead of oregano.

SALADS

Salt Cod Carpaccio with Lemon Juice and Olive Oil

Italy

This dish uses uncooked salt cod in a marinade of olive oil, garlic, and basil.

- 1 lb (450 g) salt cod, very thick pieces
- 2 cups (500 ml) olive oil, divided
- 1 garlic clove, crushed
- 4-5 fresh basil leaves, chopped
- 1/3 cup (85 ml) lemon juice
- Salt and pepper
- 1 head curly endive
- 12 black olives, pitted, chopped

1. Use watered salt cod (page 80). Drain.
2. Combine 1 1/2 cups (375 ml) olive oil with garlic and basil leaves; add cod. Marinate, refrigerated, for 24 hours.
3. Mix lemon juice and remaining 1/2 cup (125 ml) olive oil to make the salad dressing. Season with salt and pepper.
4. Clean endive; divide among 4 salad plates. Drizzle with dressing.
5. Remove cod from oil and remove any skin and bones. Cut or break cod into thin pieces and place on endive.
6. Sprinkle olives over the top.

SERVES 4

Shredded Salt Cod Salad (Chiquetaille de Morue)

Haiti

- 8 oz (225 g) salt cod
- 1/3 cup (85 ml) olive oil or canola or other light oil
- 1 small onion or 2 shallots, chopped
- 2 green onions, chopped
- 1 carrot, chopped
- 1 garlic clove, chopped
- 1/3 cup (85 ml) raw green beans, slivered
- 1 tsp (5 ml) fresh parsley, chopped
- 3 tbsp (45 ml) cider vinegar
- Freshly ground black pepper
- Dash hot pepper sauce
- 1 cucumber, peeled, sliced

1. Put salt cod in a large bowl and cover with boiling water. Allow to cool.
2. Drain. Remove skin and bones; shred. Pour boiling water over shredded cod a second time. Drain; press out all water.
3. Place cod in a salad bowl. Add oil, onions or shallots, green onions, carrot, garlic, green beans, parsley, and vinegar and mix.
4. Season to taste with black pepper and hot pepper sauce.
5. Let stand 2 hours at room temperature for flavours to develop.
6. Arrange cucumber slices around the salad bowl and serve.

SERVES 4

scalded

Salt Cod Salad (Buljol)

Trinidad

Buljol is from the French *brule gueule*, meaning "to burn your mouth." There are many variations of this dish for breakfast, lunch, or supper. Traditionally, buljol is very spicy, so it is best to experiment, letting your taste buds be your guide. This dish is most often served with slices of ripe avocado and perhaps a Trinidadian coconut bake (a biscuit-like loaf).

- 1/2 lb (225 g) salt cod
- 2 medium tomatoes, coarsely chopped
- 1 large onion, finely chopped
- 1 hot red pepper such as congo, habanero, or Scotch bonnet, seeded, chopped
- Freshly ground black pepper
- 3 tbsp (45 ml) olive oil
- 1 tbsp (15 ml) lime juice
- Lettuce leaves
- 1 avocado, sliced, for garnish
- 2 hard-boiled eggs, sliced, for garnish

1. Place salt cod in a bowl and cover with boiling water. Let cool. Drain. Remove any skin and bones; shred. Pour boiling water over a second time; let cool. Drain and press all water from cod.
2. Combine tomatoes, onion, and hot pepper with cod. Season with black pepper, olive oil, and lime juice.
3. Serve on lettuce leaves. Garnish with slices of avocado or hard-boiled eggs.

SERVES 4

VARIATION

- Add small amounts of cucumber (peeled, seeded, and chopped), chopped green onion tops, and grated cheese.

Salt Cod Salad

SALADS

Salt Cod on Onions and Cucumber Slices

Guadeloupe

Scotch bonnet peppers are a defining flavour of Caribbean cooking. They come in a variety of colours (green, yellow, orange, red, and white) and are extremely hot. The name comes from their appearance: the Scotch bonnet pepper is lantern-shaped and its crinkled top resembles a traditional Scottish hat. Many people from the Caribbean call this pepper "bonnie."

1 lb (450 g) salt cod

1 sprig fresh parsley, chopped

3 green onions, chopped

2 fresh chives, chopped

2 shallots, finely sliced

1/2 Scotch bonnet pepper, chopped

1 small red onion, finely sliced

1 cucumber, peeled, sliced

VINAIGRETTE

2 tbsp (30 ml) sunflower oil

2 limes, juiced

2 tbsp (30 ml) white wine vinegar

2 garlic cloves, finely chopped

Salt and freshly ground black pepper

1. Place salt cod in hot water and soak 5 minutes. Drain; repeat three times. Remove any skin and bones. Shred and dry cod. Place in a large bowl.
2. Add parsley, green onions, chives, shallots, pepper, and onion to shredded cod. Mix well.
3. Prepare vinaigrette by mixing sunflower oil, lime juice, white wine vinegar, and chopped garlic. Season with salt and pepper to taste.
4. Pour half the vinaigrette over cod mixture. Refrigerate for 1 hour.
5. Arrange cucumber slices on a serving platter and dress with remaining vinaigrette. Top with shredded cod mixture.

Adapted from Babette de Rozieres, *Creole*

SERVES 4

Salt Cod on Onions and Cucumber Slices

simmered

Salt Cod and Cauliflower Salad (Insalata Fredda di Baccala e Cavolfiore)

Italy

This is one of several Italian recipes for Salt Cod and Cauliflower Salad, traditionally served during Lent and occasionally on Friday nights.

- 1 1/2 lb (675 g) salt cod pieces
- 4 tbsp (60 ml) extra-virgin olive oil, divided
- 1 lemon, juiced
- 1 lb (450 g) cauliflower, cut in small florets
- 2 tbsp (30 ml) cider vinegar
- Freshly ground black pepper
- 1 sprig fresh parsley, finely chopped
- 12-16 Sicilian green olives in brine, coarsely chopped
- 1/2 red bell pepper, thinly sliced
- 1/2 small red onion, thinly sliced

1. Use watered salt cod (page 80).
2. Put cod into a medium saucepan and barely cover with water. Add 2 tbsp (30 ml) olive oil and the lemon juice. Cover; cook over medium-low heat for about 15 minutes or until cod flakes easily when pierced with a fork. Drain, remove any skin and bones, and shred cod.
3. Steam cauliflower for 5-6 minutes or cook in boiling water until tender. Drain florets and set aside to cool.
4. Transfer cod and cauliflower to a salad bowl.
5. Mix remaining 2 tbsp (30 ml) olive oil with vinegar and pepper and pour over mixture.
6. Add parsley, olives, red pepper, and onion. Toss lightly. Serve at room temperature.

SERVES 6

VARIATION

 Use black olives instead of green olives, or a combination of both.

Salt Cod and Cauliflower Salad

SALADS

Warm Salt Cod Salad with Oranges

Spain

This easy-to-make salad is not chilled, but it is still refreshing. The sweetness of the orange and the saltiness of the cod blend beautifully.

2 x 4 oz (115 g) salt cod steaks

2 oranges, peeled, thinly sliced

2 green onions, white part only, sliced

20 black olives, pitted

Olive oil

2 hard-boiled eggs, halved, for garnish

1. Use watered salt cod (page 80). Drain. Place cod in a medium saucepan, with barely enough water to cover, and simmer 10-15 minutes, until tender. Flake.
2. Arrange oranges on a salad platter. Distribute flaked cod evenly over oranges. Add green onions and olives on top. Drizzle with olive oil. Garnish with hard-boiled eggs.

SERVES 4

VARIATION

- For a cold version of this salad, dissolve 1 tsp (5 ml) sweet paprika in 1 tbsp (15 ml) white wine vinegar. Pour over salad after drizzling with olive oil. Cover and chill at least 1 hour. Garnish with sliced hard-boiled eggs.

Salt Cod Salad with Small New Potatoes

Portugal

This salad is the essence of simplicity. It is also extremely tasty. The smallest type of bacalhau, generally a salt cod weighing less than 1 lb (450 g), is typically used to make this dish. In Portugal, salt cod is classified according to size and quality: the most common are superior (*primeira*) and universal (*sortido*), each with its own range of size classifications.

1 lb (450 g) salt cod

8-12 small new potatoes, scrubbed

1/3 cup (85 ml) extra-virgin olive oil

3 garlic cloves, finely chopped

2 tbsp (30 ml) fresh parsley, chopped

2 medium tomatoes, skinned, seeded, finely chopped

1. Use watered salt cod (page 80). Drain. Place cod in a medium saucepan with just enough water to cover; simmer 10-15 minutes, or until tender. Drain, remove any skin and bones; shred cod into flakes.
2. Boil potatoes in salted water until tender; peel but keep whole.
3. Heat olive oil and garlic in a wide saucepan over medium-high heat. Add potatoes, cod, parsley, and tomatoes. Shake the pot occasionally to ensure all ingredients are mixed and heating well. Serve warm.

Adapted from Chefe Silva, *Bacalhau a Portuguesa*

SERVES 4

Salt Cod with Olive Salad (Baccala con Olive)

Italy

This salad is a welcome addition to the Christmas Eve table.

- 1 1/2 lb (675 g) salt cod
- 1 onion, quartered
- 1 tbsp (15 ml) white vinegar
- 16 black olives, sliced
- 3 anchovy fillets, rinsed, chopped
- 2 garlic cloves, finely chopped
- 1/3 cup (85 ml) capers
- 2 tbsp (30 ml) olive oil
- 2 tbsp (30 ml) lemon juice
- 3 tbsp (45 ml) fresh parsley, chopped

1. Use watered salt cod (page 80); cover with fresh water; add onion and vinegar. Bring to a boil, then simmer over low heat until tender (approximately 10-15 minutes). Drain, cool, remove any skin and bones; flake cod.
2. Combine cod, olives, anchovies, garlic, and capers in a salad bowl.
3. Combine oil, lemon juice, and parsley in a separate dish. Pour over cod mixture.
4. Refrigerate for several hours.

SERVES 4

SALADS

Salad of Salt Cod with Oranges (Ensalada de Bacalao con Naranja)

Basque Country

This recipe uses a light vinaigrette dressing with the greens and a heavier mayonnaise dressing with the salt cod—all with a colourful garnish of orange slices and parsley.

1 lb (450 g) salt cod

2 cups (500 ml) milk

1/2 cup (125 ml) mayonnaise (page 302)

1/2 orange, juiced

6 tbsp (90 ml) olive oil

2 tbsp (30 ml) cider vinegar

Salt

4 cups (1 L) mixed salad greens, such as Bibb lettuce, green and red leaf lettuce, arugula, and cress

1 orange, peeled, in wedges

1 tbsp (15 ml) fresh parsley, chopped

1. Use watered salt cod (page 80). Drain cod and transfer to a saucepan. Add enough milk to cover cod, and heat over medium-high heat until milk simmers. Do not boil. Reduce heat and simmer for 5-10 minutes, until cod is tender. Drain and set aside to cool.
2. Whisk together mayonnaise and orange juice in a small bowl; set aside.
3. Whisk together olive oil and vinegar in a second small bowl. Season to taste with salt.
4. Drizzle greens with vinaigrette. Toss gently; divide among 4 salad plates.
5. Remove any skin and bones from cod; separate into small flakes. Top greens with cod. Spoon mayonnaise mixture over cod.
6. Garnish each plate with orange slices and parsley.

SERVES 4

Salad of Salt Cod with Oranges

Orange, Red Onion, Black Olive, and Salt Cod Salad

SALADS

Orange, Red Onion, Black Olive, and Salt Cod Salad

Spain

This salad has bold, complex flavours. The oranges can be cut in slices or sections. Use 1 whole orange or more per serving. I sometimes soak a handful of raisins in orange juice for a tasty addition.

8 oz (225 g) salt cod, thick pieces
4 oranges, peeled, pith removed
2 red onions, thinly sliced
1 sprig fresh parsley, chopped
2 tbsp (30 ml) red wine vinegar
1/3 cup (85 ml) extra-virgin olive oil
16 black olives

VARIATIONS

- Simmer salt cod in step 1 with enough milk to cover. Add 2 sprigs fresh parsley, pinch dried thyme, and 1 bay leaf to the milk.
- Change the dressing in step 5: Combine 1 chopped garlic clove, 1 tbsp (15 ml) sherry vinegar, 2 tbsp (30 ml) white wine vinegar, and 2 tbsp (30 ml) freshly squeezed orange juice.

1. Use watered salt cod (page 80). Simmer cod until it flakes easily, about 20 minutes. Remove skin and bones; break into chunks. Set aside to cool.
2. Slice or section oranges. Hold in a colander; reserve juice.
3. Add red onions and parsley to oranges; toss to mix.
4. Layer orange mixture with cod in a large salad bowl.
5. Mix reserved orange juice with vinegar and pour over the layered salad.
6. Drizzle with olive oil and scatter sliced olives on top.
7. Cover with plastic wrap. Chill for 1 hour to allow flavours to develop. Toss well before serving.

SERVES 4

Salt Cod, Red Pepper, and Potato Salad

Spain

In addition to the variety of textures and tastes, this salad is a mixture of colours—yellow potatoes, red roasted peppers, and white salt cod. The variation at the end blends salt cod, juicy oranges, potatoes, and black olives. Such salads are great as a first course or a light lunch and can keep well for several days.

8 oz (225 g) salt cod

4 potatoes such as Yukon Gold or Yellow Finn, boiled, sliced

5 tbsp (75 ml) extra-virgin olive oil, divided

1 tbsp (15 ml) sherry wine vinegar

Salt and freshly ground black pepper

2 red bell peppers, roasted, peeled, cored, sliced

2 garlic cloves, thinly sliced

1. Use watered salt cod (page 80). Place in a medium saucepan with cold water to cover. Bring to a boil and simmer 10-12 minutes, until tender. Drain. Remove any skin and bones; flake cod into small pieces. Pat dry.
2. Put warm sliced potatoes in a salad bowl; add 3 tbsp (45 ml) oil, vinegar, salt, and pepper. Add peppers.
3. Add cod; toss gently to mix. Cover and set aside for 1 hour or more to meld flavours.
4. Brown sliced garlic in the remaining 2 tbsp (30 ml) oil over medium heat; pour garlic and oil over the salad.

SERVES 4

VARIATION

- Replace bell peppers with 2 Seville oranges (peeled and sliced) and 1/2 sliced red onion. Seville oranges are in season in late December or early January. Many Spanish will insist this salad should be made the day before it is to be eaten to allow the full flavour to develop.

SALADS

Salt Cod Salad with Olives and Avocado (Serenata de Bacalao)

Puerto Rico

There are many variations of Serenata de Bacalao in Puerto Rico, and similar recipes from St. Lucia, Haiti, and elsewhere in the Caribbean. I include this recipe for its variety of ingredients and contrasting colours. Ripe plantains thinly sliced crosswise and fried are an excellent accompaniment.

Some recipes use hot peppers instead of sweet; make the substitution if it is to your taste.

- 1/2 lb (225 g) salt cod
- 2 small potatoes, boiled, sliced
- 3 hard-boiled eggs, quartered
- 1 green or red bell pepper, sliced in crescents
- 1 large red onion, sliced in crescents
- 1 tomato, sliced in crescents
- 1 avocado, sliced in crescents
- 1 tsp (5 ml) capers
- 10 Spanish stuffed olives
- 1/2 tsp (2.5 ml) dried oregano, crushed (optional)
- Lettuce
- 2 tbsp (30 ml) olive oil
- 2 tbsp (30 ml) white wine vinegar
- Freshly ground black pepper

1. Use watered salt cod (page 80). Cut into 1- to 2-inch (2.5-5 cm) pieces and simmer 5 minutes. Drain and rinse. Remove any skin and bones. Shred cod and dry completely.
2. Mix potatoes, eggs, pepper, onion, tomato, avocado, capers, olives, and oregano in a large bowl. Add cod.
3. Arrange vegetables and cod on a bed of lettuce in a serving dish; drizzle with oil and vinegar to taste. Season with black pepper.
4. Refrigerate until ready to serve.

SERVES 4

Salt Cod Salad with Olives and Avocado

SALT COD CUISINE: THE INTERNATIONAL TABLE

Salt Cod Salad with Aioli

SALADS

Salt Cod Salad with Aioli

France

This salad uses a colourful mix of cooked, blanched, and raw seasonal vegetables and a pungent accompaniment called *aioli*. Aioli, a Provençal emulsion sauce of garlic and olive oil, best known in its mayonnaise form with egg yolks, comes from *ail* (garlic) and *oli* (dialect for oil). You may use the recipe for aioli in the Sauces section (page 303) or try the roasted garlic version below—the crème fraîche enlivens the vegetables.

The vegetables below are typical of the region but do not consider them a fixed list. Check for fresh vegetables such as artichokes or green or yellow beans that might be available locally.

1 1/2 lb (675 g) salt cod

1 sprig fresh parsley

1 bay leaf

1 slice lemon

ROASTED GARLIC AIOLI

3 garlic cloves

1 1/2 cups (375 ml) thick mayonnaise (page 302)

5 tsp (25 ml) crème fraîche or sour cream

SALAD

4 small new potatoes, scrubbed but not peeled

4 hard-boiled eggs, halved

12 baby carrots

4 broccoli florets, blanched 3-4 minutes

1 cup (250 ml) snow peas, blanched 2 minutes

8 cherry tomatoes

3/4 head fennel, trimmed, finely chopped

1 sprig fresh parsley, finely chopped

1. Use watered salt cod (page 80). Place in a medium saucepan, cover with water, and add parsley, bay leaf, and lemon. Bring to a gentle boil and simmer 10 minutes until cod flakes easily when touched with a fork. Drain, remove any skin and bones, flake coarsely, and allow to cool.
2. Scrub potatoes and cook in lightly salted water until tender. Bring carrots to a boil in a separate pan in lightly salted water; cook about 5 minutes (they should still be crisp). Drain; allow potatoes and carrots to cool.
3. Wrap unpeeled garlic cloves in tinfoil and bake at 400°F (200°C) for 20 minutes. Remove. When cool enough to handle, peel and mash each clove into the serving bowl. Stir in mayonnaise and crème fraiche. Refrigerate until needed.
4. Place flaked cod on a large serving platter; arrange vegetables and eggs around the edge. Sprinkle with parsley. Serve with aioli.

SERVES 4

Salt Cod Salad with Beans

Spain

The flavours of this salad develop best when it is allowed to reach room temperature before serving.

1/2 lb (225 g) salt cod

1/2 lb (225 g) white northern (or similar) beans, soaked 10-12 hours and simmered 1 1/2-2 hours

8-10 green olives, pitted

8-10 black olives, pitted

2 tomatoes, skinned, seeded

2 green onions, chopped

2 hard-boiled egg whites, chopped

1 tbsp (15 ml) fresh parsley, chopped

4 tbsp (60 ml) canned pimento or roasted red peppers, chopped

DRESSING

2 hard-boiled egg yolks, sieved

1 tsp (5 ml) Dijon mustard

3 tbsp (45 ml) sherry vinegar

1/4 cup (60 ml) extra-virgin olive oil

1 tbsp (15 ml) fish stock (page 296) or vegetable stock

1. Use watered salt cod (page 80). Dry cod and break into large pieces. Char or grill over an open fire and then shred with your fingers.
2. Place cod, beans, olives, tomatoes, onions, egg whites, parsley, and pimento in a large salad bowl.
3. Whisk egg yolks, mustard, vinegar, oil, and stock in a separate bowl for the dressing.
4. Pour dressing over cod mixture; mix gently. Taste for seasoning. Refrigerate for several hours.

SERVES 4

Tapas offer such an informal, fun, and social style of eating. You meet your friends. You chat. You have a glass of wine and order a few little plates. You share and you sample a little of everything. Maybe you don't even sit down, but lean against the bar instead.

—Simone Ortega and Ines Ortega, *The Book of Tapas*

Tapas represent a delightful way of eating with family and friends rather than a collection of particular recipes. Tapas can be hot or cold, eaten with the fingers, or served with a fork or toothpick and a piece of bread. In some cases, tapas can be small portions of main meals. Many of the dishes in the Salads, Hors d'Oeuvres, and Other Salt Cod Parts sections of this book also work well as tapas. Accompaniments are suggested with many of these recipes; turn to the Sauces section for other ideas, such as aioli, salsa verde, or salsa romesco.

Tapas ingredients should be of good quality, their preparation done carefully, and their serving and presentation immaculate but simple. The number of servings is not specified in these recipes; most give about 12 servings, except where specific numbers of avocados, tomatoes, or roasted red peppers are used.

Salt Cod with Peppers, Black Olives, Mint, and Parsley	*Spain*	Tomatoes Stuffed with Salt Cod (Tomates Rellenos de Bacalao)	*Spain*
Salt Cod with Onions (Bacalao Encebollado)	*Spain*	Blended Salt Cod (Bacalao Ligado)	*Spain*
Salt Cod with Garlic (Bacalao Al Ajo Arriero)	*Spain*	Salt Cod in Tomato Sauce, Roman Style	*Italy*
Salt Cod Slivers	*Spain*	Cod in Wine (Baccala 'Mbriache)	*Italy*
Fried Salt Cod	*Spain*	Fried Salt Cod (Baccala Fritto)	*Italy*
Salt Cod Fritters with Spinach	*Spain*	Salt Cod with Sour Cherries	*Italy*
Salt Cod and Avocado	*Spain*	Salt Cod in Vinaigrette (Escabeche de Bacalhau)	*Portugal*
Red Peppers Stuffed with Salt Cod (Pimientos Rellenos de Bacalao)	*Spain*	Salt Cod with Black Butter (Morue au Beurre Noir)	*France*
		Salt Cod Roe Pâté (Taramosalata)	*Greece*
		Avocado with Tarama	*Greece*

Salt Cod with Peppers, Black Olives, Mint, and Parsley

Spain

This versatile dish can be eaten hot or cold. Embellish with colourful peppers, salted capers, fresh chili, or sweet paprika. Spread on toast and warm under the broiler, or add a few tablespoons to an omelette.

1 lb (450 g) salt cod

1/4 cup (60 ml) extra-virgin olive oil, divided

1 large onion, thinly sliced

1 red bell pepper, thinly sliced

2 garlic cloves, thinly sliced

2 tbsp (30 ml) red wine vinegar

8 black olives

1/4 cup (60 ml) fresh mint, chopped

1/4 cup (60 ml) fresh parsley, chopped

Salad greens

1/2 lemon, juiced

Freshly ground black pepper

1. Use watered salt cod (page 80). Drain, remove any skin and bones; cut into chunks. Set aside.
2. Pour about 2 tbsp (30 ml) olive oil into a wide heavy-bottomed saucepan or frying pan, enough to cover the bottom. Add onion and pepper; simmer slowly over gentle heat for about 15 minutes until softened but not brown.
3. Add garlic and cook 3-4 minutes. Add vinegar; allow it to reduce.
4. Add cod and another 2 tbsp (30 ml) olive oil; stir gently for 5 minutes until cod flakes.
5. Add olives and cook 3-4 minutes. Add mint and parsley; stir in well.
6. Serve a small amount of the cod mixture in the middle of each plate with a mixture of salad greens. Squeeze a little lemon juice over the top and sprinkle with freshly ground black pepper.

TAPAS AND MEZES

Salt Cod with Onions (Bacalao Encebollado)

Spain

This recipe and the two that follow are adapted from *Classic Tapas* by Rafael de Haro.

1/2 lb (225 g) salt cod

Olive oil, for sautéing

1 onion, sliced in rings

1 green bell pepper, sliced in strips

3-4 thin rings of chili pepper

Crusty bread

1. Use watered salt cod (page 80). Drain. Remove any skin and bones; cut into bite-sized pieces.
2. Sauté onion rings and green pepper strips gently in oil. Add cod and cook on low heat for 10 minutes. Add chili pepper rings to taste.
3. Serve cod and vegetables on pieces of crusty bread.

Salt Cod with Garlic (Bacalao Al Ajo Arriero)

Spain

14 oz (400 g) salt cod

1 onion, chopped

3 garlic cloves, sliced

1 red bell pepper

Chili powder

6 tbsp (90 ml) tomato sauce

Olive oil, for sautéing

Fish stock (page 296)

1. Use watered salt cod (page 80). Drain. Remove any skin and bones; cut cod into bite-sized pieces.
2. Sauté onion and garlic gently in olive oil in a frying pan. Soak pepper in hot water for a few minutes, remove the flesh, and add to pan when onion begins to brown. Add a pinch of chili powder and the tomato sauce.
3. Add cod when mixture begins to cook. Fry briefly; add a little stock.
4. Cook on low heat for 10 minutes. Serve hot.

Salt Cod Slivers

Spain

8 oz (225 g) salt cod, thick steak

1 1/3 cups (335 ml) all-purpose flour

1-2 tsp (5-10 ml) baking powder

Beer

Olive oil, for frying

Salt

1. Use watered salt cod (page 80). Drain. Remove any skin and bones; break cod into thin slivers.
2. Sauté cod in a frying pan with a little olive oil.
3. Prepare batter by mixing flour, baking powder, and salt in a bowl. Add enough beer to form a thick cream; mix.
4. Add sautéed slivers to the batter. Mix well.
5. Heat enough olive oil to cover the bottom of the frying pan. Use a slotted spoon to lift out cod and fry in hot oil until golden brown. Serve hot.

Salt Cod Slivers

Fried Salt Cod

Spain

12 oz (340 g) salt cod

2 1/2 cups (625 ml) milk

All-purpose flour

Vegetable oil, for deep-frying

Salt

6 lemon slices

Salsa romesco (optional, page 304)

1. Use watered salt cod (page 80). Drain and pat dry. Cut into short strips and remove any skin and bones. Place strips in a bowl and pour cold milk over them. Cover and let soak in a cool place for 1 hour.
2. Drain cod and pat dry. Dust cod with flour, shaking off the excess.
3. Heat oil in a deep fryer or a large pan to 350°-375°F (180°-190°C). Deep-fry the cod, in batches if necessary, for 2-4 minutes.
4. Drain on paper towels and sprinkle generously with salt.
5. Transfer cod to serving plates, garnish with lemon slices, and serve with bowls of salsa romesco.

SALT COD CUISINE: THE INTERNATIONAL TABLE

TAPAS AND MEZES

Salt Cod Fritters with Spinach

Spain

The next three recipes are adapted from Jacqueline Bellefontaine, *Tapas: Greatest Ever*. For this classic Spanish tapas, prepare the salt cod, spinach, and batter separately. When everything is ready, mix the ingredients and fry. Serve with aioli.

SALT COD
- 10 oz (280 g) salt cod
- 2 lemon slices
- 2 sprigs fresh parsley
- 1 bay leaf

BATTER
- 1 cup (250 ml) all-purpose flour
- 1 tsp (5 ml) baking powder
- 1/4 tsp (1.2 ml) salt
- 1 egg, lightly beaten
- 2/3 cup (165 ml) milk

SPINACH
- 1/2 tsp (2.5 ml) garlic-flavoured olive oil
- 3 oz (85 g) fresh baby spinach, rinsed
- 1/4 tsp (1.2 ml) sweet paprika or hot paprika
- Olive oil, for frying
- Coarse sea salt (optional)
- 3/4 cup (185 ml) aioli (page 303)
- Fresh parsley, for garnish

1. Use watered salt cod (page 80). Drain. Transfer cod to a large frying pan. Add lemon, parsley, bay leaf, and enough water to cover; bring to a boil. Simmer for 10-15 minutes or until cod flakes easily. Remove cod, drain, remove skin and bones, and flake into pieces.
2. Make the batter: Sift flour, baking powder, and salt into a large bowl and make a well. Mix egg with 1/2 cup (125 ml) milk and pour into the well in the flour. Stir to make a smooth batter with a thick coating consistency. Stir in remaining milk if batter seems too thick. Let stand at least 1 hour.
3. Prepare spinach: Heat garlic-flavoured olive oil in a small saucepan over medium heat. Add spinach and cook 3-4 minutes, or until just wilted; drain. Chop finely.
4. Stir spinach and paprika into the batter. Add cod pieces to batter; mix.
5. Heat 2 inches (5 cm) olive oil in a heavy-bottomed frying pan. Use a tablespoon to drop pieces of battered cod into the oil; cook 8-10 minutes. Work in batches to avoid overcrowding. Use a slotted spoon to transfer the fritters to drain on paper towels. Sprinkle with sea salt.
6. Garnish with parsley and serve hot or at room temperature with aioli.

Salt Cod Fritters with Spinach

SALT COD CUISINE: THE INTERNATIONAL TABLE

Salt Cod and Avocado

Spain

- 12 oz (340 g) salt cod
- 2 tbsp (30 ml) olive oil
- 1 onion, finely chopped
- 1 garlic clove, finely chopped
- 3 avocados, halved lengthwise, pitted
- 1 tbsp (15 ml) lemon juice
- 1/4 tsp (1.2 ml) chili powder
- 1 tbsp (15 ml) dry sherry
- 1/4 cup (60 ml) heavy cream
- Salt and freshly ground black pepper

1. Use watered salt cod (page 80). Drain and pat dry. Break into fairly large pieces, removing any skin and bones.
2. Preheat oven to 350°F (180°C).
3. Heat oil in a large heavy-bottomed frying pan. Add onion and garlic; cook over low heat, stirring occasionally, for 5 minutes, or until softened.
4. Add cod and cook over medium heat, stirring frequently for 6-8 minutes, or until it flakes easily. Remove frying pan from the heat; let cool slightly.
5. Scoop out the avocados carefully with a teaspoon without piercing the shells. Reserve shells. Mash avocado in a bowl with lemon juice.
6. Add cod mixture to avocado mixture. Add chili powder, sherry, and cream. Beat well with a fork and season to taste with salt and pepper.
7. Spoon mixture into avocado shells and place on a baking sheet. Bake 10-15 minutes. Transfer to warm serving plates and serve.

Salt Cod and Avocado

TAPAS AND MEZES

Red Peppers Stuffed with Salt Cod (Pimientos Rellenos de Bacalao)

Spain

The Spanish usually use *pimientos de piquillo* for stuffed pepper dishes served as tapas. Piquillo peppers, grown in Northern Spain, are hand-picked and roasted over open fires for a sweet, spicy flavour. The peppers are then peeled and packed in jars or tins. You may find piquillo peppers in a Spanish-food store or the specialty section of a supermarket. Canned, bottled, or homemade roasted red peppers can be substituted.

6 oz (170 g) salt cod

3 tbsp (45 ml) olive oil, divided

1 green bell pepper, finely chopped

1 large onion, finely chopped, divided

1 cup (250 ml) béchamel sauce (light variation, page 297)

10 piquillo red peppers, canned or fresh roasted

1 sprig fresh parsley, chopped, for garnish

SAUCE

1 cup (250 ml) tomato sauce

1/2 onion, finely chopped

Freshly ground black pepper

1. Use watered salt cod (page 80). Drain, remove skin and bones, and flake.
2. Preheat oven to 375°F (190°C).
3. Heat 2 tbsp (30 ml) olive oil in a frying pan and sauté green pepper and half the onion. When lightly browned, add cod and fry 3-4 minutes.
4. Add prepared béchamel sauce; stir well.
5. Fill the red peppers and place in a baking dish.
6. Prepare tomato sauce: Heat 1 tbsp (15 ml) olive oil in a frying pan and sauté remaining onion. Add tomato sauce and black pepper. Simmer for 2-3 minutes, strain, and pour over the peppers.
7. Bake for 5-6 minutes. Serve hot.
8. Garnish with parsley.

Red Peppers Stuffed with Salt Cod

Tomatoes Stuffed with Salt Cod (Tomates Rellenos de Bacalao)

Spain

- 10 oz (280 g) salt cod
- 8 medium tomatoes
- 1 onion, chopped
- Olive oil, for sautéing
- 1 1/4 cups (310 ml) béchamel sauce (page 297)
- Medium cheddar cheese, grated

1. Use watered salt cod (page 80). Drain. Remove any skin and bones; flake.
2. Preheat oven to 350°F (180°C).
3. Wash tomatoes. Cut off tops and set aside. Scoop out seeds and part of the flesh. Season tomato shells with a little salt and pepper and place upside down to drain.
4. Sauté onion in a frying pan with a little olive oil. Add flaked cod and heat 3-4 minutes.
5. Prepare béchamel sauce in a saucepan. Remove 1/4 cup (60 ml) to pour over tomato tops. Add onion and cod to remaining 1 cup (250 ml) béchamel sauce and mix well. Keep mixture warm.
6. Fill tomatoes with sauce, onion, and cod mixture. Place tops on tomatoes. Place tomatoes in a greased baking dish. Pour a little béchamel sauce over tomatoes and sprinkle with grated cheese.
7. Bake for 20 minutes, until tomatoes soften but do not split.

VARIATION

- Instead of using tomato tops, sprinkle grated cheese on the stuffed tomatoes and bake as in step 6 above.

Tomatoes Stuffed with Salt Cod

TAPAS AND MEZES

Blended Salt Cod (Bacalao Ligado)

Spain

This recipe is similar to the Basque recipe for Salt Cod with Pil Pil Sauce (Bacalao al Pil Pil) but lacks the hot chili pepper. The cooking method, which includes shaking the pan, produces a thick *ligado* (liaison) sauce from the collagen in the thin belly parts of the cod. Passing the oil over the cod in this manner brings the gelatin out of the skin and thickens the emerging sauce.

1 1/4 lb (570 g) salt cod, thin belly/rib cage part, skin on

1 1/4 cups (335 ml) olive oil

3 garlic cloves

Fresh parsley, finely chopped

1. Use watered salt cod (page 80). Do not remove skin; remove as many bones as possible. Cut thicker fish into bite-sized squares.
2. Place fish in a frying pan; cover with cold water and bring to a boil. Remove from heat when a slight foam forms on the surface. Remove cod and place on paper towels to drain and cool. Save 1 cup (250 ml) broth and cool.
3. Put oil in a heavy frying pan (or an earthenware pan on a metal plate) over moderate heat and fry garlic until golden. Remove garlic and crush in a mortar; add to reserved broth. Let oil cool.
4. Place cold cod into the cold oil, thicker pieces first and thinnest on top.
5. Place the frying pan over moderate heat. Start shaking the pan slowly when oil begins to boil, then shake more quickly for a few minutes. Be very careful.
6. Add garlic broth slowly while continually shaking the pan. Keep moving the pan for another 15 minutes, until sauce thickens and blends. Reduce heat and cook at a slow boil until cod is tender, shaking the pan from time to time so the cod does not stick. Do not overcook. Taste for saltiness.
7. Increase the heat and shake the pan until the sauce has fully thickened.
8. Serve immediately, sprinkled with a generous amount of parsley.

VARIATION

- Add a chopped hard-boiled egg yolk to the broth before adding it to the pan.

Salt Cod in Tomato Sauce, Roman Style

Italy

This recipe was brought to my attention by Loretta Forsyth of St. John's, thanks to her Italian connections.

- 1 1/2 lb (675 g) salt cod steaks
- 1 medium onion, sliced in crescents
- 3 tbsp (45 ml) olive oil
- 1/3 cup (85 ml) butter
- 2 tbsp (30 ml) tomato paste
- 1 cup (250 ml) water
- 3/4 tsp (3.5 ml) freshly ground black pepper
- Salt
- 2 tbsp (30 ml) pine nuts
- 2 tbsp (30 ml) golden raisins

1. Use watered salt cod (page 80). Drain. Cut into 4-inch (10 cm) squares.
2. Place oil and butter in a large frying pan; add onions and brown. Add tomato paste, water, and pepper. Cook 5 minutes.
3. Add steaks, pine nuts, and raisins; simmer 20 minutes.
4. Serve small portions in tapas style.

VARIATION

- Use a 20 oz (600 ml) can plum tomatoes (chopped, with juice) and 1/2 cup (125 ml) dry white wine instead of tomato paste and water. Add 1 finely chopped garlic clove. Transfer cooked cod to warm serving dishes, and add 2 tbsp (30 ml) fresh parsley to help thicken the sauce. Taste, and adjust seasoning. Spoon sauce over cod and serve.

Cod in Wine (Baccala 'Mbriache)

Italy

- 1 lb (450 g) salt cod fillets
- 1/2 cup (125 ml) olive oil
- 1 medium onion, finely sliced
- 1 bay leaf
- 2 cups (500 ml) dry white wine

1. Use watered salt cod (page 80). Drain and pat dry. Cut into bite-sized pieces and place in a baking pan.
2. Preheat oven to 450°F (230°C).
3. Drizzle cod with olive oil. Add onion and bay leaf; pour wine over all.
4. Bake until completely cooked, approximately 20 minutes.

Fried Salt Cod (Baccala Fritto)

Italy

- 1 lb (450 g) salt cod
- All-purpose flour, for dredging
- Olive oil, for frying
- 1 lemon, juiced

1. Use watered salt cod (page 80). Drain and pat dry. Remove skin and bones. Cut, break, or shred into bite-sized pieces or strips.
2. Pound cod pieces lightly and briefly to soften them. Dredge in flour. Add olive oil to a frying pan to a depth of 0.1 inches (0.3 cm). Sauté on both sides until cod is golden.
3. Serve hot or at room temperature with a sprinkling of lemon juice.

TAPAS AND MEZES

Salt Cod with Sour Cherries

Italy

In 1928, Ada Boni's *Talismano della Felicita* was published and recognized as Italy's national cookbook. In the course of its first 21 years, 16 reprints and new editions appeared. The fifteenth edition was a monumental affair of 866 pages and more than 2,000 recipes. A condensed translation and adaptation, *The Talisman Italian Cook Book*, published in 1950, contains over a dozen recipes for salt cod. Baccala with Sour Cherries is one of those recipes.

I last made this dish for a group of 15 celebrating Canada Day 2011 at a friend's house in Paradise, Newfoundland. I served the salt cod and sour cherries in scallop shells. As the sour cherries cook, their tartness mellows to a mild sweetness.

1 1/2 lb (675 g) salt cod

1 small onion, chopped

1/2 garlic clove, chopped

1/2 cup (125 ml) olive oil

1 tbsp (15 ml) tomato paste

1/2 tsp (2.5 ml) freshly ground black pepper

1 1/2 cups (375 ml) canned sour cherries, pitted

1. Use watered salt cod (page 80). Drain. Remove skin and bones, and break into small pieces. Set aside.
2. Brown onion and garlic lightly in oil in a large frying pan. Add tomato paste and pepper; cook 4 minutes.
3. Add cherries and juice.
4. Place salt cod on cherries, cover frying pan and cook slowly for 10-15 minutes. Serve hot or cold.

Salt Cod with Sour Cherries

Salt Cod in Vinaigrette (Escabeche de Bacalhau)

Portugal

An *escabeche* is a pickle for fish. The salt cod will need 24 hours in this pickle.

1 lb (450 g) salt cod

VINAIGRETTE

2 onions, sliced

1/4 cup (60 ml) olive oil

6 garlic cloves, peeled, crushed

2 carrots, grated

1 small bunch fresh parsley, chopped

6 peppercorns

1 tsp (5 ml) sweet paprika

1 bay leaf

2 tbsp (30 ml) dry white wine

1/4 cup (60 ml) white wine vinegar

Salt

1. Use watered salt cod (page 80). Simmer cod until it flakes easily (about 10 minutes). Drain, remove any skin and bones, and allow to cool slightly. Break cod into bite-sized pieces. Put into a dish with a cover.
2. Prepare vinaigrette: Sauté onions gently in olive oil until golden. Remove from heat. Stir in garlic, carrots, parsley, peppercorns, paprika, bay leaf, wine, and vinegar. Cool and pour over cod.
3. Cover the dish and chill for 24 hours.
4. Serve the marinated cod.

Salt Cod with Black Butter (Morue au Beurre Noir)

France

Beurre noir is a French term meaning, literally, "black butter." Beurre noir is melted butter that is cooked over low heat until the milk solids turn very dark brown (not black). When this happens, acid (usually lemon juice or vinegar) is carefully added.

1 1/2 lb (675 g) salt cod

1-2 sprigs fresh parsley, coarsely chopped

2 tsp (10 ml) capers

BLACK BUTTER

8 oz (225 g) butter

2 tsp (10 ml) white vinegar, or juice from 1 lemon

1. Use watered salt cod (page 80). Simmer for 15 minutes. Drain. Remove any skin and bones; break into fairly large pieces.
2. Brown butter in a pan over low heat. Carefully add vinegar or lemon juice. Reduce by one-third and pour over cod.
3. Sprinkle with parsley and capers. Pour black butter over the salt cod.

Salt Cod Roe Pâté (Taramosalata)

Greece

Taramosalata has travelled far beyond Greece to become a favourite in many countries. It is made with *tarama*, the dried and salted roe of fish such as grey mullet or herring. Smoked (or salted) cod roe is a good alternative. In Greece, taramosalata is often eaten in the winter, and particularly during Lent, when many people fast. The Greeks import tarama from Norway.

Taramosalata is a traditional meze consisting of tarama mixed with lemon juice, bread crumbs, onions, and olive oil. *Meze* is a Greek term for a variety of small dishes, similar to the tapas of Spain.

8 oz (225 g) salt cod roe (tarama)

1 small onion, grated or finely chopped

2 slices dry bread (2 inches/5 cm thick), or 1 boiled potato

1-2 lemons, juiced

1 cup (250 ml) olive oil

Black olives, green onions, or fresh parsley, for garnish

1. Remove crusts from the bread. Soak bread in a little water for 5-10 minutes; squeeze dry. Rinse salt cod roe in a fine-meshed strainer with water to remove some of the salt.
2. Place roe in a blender; blend at low speed until creamy. Alternate adding onions and bread or potato while continuing to blend. Slowly add olive oil and lemon juice to taste. Turn blender to high speed; blend until mixture is light in colour and creamy.
3. Taste, and adjust seasoning. Add a little more bread and oil for a milder taste; if too thick, add a little water.
4. Transfer to a serving dish, cover, and chill.
5. Serve with a little oil over the surface. Garnish with black olives, chopped green onions, or chopped parsley.

Avocado with Tarama

Greece

In addition to being its own dish, as on the previous page, taramosalata can be served as a garnish or a dip. It is used in this recipe as a filling for avocado and served as a meze. Known in Greece as *cos*, Romaine lettuce is said to have originated on the Greek island of Cos (Kos).

2 avocados, halved, pitted

8 leaves romaine lettuce or arugula

4 tbsp (60 ml) taramosalata (page 137)

8 lemon wedges

16 kalamata olives

1 tsp (5 ml) fresh parsley, chopped

1. Remove avocado from the shells. Slice and arrange on chilled romaine or arugula leaves on 4 salad plates.
2. Fill each avocado half shell with taramosalata.
3. Garnish each serving with 2 lemon wedges and 4 olives; sprinkle with parsley. Serve immediately.

Adapted from Eva Zane, *Greek Cooking for the Gods*

Kalamata olives.

Romaine lettuce.

HORS D'OEUVRES

Most of these recipes require that a mixture of salt cod and other ingredients (oil, herbs, spices, potatoes, yams, pumpkin, or avocado) be shaped into bite-sized pieces: croquettes, small cakes, balls, fritters, puffs, patties, or larger cod cakes. The terminology itself is not terribly important—you can give any mixture the shape of a cake, croquette, or ball. These morsels are most often fried (sometimes deep-fried) and served with a dipping sauce.

BRANDADE, SPREADS, DIPS

Salt Cod Brandade	*France*
Hot Avocado with Salt Cod (Féroce d'Avocat)	*Martinique-Guadeloupe*
Beaten Dried Cod (Baccala Mantecato)	*Italy*
Salt Cod with Bananas	*Newfoundland and Labrador*
Salt Cod Parfait	*Newfoundland and Labrador*

CROQUETTES, CAKES, PATTIES, PUFFS

Salt Cod Fish Cakes	*Newfoundland and Labrador*
Hairy Tatties	*Scotland*
Brazilian Cod Cakes	*Brazil*
Salt Cod Fritters	*Newfoundland and Labrador*
Salt Cod Acra	*Guadeloupe*
Cod Cakes (Accra)	*Trinidad*
Stamp and Go (Cod Fritters)	*Jamaica*
Salt Cod Cakes / Croquettes / Fritters (Bolinhos de Bacalhau)	*Portugal*

CROQUETTES, CAKES, PATTIES, PUFFS (CONT'D)

Salt Codfish Cakes	*Bermuda*
Saltfish and Yam Cakes	*Anguilla*
Cod Fritters (Frituras de Bacalao)	*Cuba*
Curried West Indies Saltfish Cakes	*Jamaica*
Saltfish Balls	*St. Lucia*
Salt Cod Puffs	*Newfoundland and Labrador*
Salt Cod Croquettes	*Italy*
Salt Cod Patties with Garlic Sauce (Bakaliaros Kefte Skordalia)	*Greece*
Salt Cod Balls	*Scotland*
Baked Cod Cakes (Bakalioros Keftedes)	*Greece*
Salt Cod in Potato Jackets (Bacalhau Numa Casca de Batata)	*Portugal*

DUMPLINGS

Salt Cod Dumplings	*Newfoundland and Labrador*

brandade, spreads, dips

Salt Cod Brandade

France

The variations at the end of this recipe show the versatility of this dish. Brandade can be used in eggs Benedict, vol-au-vents, or stuffed piquillo peppers.

1 lb (450 g) salt cod
1/2 cup (125 ml) olive oil
1/2 cup (125 ml) heavy cream
2-3 garlic cloves, crushed
Pinch nutmeg (optional)
1 tsp (5 ml) lemon juice
White pepper
French bread

1. Use watered salt cod (page 80). Poach in water 10-15 minutes until just tender. Drain; remove skin and bones. Shred and mash into very small pieces.
2. Heat oil in a small saucepan until hot. Warm cream in a separate saucepan; do not boil.
3. Transfer cod to a large mixing bowl (or blender or food processor). Stirring continuously with a wooden spoon, gradually alternate adding small amounts of oil and cream.
4. Add garlic. (Some cooks prefer to put the crushed garlic in the heated oil. If so, do not let it burn.) Stir until mixture reaches a smooth, creamy consistency; use as much cream and olive oil as necessary. Season with nutmeg, lemon juice, and white pepper.
5. Spoon brandade into a shallow serving bowl.
6. Surround with thin, buttered slices of French bread that have been toasted on both sides on a cookie sheet in a preheated 375°F (190°C) oven.
7. Serve brandade warm, at room temperature, or cool. Reheat slowly, if desired, in a double boiler or under a broiler.

Salt Cod Brandade

VARIATIONS

- Add a potato, boiled in its skin, then peeled and mashed.
- Mark Kurlansky in *Cod* describes an early French recipe, Morue en Brandade, in which the skin is kept on the salt cod, as "especially flavourful."
- Eggs Benedict: Use Salt Cod Brandade as the base (instead of ham) on which to serve poached eggs, covered with hollandaise sauce. Eggs Benedict could be sprinkled with grated cheese and broiled.
- Vol-au-vents: Serve brandade hot in vol-au-vents (small, hollow cases of puff pastry).
- Piquillo peppers: Fill peppers with brandade, using a small spoon and taking care not to tear the flesh. Place filled peppers on their sides in a lightly oiled baking dish. Bake about 20 minutes in a preheated 300°F (150°C) oven until filling is heated through.
- Potato slices: Scrub red potatoes and boil until just tender. Immediately drain and immerse in ice water to stop further cooking. When potatoes have cooled, cut into 0.3-inch (0.8 cm) slices. Top each slice with a spoonful of brandade, a dollop of crème fraîche (or sour cream), and a small garnish of caviar.
- Toast with olives and tomatoes: Roughly chop 1 tomato and 12 small Niçoise olives; mix with 2 tbsp (30 ml) extra-virgin olive oil. Spread brandade on each piece of toast or canapé and top with olive-tomato mixture.

Salt Cod Brandade (with Eggs Benedict)

Salt Cod Brandade (with Olives and Tomatoes)

Hot Avocado with Salt Cod (Féroce d'Avocat)

Martinique-Guadeloupe

Féroce refers to how much hot fresh pepper has been used in the dish. Traditionally, this is a highly seasoned dish, but ultimately the hot pepper is added to taste.

Meal or flour made from cassava, a white-fleshed tropical root vegetable, can be bought ready-made—it is also known as manioc meal or tapioca flour. In the Caribbean, a barbecue is often used to brown the cod slightly and give it a hint of smokiness.

8 oz (225 g) salt cod

2 avocados, peeled, cubed

1 small onion, finely chopped

1 garlic clove, crushed

2/3 cup (165 ml) vegetable oil

5 tbsp (75 ml) lime or lemon juice

1 tbsp (15 ml) white wine vinegar

1 or more habanero peppers, red or green, seeded, chopped

Freshly ground black pepper

1 sprig fresh parsley, chopped

Pinch white sugar

6 tbsp (90 ml) coconut milk or milk

4 oz (115 g) cassava meal or cassava flour

1. Use watered salt cod (page 80). Drain. Rinse with cold water, pat dry, and barbecue or broil until lightly coloured on both sides.
2. Remove any skin and bones; shred cod as finely as possible. Place in a bowl with avocado.
3. Prepare seasoning: Mix together onion, garlic, oil, lime or lemon juice, vinegar, peppers, ground pepper, parsley, and sugar. Pour over cod and avocado.
4. Mix cassava meal with just enough coconut milk to moisten; add to cod, avocado, and seasoning. Mix all together to a smooth paste.
5. Cool before serving as a spread, a dip spooned onto lettuce or spinach leaves, or shaped into balls or canapés to accompany drinks. Garnish with slices of cucumber and tomatoes. Refrigerate if not serving immediately.

Adapted from Elisabeth Lambert Ortiz, *Caribbean Cooking*

HORS D'OEUVRES

Beaten Dried Cod (Baccala Mantecato)

Italy

Traditionally, baccala mantecato was made with stockfish, the dried cod from Norway that is still favoured by Venetians above the baccala (salt cod). However, baccala is used extensively to make this dish as it is easier to obtain.

Throughout Italy, small bars serve dishes of sardines in salt, marinated eggplant, anchovies, and baccala mantecato on grilled sliced polenta (page 214) or crostini. Crostini are made by thinly slicing bread, typically plain white bread, and toasting or grilling until crispy.

1 lb (450 g) salt cod

1 medium carrot, chopped

1 medium onion, chopped

1 celery stalk, chopped

1 cup (250 ml) milk or half and half, warmed

1 cup (250 ml) extra-virgin olive oil

Freshly ground black pepper

Fresh parsley, chopped, for garnish

1. Use watered salt cod (page 80). Drain. Place in a medium saucepan.
2. Add carrot, onion, and celery to cod and cover with cold water. Simmer for 10 minutes, or until cod is tender.
3. Remove cod and drain on paper towels. Remove all bones while cod is still warm. Keep the skin on for additional flavour (optional). Flake cod into small pieces and place in a bowl.
4. Stir cod with a pestle and/or whisk thoroughly, alternately adding trickles of warm milk and olive oil. Continue for 15-20 minutes, or until creamy smooth. Season with pepper. Serve sprinkled with parsley.

VARIATIONS

- When simmering the watered salt cod, add 1 bay leaf, 1 tsp (5 ml) dried thyme, and 1/2 tsp (2.5 ml) dried sage.
- Add 3 chopped anchovy fillets and 1 finely chopped garlic clove to the salt cod spread.
- Serve baccala mantecato on croutons of fried white bread or fried polenta.
- Cook lasagna noodles. Drain and cool. Lay the noodles on a cutting board. Spread each with 1/4 cup (60 ml) salt cod mixture. Roll up like a jelly roll and cut into bite-sized pieces.

Salt Cod with Bananas

Newfoundland and Labrador

This recipe is adapted from one submitted to *The Evening Telegram* in 1975 by Dorothy Duff Moores. It was brought to my attention by Margaret Walsh Best, who has made the dish part of her Christmas tradition. These ingredients combine for an extremely delicate flavour.

1 lb (450 g) salt cod

1 1/2 bananas

1 tsp (5 ml) lemon juice

2/3 cup (165 ml) whipping cream

2 tbsp (30 ml) fresh chives, chopped, divided

2 tbsp (30 ml) fresh parsley, chopped, divided

2 egg yolks

1. Use watered salt cod (page 80). Simmer gently for about 15 minutes until it becomes tender and flaky. Drain; remove any skin and bones.
2. Add half of the chives and parsley to the cod. Season to taste. Stir in cream.
3. Beat egg yolks and add gradually to mixture. Heat almost to boiling.
4. Peel and slice bananas. Sprinkle with lemon juice. Add to cod mixture.
5. Serve in scallop shells. Garnish with remaining chives and parsley.

Salt Cod with Bananas

HORS D'OEUVRES

Salt Cod Parfait

Newfoundland and Labrador

The cod I used to create this dish was caught in the waters off Cape Spear, Newfoundland. I went back to the rocks at Cape Spear to photograph the finished parfait.

- 3/4 lb (345 g) salt cod, thick pieces
- 2/3 cup (165 ml) sour cream, divided
- 1/3 cup (85 ml) mayonnaise (page 302)
- 2/3 cup (165 ml) red onion, finely chopped
- 1 cup (250 ml) cucumber, chopped
- 1/4 cup (60 ml) fresh chives, chopped
- 1/4 cup (60 ml) fresh dill, chopped
- 1 lemon, juiced
- Salt
- 4 lemon slices
- Caviar

1. Use watered salt cod (page 80). Simmer until cooked. Drain. Remove any skin and bones; finely sliver cod.
2. Mix mayonnaise and 1/3 cup (85 ml) sour cream in a bowl. Add salt cod and onion and mix to coat thoroughly. Keep chilled.
3. Mix cucumber, chives, dill, lemon juice, and salt in a separate bowl.
4. Spoon a layer of cucumber mixture into the bottoms of 4 parfait glasses. Place a layer of salt cod mixture on top of the cucumber.
5. Repeat layers. Finish with a splash of sour cream.
6. Garnish with lemon slices and salmon caviar, lumpfish caviar, or herring roe.

SERVES 4

Salt Cod Parfait

croquettes, cakes, patties, puffs

Salt Cod Fish Cakes

Newfoundland and Labrador

The use of fatback pork and savoury distinguishes this recipe from the cakes and croquettes of other recipes in this section.

- 1 1/4 lb (570 g) salt cod
- 4 medium potatoes, peeled, boiled, mashed
- 2 onions, chopped
- Butter, for sautéing
- 1 tbsp (15 ml) dried savoury, finely crushed
- Freshly ground black pepper
- 1 egg, beaten (optional)
- All-purpose flour or fine bread crumbs
- 4 oz (115 g) fatback pork

1. Use watered salt cod (page 80). Simmer cod until it flakes easily, about 10 minutes. Remove from the heat. Drain. Remove any skin and bones; flake fish into small pieces.
2. Sauté onions in a small amount of butter.
3. Combine cod, potatoes, sautéed onions, savoury, and pepper in a mixing bowl. Stir well. If mixture requires extra binding, add beaten egg and mix well.
4. Shape into round cakes about 2.5-3 inches (6-7.5 cm) in diameter and coat lightly with flour or bread crumbs.
5. Prepare scrunchions (page 300) with fatback. Fry cakes in scrunchions over a moderate-high heat for 6-7 minutes on each side, or until crusty and golden. Turn once.
6. Garnish with warm scrunchions.

VARIATIONS

 Use parsley or sage (fresh or dried) instead of savoury.

 Add cooked parsnip or turnip to potatoes.

 For party appetizers, make 1-inch-diameter (2.5 cm) patties.

Salt Cod Fish Cakes

HORS D'OEUVRES

Hairy Tatties

Scotland

Hairy Tatties, also known as Hairy Willies, is a traditional Scottish dish. The flakes of salt cod are broken into strands not much thicker than hairs, which explains the name.

Serve these with a mustard-zapped salsa verde (page 303) for great comfort food on a winter evening.

1 lb (450 g) salt cod	Freshly ground black pepper
5 medium potatoes, peeled, boiled	2 tbsp (30 ml) fresh parsley, chopped
2 tbsp (30 ml) butter	Oatmeal
1/2 cup (125 ml) milk, heated	Vegetable oil, for frying
Dijon mustard	

1. Use watered salt cod (page 80). Cover cod with fresh cold water, bring slowly to a boil; reduce heat to simmer. Cover the pan; cook slowly for 8-10 minutes; drain. Remove any skin and bones and flake cod into small pieces.
2. Mash potatoes with butter and milk; add mustard and pepper to taste.
3. Stir in flaked cod and parsley. Allow mixture to cool. Form into cakes; roll in oatmeal. Chill. Fry cakes in hot oil until golden brown on both sides.

Brazilian Cod Cakes

Brazil

This recipe has an abundance of herbs and spices—experiment or use carefully. The poached eggs on top are a Brazilian touch.

1/2 lb (225 g) salt cod	2 tbsp (30 ml) fresh parsley, chopped
1/4 cup (60 ml) olive oil	3 garlic cloves, crushed
2 cups (500 ml) dry bread crumbs	3 tsp (15 ml) sweet paprika
1 medium onion, chopped	3 dashes piri piri or other hot pepper sauce
3 tbsp (45 ml) fresh mint, chopped	4 eggs, poached, for garnish
1/4 cup (60 ml) fresh coriander, chopped	

1. Use watered salt cod (page 80). Simmer cod in water. Drain. Remove skin and bones. Flake.
2. Combine all ingredients except eggs in a large bowl. Mix thoroughly. Divide into 4 patties, each about 0.5 inches (1.2 cm) thick.
3. Brown patties on both sides in a frying pan. Use a little olive oil and, if desired, a little butter.
4. Poach eggs. Top patties with eggs and serve.

Salt Cod Fritters

Newfoundland and Labrador

Served as an appetizer at Nicole's Café in Joe Batt's Arm, Fogo Island, Newfoundland and Labrador, these fritters are distinguished by the locally made partridgeberry mayonnaise that accompanies them.

The partridgeberry, internationally known as the lingonberry, is a relative of the cranberry and grows in the dry acidic soils of Newfoundland and Labrador's barrens and coastal headlands. It is tart and high in vitamin C, tannin, anthocyanin, and antioxidants. It is also the centre of attention for the annual Fogo Island Partridgeberry Harvest Festival.

1/2 lb (225 g) salt cod
1 cup (250 ml) all-purpose flour
1 egg
1/4 cup (60 ml) green onions, chopped
1/2 cup (125 ml) milk
Salt and freshly ground black pepper
Olive oil, for deep-frying
Partridgeberry mayonnaise (page 302), to serve

1. Use watered salt cod (page 80). Drain. Remove any skin and bones; flake or finely shred cod.
2. Combine flour, egg, green onion, milk, salt, and pepper; add cod. Mix thoroughly.
3. Heat enough olive oil in a deep fryer on high heat to cover and cook the fritters.
4. Shape mixture with a teaspoon into uniform shapes. Cook in batches for 5 minutes or until crispy.
5. Serve with partridgeberry mayonnaise.

Courtesy of Nicole Torraville, Nicole's Cafe, Fogo Island

Salt Cod Fritters

HORS D'OEUVRES

SALT COD CUISINE: THE INTERNATIONAL TABLE

Salt Cod Acra

Guadeloupe

Akkra, originally West African fritters made from black-eyed peas, spread to the Caribbean and Brazil through the slave trade. Crispy on the outside and creamy in the middle, they are various known as *akra*, *acra*, *accra*, *acrat*, and *acaraje*. The name *accra* is also used for fritters, sometimes made with a heavy batter, into which other ingredients are mixed, the most popular being salt cod.

12 oz (340 g) salt cod

1 cup (250 ml) all-purpose flour

3/4 cup (185 ml) milk

1 tbsp (15 ml) fresh coriander, chopped

2 green onions, chopped

1 medium onion, chopped

2 garlic cloves, finely chopped

3 fresh garlic chives or chives, chopped

Freshly ground black pepper

1/3 red chili pepper, chopped

1 tbsp (15 ml) baking powder

Sunflower oil, for deep-frying

1. Use watered salt cod (page 80). Cover cod with water and simmer gently, covered, until tender, about 15 minutes. Drain. Remove any skin and bones. Finely shred cod. Purée in a food processor.
2. Mix flour and milk in a large bowl. Stir in puréed cod, coriander, green onions, onion, garlic, and chives. Season to taste with pepper. Add chili pepper. Stir vigorously. Refrigerate until well cooled.
3. Add baking powder to the mixture; stir well.
4. Heat oil in a deep fryer. Drop in teaspoonfuls of the mixture and fry until golden. The acras will take shape and rise to the surface of the oil. Remove, drain on paper towels, and serve hot.

Adapted from Babette de Rozieres, *Creole*

HORS D'OEUVRES

Cod Cakes (Accra)

Trinidad

In contrast to the previous recipe, which uses baking powder and milk, this one uses yeast and water.

- 1/2 lb (225 g) salt cod
- 2 tsp (10 ml) active dry yeast
- 6 tbsp (90 ml) warm water
- 1 cup (250 ml) all-purpose flour
- 1 tsp (5 ml) white sugar
- 1 onion, finely chopped
- 1 garlic clove, finely chopped
- 1 tbsp (15 ml) habanero peppers, chopped
- 1 tbsp (15 ml) fresh chives, chopped
- Freshly ground black pepper
- Vegetable oil, for deep-frying

1. Use watered salt cod (page 80). Pour boiling water over cod; allow to cool. Rinse in cold water; remove any skin and bones. Shred.
2. Sprinkle yeast on warm water and let stand 10 minutes.
3. Mix cod with flour, sugar, onion, garlic, peppers, chives, and pepper.
4. Add yeast mixture and beat until smooth. Allow to rise for 1 1/2-2 hours in a warm draft-free place.
5. Drop by tablespoonfuls into hot oil and fry until golden brown. Drain on paper towels and serve hot.

Adapted from Elisabeth Lambert Ortiz, *Caribbean Cooking*

Stamp and Go (Cod Fritters)

Jamaica

There are many interpretations of the meaning of the fanciful name Stamp and Go, but most centre on the sale of these cod cakes at bus stops. The rider would quickly hop off the bus, get a cake or two, return to the bus, and go.

- 1/2 lb (225 g) salt cod
- 1 onion, finely chopped
- 1 garlic clove, chopped
- 2 green onions, chopped
- 1 tbsp (15 ml) Scotch bonnet peppers, seeds removed, chopped
- 1 tomato, chopped
- 1/2 tsp (2.5 ml) dried thyme
- Freshly ground black pepper
- Pinch sweet paprika
- 2 tbsp (30 ml) vegetable or annatto oil
- 1 tbsp (15 ml) baking powder
- 1 cup (250 ml) all-purpose flour (more, if needed)
- Vegetable oil, for frying

1. Use watered salt cod (page 80). Simmer gently, covered, until cod is tender, about 15 minutes. Drain. Remove any skin and bones. Finely shred cod.
2. Combine chopped onion, garlic, green onions, peppers, and tomato. Add thyme, black pepper, and paprika. Sauté in a small amount of oil.
3. Place cod in a mixing bowl. Add flour, mixed with baking powder, and sufficient cold water to make a soft sticky batter; stir until smooth. Add cooked ingredients; stir until mixed.
4. Make fritters (or small flattened cakes) of the desired size and shape. Fry on both sides on medium heat until golden brown.
5. Drain on paper towels. Serve hot.

Salt Cod Cakes / Croquettes / Fritters (Bolinhos de Bacalhau)

Portugal

These cakes lend themselves to a light first course or snack and can be used as *peticos*, "little tastes." They could also be combined with rice and greens for a simple meal. They are often served on Christmas Eve.

- 1 lb (450 g) salt cod
- 3 potatoes, peeled, boiled, mashed
- 1 tbsp (15 ml) olive oil
- 1 medium onion, finely chopped
- 3 eggs, lightly beaten, divided
- 1/4 cup (60 ml) fresh parsley, chopped
- 2 tsp (30 ml) pimento paste or roasted red peppers, mashed
- Pinch white pepper
- Bread crumbs
- Vegetable or olive oil, for frying or deep-frying

1. Use watered salt cod (page 80). Drain cod and rinse.
2. Place cod and potatoes in a medium saucepan; cover with water. Bring to a boil and simmer 15 minutes. Remove cod, and remove any skin and bones. Flake or shred cod. Drain and dice potatoes when cooked.
3. Heat olive oil in a small saucepan over medium heat and cook onion, stirring occasionally, for 3 minutes, or until tender.
4. Mix cod, potatoes, and onions. Add 2 eggs, one at a time, stirring until mixture holds together and is well blended. Stir in parsley, white pepper, and pimento. (For a lighter, fluffy interior, some cooks beat the egg whites to soft peaks before adding with yolks to the mixture.)
5. Shape mixture into 1-inch (2.5 cm) ovals, finger shapes, or croquettes. Keep them uniform. Dip into remaining beaten egg and roll in bread crumbs, coating all over.
6. Heat 1 inch (2.5 cm) oil in a heavy frying pan. Cook cakes in batches over medium-high heat for 2-3 minutes until evenly browned and heated through.
7. Drain on paper towels; keep warm in oven until serving.

VARIATIONS

- Add finely chopped garlic cloves and fresh coriander to the mixture.
- Use 1/2 tsp (2.5 ml) hot pepper sauce instead of pimento paste for a hotter cake.
- At step 4 above, substitute 1/2 tsp (2.5 ml) nutmeg for the pimento and add 2/3 cup (165 ml) port to cod, potato, and onion mixture.

HORS D'OEUVRES

Salt Codfish Cakes

Bermuda

Recipes for Bermuda's cod cakes vary but, in general, they are crispy on the outside; inside they are soft and creamy or firm and chunky, depending on how finely the potatoes and cod are chopped. They are always moist. As with cod cakes anywhere, the herbs provide the taste.

These cakes are traditionally eaten in sweet hot cross buns with a little mayonnaise on Good Friday. A sprinkle of hot pepper sauce can be added to the sandwich or the cod mixture.

- 1 1/4 lb (570 g) salt cod
- 5 medium potatoes, peeled, boiled, mashed
- 1 medium onion, chopped
- 2 tsp (10 ml) fresh parsley, chopped
- 1 tsp (5 ml) dried thyme
- Freshly ground black pepper
- 1 egg, beaten
- All-purpose flour, for dusting
- Salt
- Olive oil, for frying

1. Use watered salt cod (page 80). Drain.
2. Cover cod and potatoes with fresh water in a large saucepan. Bring to a boil and simmer until potatoes are cooked. Drain.
3. Remove any skin and bones; break or flake cod into small pieces. Mash potatoes and cod together.
4. Add onion, parsley, thyme, black pepper, and egg. Mix well.
5. Form mixture into patties, dust with flour and a little salt. Fry in oil until golden brown and crispy.

Saltfish and Yam Cakes

Anguilla

These salty, sweet cakes are great at lunch with a lightly dressed salad, or as hors d'oeuvres with spicy chutney or sour cream. This is an adaptation of a recipe by Chef Daniel Orr of Anguilla, published in *The Anguillian* newspaper. His recipe leaves plenty of room for experimenting.

- 1 lb (450 g) salt cod
- 1 1/2 cups (375 ml) grated yam or sweet potato
- 1 egg
- 1/2 tsp (2.5 ml) freshly ground black pepper
- 2 tbsp (30 ml) all-purpose flour
- Olive oil, for frying
- Salt (optional)
- 1 tbsp (15 ml) fresh thyme, finely chopped
- 1 tbsp (15 ml) fresh parsley, finely chopped
- Assorted chilies, for garnish
- Hot pepper sauce

1. Use watered salt cod (page 80). Cover with fresh water and simmer gently until cod is tender, about 15 minutes. Drain. Remove any skin and bones. Finely shred cod.
2. Grate yam. Mix with remaining ingredients immediately, before it discolours.
3. Check seasoning by forming a test cake and cooking it in heated oil until brown and crispy. Taste, adjust seasoning if necessary; add water if too dry.
4. Shape and cook remaining cakes.
5. Garnish with chilies and serve hot.

Cod Fritters (Frituras de Bacalao)

Cuba

> Cod was part of the slaves' basic diet during colonial times being a cheap and easily conserved protein. In the sugar mills, one person was charged with distributing the salt cod ration and such was the importance of the job that the expression "he who cuts the cod" is still used to indicate a person with power.
>
> —Beatriz Llamas, *A Taste of Cuba*

Although salt cod is not as cheap as it once was, it is still enjoyed with enthusiasm in Cuba. In this basic recipe for cod fritters, the cod is left uncooked until it reaches the stage for deep-frying; in some recipes, the cod is cooked before being added to the batter.

3/4 lb (340 g) salt cod

3 eggs, beaten

1/3 cup (85 ml) whole wheat flour

2 tbsp (30 ml) onion, finely chopped

1 tbsp (15 ml) red bell pepper, finely chopped

1 tbsp (15 ml) green bell pepper, finely chopped

1 garlic clove, crushed

1 tbsp (15 ml) fresh parsley, chopped

Freshly ground black pepper

Vegetable oil, for deep-frying

1. Use watered salt cod (page 80). Remove any skin and bones; flake.
2. Mix flour into beaten eggs until smooth. Add onion, peppers, garlic, parsley, and cod. Season with black pepper.
3. Heat oil in a frying pan. Drop mixture by tablespoonfuls into the oil to cook the fritters. Deep-fry until golden. Drain on paper towels. Serve immediately.

Adapted from Beatriz Llamas, *A Taste of Cuba*

HORS D'OEUVRES

Curried West Indies Saltfish Cakes

Jamaica

- 8 oz (225 g) salt cod
- 1 cup (250 ml) all-purpose flour
- 5 garlic cloves, chopped
- 1 tsp (5 ml) curry powder
- 1/2 tsp (2.5 ml) cayenne pepper
- 2 tsp (10 ml) baking powder
- 3 green onions, chopped
- 2 eggs
- 1 cup (250 ml) water
- Vegetable oil, for frying
- Lemon slices, for garnish
- Curry garlic mayonnaise or tartar sauce (page 302), to serve

1. Use watered salt cod (page 80). Cover with water and bring to a boil; simmer until tender, about 15 minutes. Drain. Remove any skin and bones. Flake.
2. Mix flour, garlic, curry powder, cayenne pepper, baking powder, onions, eggs, and water with cod in a mixing bowl until well blended. Adjust water and/or flour as necessary to achieve the consistency of a fairly thick pancake batter.
3. Make cakes into the desired shape and size and fry in heated oil in a large frying pan, being careful not to overcrowd. Cook about 2-4 minutes per side, or until the cakes are golden and firm. Drain on paper towels.
4. Serve hot with curry garlic mayonnaise or tartar sauce and lemon slices.

Saltfish Balls

St. Lucia

- 1 lb (450 g) salt cod
- 1 lb (450 g) pumpkin, peeled, seeded, cubed
- Salt
- 1 tbsp (15 ml) butter, softened
- 2 eggs, lightly beaten
- Freshly ground black pepper
- 1/2 cup (125 ml) soft fresh white bread crumbs, finely shredded, divided
- Vegetable oil, for frying

1. Use watered salt cod (page 80). Drain, add fresh water, bring to a boil; simmer 15 minutes. Drain. Remove any skin and bones. Separate cod into fine flakes. Set aside.
2. Boil pumpkin cubes in lightly salted water for 20 minutes, until tender. Drain, and completely dry pumpkin pieces. Purée pumpkin or mash with a fork.
3. Add butter, cod, eggs, and a little pepper. Stir with a wooden spoon until the mixture is smooth. Beat in a few tablespoons of bread crumbs if mixture is too thin.
4. Make balls into desired shape and size. Dip in remaining bread crumbs and place on parchment paper.
5. Fry balls in oil in a heavy frying pan over moderate heat for 3-4 minutes, turning occasionally and adjusting the heat so they brown evenly without burning. Do not overcrowd the pan. Serve warm.

Salt Cod Puffs

Newfoundland and Labrador

1 lb (450 g) salt cod

1 lb (450 g) potatoes, peeled, boiled, mashed

1 medium onion, finely chopped

1/4 cup (60 ml) fresh parsley, finely chopped

1/4 tsp (1.2 ml) freshly ground black pepper

6 eggs, separated

Vegetable oil, for deep-frying

1. Use watered salt cod (page 80). Simmer 15 minutes, until tender. Drain, remove skin and bones. Flake and finely shred cod.
2. Mix cod with potatoes. Add onion, parsley, and pepper. Mix well.
3. Add egg yolks and mix.
4. Whip egg whites in separate bowl and add to mixture.
5. Form into puffs. Deep-fry until golden brown.

Courtesy of Sharon Coady, Aquaforte, and Wilf Curran, Ferryland

Salt Cod Puffs

HORS D'OEUVRES

Salt Cod Croquettes

Italy

- 1 1/2 lb (675 g) salt cod
- 3 anchovy fillets, chopped
- 1 tbsp (15 ml) fresh parsley, chopped
- 1 1/2 tsp (7.5 ml) freshly ground black pepper
- 1 tbsp (15 ml) Parmesan cheese, grated
- 2 slices white bread, soaked in water and squeezed dry
- 3 eggs, lightly beaten, divided
- 1/2 cup (125 ml) all-purpose flour
- 1 cup (250 ml) bread crumbs
- 1 cup (250 ml) olive oil

1. Use watered salt cod (page 80). Simmer for 30 minutes. Drain. Remove any skin and bones. Chop fine.
2. Add anchovies, parsley, pepper, cheese, bread, and 2 eggs; mix well.
3. Shape into croquettes. Roll in flour, dip into the remaining beaten egg, roll in bread crumbs, and fry in olive oil until brown all over. Frying time will be about 4 minutes on each side.

Adapted from Ada Boni, *The Talisman Italian Cook Book*

Salt Cod Patties with Garlic Sauce (Bakaliaros Kefte Skordalia)

Greece

Skordalia is a thick sauce in Greek cuisine made by combining crushed garlic with a bulky base (a purée of potatoes, walnuts, and almonds, or liquid-soaked stale bread) and then beating in olive oil to make a smooth emulsion.

- 1 lb (450 g) salt cod
- 1 bay leaf
- 1 onion, quartered
- 2 cups (500 ml) potatoes, peeled, boiled, mashed
- 2 green onions, finely chopped
- 2 tbsp (30 ml) fresh parsley, finely chopped
- 1 egg
- All-purpose flour
- 2 tbsp (30 ml) olive oil
- 2 tbsp (30 ml) butter
- Skordalia (page 299), to serve

1. Use watered salt cod (page 80). Simmer cod for 20 minutes in a medium saucepan with bay leaf and quartered onion.
2. Remove cod. Drain, remove skin and bones, flake, and mash completely.
3. Combine cod, potatoes, green onions, parsley, and egg. Knead thoroughly and shape into patties on a floured board, dusting with flour.
4. Heat olive oil and butter in a frying pan; fry patties on both sides until golden brown.
5. Serve on a platter with a bowl of skordalia.

Adapted from Eva Zane, *Greek Cooking for the Gods*

Salt Cod Balls

Scotland

1 lb (450 g) salt cod

6 medium potatoes, peeled, boiled, mashed

Freshly ground black pepper

2 tbsp (30 ml) butter

1/4 cup (60 ml) milk, heated

2 eggs

All-purpose flour

Vegetable oil, for deep-frying

Sprigs fresh parsley, for garnish

1. Use watered salt cod (page 80). Bring to a boil and simmer until tender, about 15 minutes. Drain. Remove any skin and bones. Flake cod finely while hot.
2. Season potatoes with pepper; cream potatoes with milk and butter until fluffy.
3. Measure potatoes and cod. Allow twice as much mashed potato as flaked cod. Stir potatoes and cod until blended; add butter to taste. Beat eggs lightly and stir into mixture.
4. Refrigerate until cold and firm. Shape into small balls and roll in flour. Deep-fry in hot oil until golden brown. Drain on paper towels.
5. Garnish with parsley and serve.

Baked Cod Cakes (Bakalioros Keftedes)

Greece

This is the only dish in this section in which the cakes are baked instead of fried or deep-fried. As in the recipe on the previous page, they are served with a bowl of garlicky skordalia.

1 lb (450 g) salt cod

4 medium potatoes, peeled, boiled, mashed, dry

1/4 cup (60 ml) milk

1 tbsp (15 ml) chopped onion

Cayenne pepper

1 egg, slightly beaten

Skordalia (page 299), to serve

1. Use watered salt cod (page 80). Place in a pan; cover with boiling water. Cover pan and let stand 20 minutes; drain. Cover cod with more boiling water and let stand for another 20 minutes; drain.
2. Preheat oven to 350°F (180°C).
3. Flake cod and mix with mashed potatoes, milk, onion, cayenne, and egg.
4. Shape the mixture into 2-inch (5 cm) cakes. Place on a well-greased baking sheet; bake for 35 minutes or until brown.
5. Serve with skordalia.

Adapted from Recipe Club of Saint Paul's Greek Orthodox Cathedral, *The Complete Book of Greek Cooking*

HORS D'OEUVRES

Salt Cod in Potato Jackets (Bacalhau Numa Casca de Batata)

Portugal

Chestnuts were popular in the days of the Roman Empire and today are often used in dishes from Spain, Italy, France, Portugal, and other countries. Their sweetness provides a foil for the saltiness of the bacalhau. Although chestnuts can be difficult to get outside of specialty food shops, they can at times be found either vacuum-packed or in jars (look for those without sugar). Walnuts or pecans could be used as substitutes.

- 3/4 lb (340 g) salt cod
- 10 small potatoes
- 1 tbsp (15 ml) olive oil
- 1/4 cup (60 ml) warm water
- 2 cups (500 ml) baby spinach, tightly packed
- 3/4 cup (185 ml) chestnuts, roasted, finely chopped
- 1 garlic clove, finely chopped
- 1 cup (250 ml) mayonnaise (page 302), divided
- 1/2 cup (125 ml) dried bread crumbs, finely crushed
- Salt and freshly ground black pepper

1. Use watered salt cod (page 80). Simmer for about 15 minutes, until tender. Drain. Remove any skin and bones. Flake or shred cod. Set aside and keep warm.
2. Preheat oven to 450°F (230°C). Scrub potatoes and bake until tender, about 45-50 minutes. Let cool until easy to handle. Split potatoes lengthwise. Scoop out flesh and mash thoroughly; leave a thin layer inside the skin. Set aside mashed potato and keep warm.
3. Heat olive oil in a frying pan and sauté garlic briefly. Add spinach and 1/4 cup (60 ml) warm water; sauté 4-5 minutes. Transfer spinach to a colander. Press out all the liquid. Chop spinach into small pieces.
4. Place three-quarters of the mashed potato into a large bowl. Stir in shredded cod, spinach-garlic mixture, chestnuts, and 1/2 cup (125 ml) mayonnaise.
5. Mound mixture into potato skins and top with remaining mayonnaise. Sprinkle with bread crumbs, place on a baking sheet, and roast until golden brown, about 15 minutes. Serve hot.

Adapted from David Leite, *The New Portuguese Table*

Salt Cod in Potato Jackets

dumplings

Salt Cod Dumplings

Newfoundland and Labrador

My inspiration for this recipe came from Andreas Viestad's *Kitchen of Light: New Scandinavian Cooking*. Although dumplings can be cooked in some salt cod soups and stews, these are made with salt cod and cooked in fish stock. They are served on their own, accompanied by drawn butter or a dill-flavoured béchamel sauce. Make the dumplings as light as possible.

1 lb (450 g) salt cod fillets

2 eggs

3 tbsp (45 ml) cornstarch

1 cup (250 ml) flour

1 tsp (5 ml) white pepper

2 cups (500 ml) whipping cream, whipped

Water

1 cup (250 ml) fish stock (page 296)

1. Use watered salt cod (page 80). Drain. Remove any skin and bones. Break cod into pieces.
2. Run cod through a meat grinder twice or blend in a food processor; it should be smooth.
3. Beat eggs lightly in a large bowl. Add cornstarch, flour, pepper, and cod; mix well. Fold whipped cream gently into the mixture, trying not to deflate it.
4. Use a tablespoon to form dumpling mixture into small balls.
5. Bring a stockpot or deep frying pan of water and fish stock to a boil. Add dumplings, reduce heat and simmer about 7 minutes, until cooked through.
6. Remove with a slotted spoon and serve with drawn butter (page 300), béchamel sauce (page 297), with dill, or a sauce of your choice.

Salt Cod Dumplings

SOUPS AND CHOWDERS

> Seven virtues has soup:
> It calms thirst and diminishes hunger,
> Aids in sleeping and digestion,
> Tastes good and never offends,
> And brings color to the face.
> —Jose Maria Busca Isusi,
> *Traditional Basque Cooking*

The use of fish stock (page 296) rather than water will greatly enhance many salt cod soups and chowders and offers an opportunity to add an extra creative touch. If you make large quantities of stock, freeze it in small portions in ice-cube trays or 1-cup packages. Ready-made fish stock is also available in cubes and bottles of concentrated fish sauce.

The three chowder recipes are similar in name but have only two ingredients in common: salt cod and onions. The first chowder recipe, from Newfoundland and Labrador, includes among its 17 ingredients a range of spices; the second recipe includes, in its 8 ingredients, fatback pork, carrots, and potatoes. Chili pepper, sausage, kale, and fresh mint are used in the recipe from Portugal.

Salt Cod, Leek, and Chickpea Soup	*Spain*	Salt Cod, Okra, and Yam Soup	*Caribbean*
Green Broth with Salt Cod		Bouillabaisse	*France*
(Caldo Verde with Salt Cod)	*Portugal*	Bathed Bread (Pan Bagna)	*Italy*
Bread Soup with Salt Cod (Acorda de Bacalhau)	*Portugal*	Salt Cod and Tomato Soup	*Newfoundland and Labrador*
Bread Soup with Cod (Migas a Lagareiro)	*Portugal*	Salt Cod Chowder	*Newfoundland and Labrador*
Baccala Soup	*Italy*	Traditional Salt Cod Chowder	*Newfoundland and Labrador*
Herdsmen's Dried Cod Soup		Kale and Salt Cod Chowder	*Portugal*
(Sopa de Bacalhau dos Campinos)	*Portugal*		

SALT COD CUISINE: THE INTERNATIONAL TABLE

To the Salt Cod, Leek & Chickpea

"As much from the land as the sea
has come this potion; this eclectic bounty
We lift a glass to the ally of the onion;
the Atlantic wonder;
the Europe and Asian seed
and honour this salted elixir,
this purée of mysterious
desire and need"

— Bru Chubbs
November 5th · MMXI

SOUPS AND CHOWDERS

Salt Cod, Leek, and Chickpea Soup

Spain

This purée with its hint of smokiness is used to celebrate the culture of the salt cod in a toast proposed by Boyd W. Chubbs, a Newfoundland and Labrador poet, musician, and artist (see facing page).

Leeks are often the vegetable of choice to add to salt cod soups and stews, particularly in Spanish recipes. On a very modest scale, I grow about four dozen leeks each year for this purpose.

- 8 oz (225 g) salt cod
- 4 oz (115 g) smoked cod
- 2 1/2 cups (625 ml) milk
- 1/2 cup (125 ml) water
- 1/2 cup (125 ml) chicken stock
- 4 oz (115 g) chickpeas, soaked 12 hours
- 2 cups (500 ml) leeks
- 1 cup (250 ml) green onions
- 3 garlic cloves
- 3 tbsp (45 ml) olive oil
- 1 medium potato, chopped
- 1 red bell pepper, chopped
- 1 carrot, chopped
- 1 cup (250 ml) heavy cream, warmed
- White pepper
- Fresh parsley, chopped, for garnish
- Truffle oil

1. Use watered salt cod (page 80). Drain well.
2. Place salt cod and smoked cod in a frying pan with milk. Simmer 10 minutes; remove cod and reserve milk. Remove any skin and bones. Flake or shred cod.
3. Combine water and chicken stock with 2 cups (500 ml) reserved milk from step 2 in a stockpot. Add cod and chickpeas; simmer 20 minutes.
4. Roughly chop leeks, green onions, and garlic; sauté in olive oil for 5 minutes and add to the stockpot.
5. Add potato, red pepper, and carrot. Simmer 40 minutes. Mix in warmed cream thoroughly.
6. Cool soup slightly. Blend in batches, until smooth. Season with white pepper and gently reheat if necessary.
7. Serve in warmed soup bowls, garnish with parsley, and drizzle with a little truffle oil.

SERVES 4

VARIATION

- Serve the purée from step 6 cold in small glasses or bowls, topped with a few drops of parsley-infused olive oil and 1/4 tsp (1.2 ml) herring roe. Decorate with small pieces of chervil and propose a toast to the culture of the salt cod.

Green Broth with Salt Cod (Caldo Verde with Salt Cod)

Portugal

Caldo verde, a national dish in Portugal, is very versatile. Finely sliced greens are a basic ingredient—sliced kale, collard greens, Savoy cabbage, or the leaves of a very large cabbage known as *couve*. It is important that the stalks and tough parts of the greens are removed and the rest finely shredded. Caldo verde is traditionally served with slices of *broa*, Portuguese corn bread, to soak up the broth.

- 12 oz (340 g) salt cod, divided
- 2 tbsp (30 ml) olive oil
- 1 large onion, chopped
- 3 garlic cloves, finely chopped
- 5 cups (1.2 L) water
- 1 cup (250 ml) fish stock (page 296)
- 4 medium potatoes, peeled, chopped
- 7 oz (200 g) kale, collard greens, or cabbage, finely shredded

1. Use watered salt cod (page 80). Remove any skin and bones; flake cod.
2. Heat oil in a medium saucepan over medium-high heat. Add onions and cook until translucent. Add garlic and half the salt cod. Sauté about 5 minutes until garlic starts to brown. Add water, fish stock, and potatoes. Simmer gently for 15-20 minutes, until potatoes are soft.
3. Mash salt cod, potatoes, and onions in the saucepan; or let the soup cool, purée, and return to the pot.
4. Add greens and remaining salt cod to the soup. Simmer 5-10 minutes, until greens and cod are tender.
5. Taste for seasoning; serve in warmed soup bowls.

SERVES 4

Green Broth with Salt Cod

Bread Soup with Salt Cod (Acorda de Bacalhau)

Portugal

While I was in Portugal in the mid-1980s, I enjoyed a variety of salt cod and bread soups, and I have since collected many such recipes. These two are adapted from Maria de Lourdes Modesto's *Traditional Portuguese Cooking*.

This *acorda* is a soup of broken 1-2-day-old dense bread moistened with boiling water or broth and flavoured with garlic and coriander. The bread soaks up most of the broth and becomes very wet. Use crusty, peasant-style bread—Portuguese, Italian, French, or Greek.

- 8 oz (225 g) salt cod
- 4 cups (1 L) water
- 5 garlic cloves, coarsely chopped
- 5 tbsp (75 ml) olive oil
- 3/4 cup (185 ml) fresh coriander, finely chopped
- 3/4 green bell pepper, coarsely chopped (optional)
- Freshly ground black pepper
- 5 slices dry bread, torn into chunks
- 4 eggs

1. Use watered salt cod (page 80). Rinse.
2. Bring water to a boil and turn off heat. Add cod to the hot water. Cover and leave for 15-20 minutes, until cod flakes easily.
3. Crush garlic to a paste. Combine garlic and olive oil in a large serving bowl. Mix in coriander and green pepper.
4. Remove cod from the hot water, reserving the water. Remove skin and bones from the cod; shred or flake into small pieces. Add to the serving bowl. Sprinkle with black pepper.
5. Pour half the hot broth into the same bowl. Add bread chunks, letting them soak up the broth. Add more liquid if the mixture is too dry (it should be a fairly thick soup, but there should be some broth). Stir gently.
6. Poach or soft-boil the eggs. Serve one-quarter of the soup and 1 egg to each person.

SERVES 4

Bread Soup with Salt Cod

Bread Soup with Cod (Migas a Lagareiro)

Portugal

Migas has a drier texture than acorda, like bread stuffing without the turkey. This recipe is from the Beira Alta province of Portugal and is often cooked by those working in the olive presses. Shaking the ingredients in the saucepan in the later stages of cooking is called *baquear* (tumbling).

1 lb (450 g) salt cod steaks
1 small white cabbage, shredded
6 medium potatoes, peeled, chopped
2 medium onions, chopped
2 cups (500 ml) maize bread crumbs or cornmeal
1 1/2 cups (375 ml) olive oil

1. Use watered salt cod (page 80). Remove any skin and bones; flake cod into small pieces.
2. Combine cabbage, potatoes, onions, and salt cod in a large saucepan. Add enough water to cover ingredients. Bring to a boil; cook approximately 20 minutes.
3. Add bread crumbs and olive oil. Shake saucepan while continuing to cook for a few minutes so the contents mix together and resemble a traditional bread soup.

SERVES 4

Baccala Soup

Italy

This is a simple Italian way of preparing salt cod soup. Many variations exist.

1 1/2 lb (675 g) salt cod
1/2 cup (125 ml) olive oil
2 small onions, sliced
2 garlic cloves, chopped
1 stalk celery, chopped
1 bay leaf
1/2 tsp (2.5 ml) dried thyme
1 tsp (5 ml) fresh parsley, chopped
1 1/2 cups (375 ml) canned tomatoes
1/2 cup (125 ml) dry white wine
3 medium potatoes, sliced
3 cups (750 ml) water
1/2 tsp (2.5 ml) freshly ground black pepper
4 slices Italian bread, toasted, rubbed with garlic

1. Use watered salt cod (page 80). Drain. Remove skin and bones; break into chunks.
2. Place oil, onions, and garlic in a large saucepan and brown gently. Add celery, bay leaf, thyme, and parsley; continue browning. Add tomatoes; cook 5 minutes. Add wine, potatoes, and water. Cook 10 minutes.
3. Add cod. Reduce heat, cover, and cook slowly 30-40 minutes, or until potatoes are cooked.
4. Add pepper and taste for seasoning.
5. Pour soup over garlic toast in soup dishes.

SERVES 4

SOUPS AND CHOWDERS

Herdsmen's Dried Cod Soup (Sopa de Bacalhau dos Campinos)

Portugal

According to tradition, this soup was prepared in an earthenware bowl and eaten with a wooden spoon. It is from Azambuja, a Portuguese municipality in the District of Lisbon, in the historic region of Ribatejo.

1 1/4 lb (570 g) cod steaks, skinned

2 large onions, sliced

4 tomatoes, seeded, cut in pieces

4 medium potatoes, peeled, sliced

1 garlic clove, chopped

4 slices whole wheat bread

6 tbsp (90 ml) olive oil

White pepper

1. Do not soak cod. Wash it in several changes of water to remove as much salt as possible.
2. Place onions, tomatoes, potatoes, and garlic in a stockpot. Lay cod steaks on top. Add enough water to cover all ingredients. Bring to a boil; simmer 20 minutes.
3. Place bread slices in a baking dish. Pour some of the hot broth over the bread. Cover, and leave the bread to soak up the broth.
4. Remove cod when cooked.
5. Drain excess stock from the bread; pour enough olive oil over the top to ensure the bread absorbs the taste. Turn the slices over several times; place onions, potatoes, and tomatoes on top. Sprinkle with pepper.
6. Serve cod separately.

SERVES 4

Salt Cod, Okra, and Yam Soup

SOUPS AND CHOWDERS

Salt Cod, Okra, and Yam Soup

Caribbean

Although okra is native to Africa, it has found its way into practically every Caribbean country and is very much a part of the everyday cuisine. When cleaning okra, be sure to top and tail it, as the extremities are tougher than the rest.

In this recipe, salt cod, spinach, and okra in a tomato-wine broth surround a serving of mashed yams placed in the middle of individual soup bowls.

3/4 lb (340 g) salt cod

1 tbsp (15 ml) olive oil

3 garlic cloves, chopped

1 medium onion, chopped

1 jalapeno pepper, seeded, chopped

3 cups (750 ml) canned tomatoes, drained, chopped

1 cup (250 ml) white wine

2 bay leaves

3 1/2 cups (840 ml) water

8 oz (225 g) okra, trimmed, quartered

8 oz (225 g) spinach

Salt and freshly ground pepper

YAM PURÉE

1 1/2 lb (675 g) yams, peeled, chopped

1 lemon, juiced

1/4 cup (60 ml) butter

2 tbsp (30 ml) heavy cream

1 tbsp (15 ml) fresh chives, chopped

1. Use watered salt cod (page 80). Remove skin and bones; cut into bite-sized pieces. Set aside.
2. Prepare yam purée: Place yams in a saucepan with lemon juice; cover with cold water. Bring to a boil and cook 25 minutes, or until tender.
3. Drain yams well and allow to dry. Mash; add butter and cream. Season to taste. Add chives.
4. Heat oil in a heavy saucepan. Add garlic, onion, and jalapeno pepper. After 5 minutes, add salt cod; simmer another 5 minutes.
5. Stir in tomatoes, wine, and bay leaves; bring to a boil. Add water, return to the boil, reduce heat, and simmer 10 minutes.
6. Add okra. Cook for 10 minutes. Stir in spinach and cook 5 more minutes, or until okra is tender. Season to taste.
7. Place a dollop of yam purée in the centres of 4 warmed soup bowls. Carefully add soup to fill bowls.

Adapted from Anne Sheasby, *The Ultimate Soup Bible*

SERVES 4

Bouillabaisse

France

Bouillabaisse is thought to have originated in Marseilles but can be found all along the coast of the Provence region of France on the Mediterranean coast. Traditionally, bouillabaisse uses several kinds of fish, shellfish, and vegetables flavoured with herbs and spices such as garlic, basil, bay leaf, fennel, and saffron. This recipe is a variation of the traditional bouillabaisse: salt cod is the only fish used.

1 1/2 lb (675 g) salt cod

1 leek, chopped

1 small onion, chopped

2 tomatoes, seeded, chopped

2 garlic cloves, chopped

2 tsp (10 ml) orange rind, grated

1/4 cup (60 ml) olive oil

1/2 tsp (2.5 ml) dried thyme

1 tsp (5 ml) fennel seeds

Pinch saffron threads

3 cups (750 ml) water

1 1/2 cups (375 ml) dry white wine

3 tbsp (45 ml) Pernod

3 potatoes, cubed

2/3 cup (165 ml) fresh parsley, chopped

Salt and freshly ground black pepper

1. Use watered salt cod (page 80). Drain; remove skin and bones. Cut into small pieces.
2. Sauté leek and onion in olive oil until soft.
3. Add tomatoes, garlic, orange rind, thyme, fennel, and saffron. Stir, while cooking, for 5 minutes.
4. Add water, wine, and Pernod. Bring to a boil; simmer 5 minutes. Add potatoes. Cook for 3-4 minutes.
5. Add cod and simmer 10-15 minutes until cod and potatoes are cooked.
6. Stir in chopped parsley. Check seasoning and add salt and pepper.

SERVES 4

SOUPS AND CHOWDERS

Bathed Bread (Pan Bagna)

Italy

Traditionally, *pan bagna*, or bathed bread, is a layered vegetable (tomatoes, raw onions, black olives) and fish (tuna, anchovy) sandwich made with crusty Italian bread and drizzled with olive oil.

Here the bread is bathed or moistened with the liquid used in cooking the salt cod. The bread is then drizzled with olive oil, sprinkled with black pepper, topped with chunks of salt cod, and served in a soup bowl.

1 1/2 lb (675 g) salt cod steaks

2 garlic cloves, chopped

6 sun-dried tomatoes

2 bunches dried fennel fronds, 1/4 cup (60 ml) chopped fresh fennel bulb, or 1 tsp (5 ml) fennel seeds

4 slices dried bread (0.7 inches/ 2 cm thick, or more)

Olive oil, for drizzling

Freshly ground black pepper

1. Use watered salt cod (page 80).
2. Combine garlic, tomatoes, fennel, and cod in a saucepan; cover with water.
3. Cover and cook for 1 hour over low heat to blend flavours, adding water if necessary to keep ingredients well covered; there should be enough broth to pour over the bread.
4. Remove cod. Place a slice of bread in each of 4 serving bowls. Strain liquid and pour enough over bread to saturate. Allow 10 minutes for the bread to soak up the liquid. Drizzle with olive oil; top with black pepper. Add cod.

SERVES 4

VARIATION

At step 2, add 12 pearl onions or 2 sliced leeks.

Fennel fronds.

SALT COD CUISINE: THE INTERNATIONAL TABLE

Salt Cod and Tomato Soup

Newfoundland and Labrador

This is a favourite salt cod soup of Pat, a friend of mine, who brings it to many parties. He sometimes uses "pot liquor"—reserved liquid from cooking a boiled dinner—to replace the chicken stock or light broth.

1 lb (450 g) salt cod

1 tbsp (15 ml) olive oil

1 medium onion, chopped

4 tomatoes, chopped

2 garlic cloves, chopped

5 cups (1.2 L) chicken stock, light broth, or fish stock (page 296)

8 black olives, chopped

1 sprig fresh parsley, chopped

Salt and freshly ground black pepper

1. Use watered salt cod (page 80). Put cod in a saucepan with fresh water; simmer for 15 minutes. Drain, remove skin and bones, and shred cod.
2. Heat olive oil in a stockpot. Add onion and simmer 3 minutes; add tomatoes and garlic and simmer another 5 minutes. Add stock, bring to a boil, and simmer 30 minutes.
3. Purée the base (oil, onions, tomatoes, garlic, and stock) until smooth. Return to heat and add cod, olives, and parsley. Season soup with salt and freshly ground black pepper.

SERVES 4

Salt Cod Chowder

Newfoundland and Labrador

Homemade fish stock is ideal for this recipe.

1 1/2 lb (675 g) salt cod

All-purpose flour

5 tbsp (75 ml) olive oil, divided

3 onions, coarsely chopped

3 garlic cloves, finely chopped

1 green bell pepper, sliced

1 red bell pepper, sliced

5 cups (1.2 L) fish stock (page 296)

1 2/3 cups (415 ml) canned tomatoes, coarsely chopped

1/4 tsp (1.2 ml) dried chili pepper flakes, crushed

1/2 tsp (2.5 ml) dried basil

1 tbsp (15 ml) fresh parsley, chopped

1/2 tsp (2.5 ml) curry powder

1/2 tsp (2.5 ml) dried thyme

Salt and freshly ground black pepper

1/2 cup (125 ml) white wine

1. Use watered salt cod (page 80). Remove any skin and bones; cut into small pieces about 1 inch (2.5 cm) square.
2. Dip cod in flour; fry in 3 tbsp (45 ml) olive oil over medium heat until tender but not browned. Set aside.
3. Sauté onions, garlic, and red and green peppers in remaining olive oil. Add fish stock, tomatoes, and spices. Cover and simmer 15 minutes. Add wine and simmer 5 minutes.
4. Add cod, being careful not to let it boil. Serve immediately. This chowder does not improve with age.

Used with permission from Kitty Drake and Ned Pratt, *Rabbit Ravioli*

SERVES 6-8

SOUPS AND CHOWDERS

Traditional Salt Cod Chowder

Newfoundland and Labrador

Salt pork, salt cod, and ship's biscuit were part of the bulk provisions of fishermen from Brittany, Normandy, and the Basque country, so it was relatively easy for them to make chowder. Since then, fresh cod chowder and salt cod chowder have remained traditions in Newfoundland and Labrador cooking.

The salt pork gives the chowder its characteristic flavour.

- 12 oz (340 g) salt cod
- 3 oz (85 g) fatback pork, finely chopped
- 1 medium onion, chopped
- 3 medium potatoes, peeled, chopped
- 2 carrots, chopped
- 3 cups (750 ml) milk, heated
- Freshly ground black pepper
- 3/4 cup (185 ml) canned or frozen corn (optional)

1. Use watered salt cod (page 80). Remove any skin and bones. Cut into 1-inch-square (2.5 cm) pieces. Set aside.
2. Sauté fatback pork until lightly browned and crisp. Remove pork (scrunchions) and reserve for garnish.
3. Add chopped onion and sauté until golden.
4. Add potatoes, carrots, and pepper with enough boiling water to cover vegetables. Bring to a boil and simmer until vegetables are tender.
5. Add heated milk, corn, and flaked cod. Bring soup back to a simmer, until cod is tender.
6. Serve hot with freshly baked homemade bread and butter, or soda crackers.

SERVES 4

Kale and Salt Cod Chowder

Portugal

Portuguese *chourico*, similar to Spanish chorizo, is a pork sausage seasoned with garlic, fat, paprika, spices, and wine. It is stuffed into natural or artificial casings and slowly dried or smoked. *Linguica* is similar to chourico, but not as thick, and made with a different cut of pork than that used in chourico. Milder in taste, linguica is usually seasoned with garlic, onions, wine, paprika, or sweet red pepper paste, depending on the region.

- 8 oz (225 g) boneless and skinless salt cod
- 2 tsp (10 ml) olive oil
- 8 oz (225 g) linguica or chourico sausage, sliced
- 1 small onion, chopped
- 2 medium potatoes, peeled, chopped
- 8 cups (2 L) chicken broth
- 3 cups (750 ml) kale, rinsed, coarsely chopped
- 1 bay leaf
- 1/4 tsp (1.2 ml) dried chili pepper flakes
- 1/4 cup (60 ml) fresh mint, finely chopped

1. Use watered salt cod (page 80). Drain and shred into bite-sized pieces, removing any bones. Cover cod with fresh water; bring nearly to a boil. Remove from heat, cover, and let sit 15 minutes. Drain and set aside.
2. Warm olive oil in a stockpot over high heat. Add sausage and cook, stirring constantly, for 3 minutes to lightly brown.
3. Reduce heat to medium. Add onions and cook, stirring frequently, about 5 minutes or until onions are nearly soft. Add potatoes and toss.
4. Add chicken broth and bring to a boil. Add kale, bay leaf, and chili flakes. Return to a boil; simmer 30 minutes.
5. Skim fat off the soup. Add cod, adjust seasoning, ladle into bowls, and sprinkle each with fresh mint.

SERVES 4

Kale and Salt Cod Chowder

STEWS AND RAGOUTS

There are as many varieties of salt cod stew as there are combinations of supporting ingredients available in a particular region or country; however, the preparation is generally similar. In most recipes, salt cod stews are made by first preparing an aromatic liquid with vegetables and herbs, in which pieces of salt cod are poached. In a few recipes, the cod is first browned in a small amount of butter or oil.

Pan-Cooked Salt Cod (Baccalà al Tegame)	*Naples, Italy*
Sicilian Salt Cod Stew	*Italy*
Sweet and Sour Cod Stew (Zuppa Di Baccala Agrodolce)	*Campania, Italy*
Salt Cod Stew (Bacalhoada)	*Portugal*
Salt Cod Stew (Stuffat tal-Bakkaljaw)	*Malta*
Salt Cod with Leeks in Lemon Sauce	*Greece*
Salt Cod with Spinach and Leeks	*Greece*
Salt Cod Stew	*Greece*
Brazilian Fish Stew (Moqueca de Peixe)	*Brazil*
Salt Cod with Coconut Milk (Bacalhau com Leite de Coco)	*Brazil*
Salt Cod Bahia Style (Bacalhau a Baiana)	*Brazil*
Stewed Saltfish	*Jamaica*
Baked Breadfruit and Saltfish Stew	*St. Vincent and the Grenadines*
Norwegian Salt Cod over Stew of Grapes (Bacalao Noruego Sobre Estofado de Uvas)	*Dominican Republic*
Saltfish Stew	*Trinidad*
Saltfish Stew	*Puerto Rico*
Spinach and Chickpeas with Salt Cod Dumplings	*Spain*
Bacalao Stew	*Norway*
Salt Cod and Squid Stew	*Newfoundland and Labrador*

Pan-Cooked Salt Cod (Baccalà al Tegame)

Naples, Italy

These three Italian stews reveal much of the regional nature of Italian cooking. If you read the recipes as a group, you'll note the variety of dried fruit and herbs used—you might also be inspired to experiment. The first recipe is from the 1800s and sets the tone for this section. It was recorded by Mark Kurlansky in *Salt*:

> Always select the largest cod and the one with black skin, because it is the most salted. Soak it well. Then take a pan, add delicate oil and minced onion, which you will sauté. When it turns dark, add a bit of water, raisins, pine nuts, and minced parsley. Combine all these ingredients and just as they begin to boil, add the cod.
>
> When tomatoes are in season, you can include them in the sauce described above, making sure that you have heated it thoroughly.
>
> —Ippolito Cavalcanti (1787-1860), Cucina casereccia in dialetto Napoletano, Home cooking in Neapolitan dialect

Whole salt cod.

Pan-Cooked Salt Cod

STEWS AND RAGOUTS

Sicilian Salt Cod Stew

Italy

This recipe is adapted from several Sicilian recipes for salt cod stew. One of the original recipes from Messina (Sicily's third largest city) uses stockfish. I've substituted salt cod, as stockfish is difficult to find. Sicilian Salt Cod Stew came to my attention courtesy of Jeff Gilhooly, when he was host of the St. John's Morning Show on CBC Radio.

1 x 6 oz (170 g) skinless salt cod steaks

1/2 cup (125 ml) extra-virgin olive oil

1 medium onion, finely chopped

2 garlic cloves, crushed

2 tbsp (30 ml) all-purpose flour

16 oz (450 g) can plum tomatoes, coarsely chopped, or fresh tomatoes, skinned, chopped

Freshly ground black pepper

2 baking potatoes, peeled, sliced

2 slightly underripe pears, peeled, cored, sliced

16 oil-cured black or green olives, pitted, halved

2 small, tender celery stalks, sliced

1 bay leaf

1 sprig fresh thyme

4 tsp (20 ml) capers

2 tbsp (30 ml) pine nuts

1/3 cup (85 ml) golden raisins, soaked, drained

1. Use watered salt cod (page 80). Drain.
2. Pour oil into a baking dish or a heavy pot and sauté onion and garlic gently.
3. Coat pieces of cod lightly with flour and cook for 4 minutes over a slightly higher heat, turning once. Season with pepper.
4. Add tomatoes and sufficient hot water to just cover the cod. Cover, and simmer over a moderate heat for 30 minutes.
5. Add potatoes, pears, olives, celery, bay leaf, thyme, capers, nuts, and raisins. Stir carefully, cover, and cook for 40 minutes. Moisten with hot water, if required.

Adapted from Mariapaola Dettore, *Flavours of Italy: Sicily*

SERVES 4

Sweet and Sour Cod Stew (Zuppa Di Baccala Agrodolce)

Campania, Italy

The quantity and variety of dried fruit in this recipe can be varied to taste. To get the sweet and sour taste, some versions of this recipe use dried apples and dried mushrooms, along with lemon zest, tomato paste, white wine, and white vinegar. Experiment!

- 1 1/2 lb (675 g) salt cod
- 1/4 cup (60 ml) extra-virgin olive oil
- 1 garlic clove, finely chopped
- 2 chili peppers, sliced
- 16 walnut halves, chopped
- 4 dried figs
- 4 prunes, pitted
- 1 tbsp (15 ml) golden raisins
- 1 tbsp (15 ml) pine nuts
- 1 cauliflower head, separated in florets
- 4 cups (1 L) plum tomatoes, coarsely chopped
- 4 slices of heavy-textured or crusty bread, toasted

1. Use watered salt cod (page 80). Drain, remove skin and bones. Break into large flakes.
2. Heat oil in a large saucepan and sauté garlic.
3. Add chili peppers, walnuts, figs, prunes, raisins, pine nuts, cauliflower, and tomatoes. Bring to a boil; cook 20 minutes.
4. Add cod when mixture seems well blended. Simmer 10-15 minutes.
5. Serve over slices of toasted bread.

Adapted from Accademia Italiana della Cucina, *La Cucina*

SERVES 4

Salt Cod Stew (Bacalhoada)

Portugal

This is a basic bacalhoada recipe with salt cod, potatoes, and onions as the base.

- 1 lb (450 g) salt cod
- 4 potatoes, peeled, boiled, sliced
- 2 large onions, sliced
- 2 tomatoes, sliced (optional)
- 3/4 cup (185 ml) extra-virgin olive oil, divided
- Freshly ground black pepper
- 20 black or green olives, pitted
- 4 hard-boiled eggs, sliced

1. Use watered salt cod (page 80). Simmer in water for 2-3 minutes. Remove skin and bones. Cut or break cod into small chunks or flakes.
2. Preheat oven to 350°F (180°C).
3. Coat the bottom of a baking dish with olive oil. Combine half the potatoes, onions, tomatoes, and cod as a bottom layer in the dish. Drizzle with olive oil. Sprinkle with pepper. Make a second layer with the remaining onions, potatoes, tomatoes, and cod. Drizzle with remaining olive oil.
4. Cover and bake for 30 minutes. Add hard-boiled eggs and olives for the last 5 minutes.

SERVES 4

VARIATIONS

- Simmer salt cod in water, milk, or a combination of both.
- In step 2, place ingredients in a heavy saucepan. Cover and cook over medium heat for 30 minutes.

STEWS AND RAGOUTS

Salt Cod Stew (Stuffat tal-Bakkaljaw)

Malta

Maltese cuisine is influenced by other nearby Mediterranean traditions, including Italian (particularly Sicilian) and Arabic cuisine. There is also a noticeable British influence. This salt cod stew changes with the season and the availability of local vegetables. A winter variation of this recipe could include pumpkin, cauliflower, and black olives. In some recipes anchovies, raisins, and nutmeg are added.

In the nineteenth and the first half of the twentieth century, Malta was a market for Newfoundland dried salt cod.

- 1 1/2 lb (675 g) salt cod
- 2 tsp (10 ml) olive oil
- 3 garlic cloves, chopped
- 1 medium onion, chopped
- 2 tsp (10 ml) fresh mint, chopped
- 1 tbsp (15 ml) fresh marjoram, chopped
- 2 bay leaves
- 10 black olives, pitted
- 6 artichoke hearts, fresh or canned, quartered
- 1-2 chili peppers, finely chopped
- 3 tbsp (45 ml) tomato paste
- 1 tsp (5 ml) white sugar
- 2 potatoes, peeled, chopped
- 2 carrots, peeled, chopped
- 2/3 cup (165 ml) dry white wine
- 2 cups (500 ml) canned tomato purée or diced tomatoes
- Fish stock (page 296) or chicken stock
- 1 tsp (5 ml) dried rosemary
- 1/2 cup (125 ml) fresh lima beans (if available) or dried, soaked

Halved artichokes.

1. Use watered salt cod (page 80). Drain and rinse the cod. Simmer 15 minutes. Remove any skin and bones; break or flake the cod.
2. Heat olive oil and fry garlic and onion. Add mint, marjoram, and bay leaves, stirring continuously. Add olives, artichoke hearts, chili peppers, tomato paste, and sugar.
3. Add potatoes, carrots, wine, tomato purée, and enough stock to cover the contents when onions are soft.
4. Simmer until the liquid is reduced by half. Add beans, rosemary, and cod. Simmer an additional 10 minutes, or until stew has thickened. Serve.

SERVES 4

Salt Cod with Leeks in Lemon Sauce

Greece

The three Greek stew recipes use progressively more ingredients. All use olive oil and lemon juice from the Greek countryside; the third adds dry white wine, a welcome addition to the Greek table.

1 lb (450 g) salt cod

1/4 cup (60 ml) olive oil

1 lb (450 g) leeks, sliced

1 medium onion, chopped

1/3 cup (85 ml) water

3 tbsp (45 ml) fresh lemon juice, strained

1 tbsp (15 ml) all-purpose flour

Freshly ground black pepper

1. Use watered salt cod (page 80). Drain, remove skin and bones. Cut into serving-size portions.
2. Heat oil over medium heat in a stockpot or large saucepan. Add leeks, onions, and water; cover and simmer over low heat for approximately 10 minutes.
3. Place cod on top of vegetables. Simmer for 15 minutes over low heat until cod is flaky.
4. Combine lemon juice and flour in a small bowl until it is an even paste; combine gently with cod and leeks. Simmer for a few minutes to even out the sauce. Sprinkle with pepper. Serve.

SERVES 4

Salt Cod with Leeks in Lemon Sauce

Salt Cod with Spinach and Leeks

Greece

Newfoundland and Labrador variations of the recipe could substitute, for example, turnip greens, rape, or dandelion greens for the spinach.

- 1 lb (450 g) salt cod
- 1 lb (450 g) leeks, thinly sliced
- 1 lb (450 g) fresh spinach, trimmed, washed
- 1/3 cup (85 ml) olive oil
- 3-4 green onions
- 1 medium onion, chopped
- 2 medium potatoes, sliced
- 1 tomato, peeled, grated or 1/2 cup (125 ml) canned tomatoes
- 1/4 cup (60 ml) fresh parsley, chopped
- 1/4 cup (60 ml) fresh dill, chopped
- 1 tbsp (15 ml) all-purpose flour
- 2 tbsp (30 ml) fresh lemon juice, strained
- Freshly ground black pepper

1. Use watered salt cod (page 80). Drain, remove skin and bones. Cut into serving-size portions.
2. Bring 2/3 cup (165 ml) water to a boil and parboil leeks for 4-5 minutes. Lift out leeks and place in a colander.
3. Add spinach gradually to the same pot and cook for several minutes until leaves are limp. Drain; reserve broth.
4. Heat oil in a large stockpot and sauté onions gently until wilted, about 10 minutes.
5. Add leeks, spinach, and potatoes, stirring to coat with oil. Pour in grated tomato and reserved broth; cover and simmer 10 minutes.
6. Add parsley and dill. Place cod on top of the vegetables. Cover and cook for 20 minutes, or until cod is flaky and potatoes are tender.
7. Mix flour with lemon juice in a small bowl, a little at first, to remove lumps.
8. Add 5-6 tbsp (75-90 ml) cooking liquid to the sauce. Stir briskly with a fork and add contents of the bowl to the saucepan. Mix in gently and simmer another few minutes. Season with pepper and serve.

SERVES 6-8

Dill and salt cod.

Salt Cod Stew

Greece

Aristedes Pasparakis, "an ambassador of Greekness" and one of the authors of *New Greek Cuisine*, owns several Greek restaurants in Canada. He strives for flavourful and healthful food by adding many ingredients at the end of the cooking so they remain full-bodied in the dish. Note that the salt cod is cooked in a dry white wine rather than olive oil.

4 x 4 oz (115 g) salt cod, skin on

2 cups (500 ml) dry white wine

2 potatoes, thinly sliced

1 small carrot, thin strips

2 zucchini, thinly sliced

2 small leeks, cut in 1-inch (2.5 cm) chunks

16 Greek olives, pitted, halved

2 cups (500 ml) tomatoes, chopped

1 1/2 cups (375 ml) celery leaves, chopped

1/2 red bell or banana pepper, cut in rings

2 tbsp (30 ml) chili peppers, thinly sliced, or 1 tsp (5 ml) dried chili pepper flakes

2 tbsp (30 ml) sultanas

2 tbsp (30 ml) olive oil

Fresh parsley, chopped, for garnish

GARLIC-WALNUT SAUCE

1 cup (250 ml) walnut pieces

3 garlic cloves, smashed

2 tbsp (30 ml) lemon juice

2 tbsp (30 ml) olive oil

Salt and freshly ground pepper

1/4 cup (60 ml) water

1. Use watered salt cod (page 80). Drain. Keep the skin on.
2. Heat a large frying pan on medium-high heat. Add wine and cod, skin side down. Cover and simmer 8-10 minutes, until tender. Transfer cod to a warm plate and keep warm. Reserve liquid.
3. Prepare garlic-walnut sauce: Use a food processor or blender on medium speed to combine walnut pieces and garlic. Add lemon juice, 2 tbsp (30 ml) olive oil, salt, and pepper until just a little chunky. Add water and blend until smooth. Set aside.
4. Boil a stockpot of salted water over high heat. Add potatoes and carrots; cook 5 minutes. Add zucchini and leeks; cook 3 minutes. Drain vegetables and return to pan. Add reserved cooking wine.
5. Add olives, tomatoes, celery leaves, red pepper, chilies, and sultanas. Cook, stirring, 3-4 minutes. Remove from heat and stir in 2 tbsp (30 ml) olive oil.
6. Serve vegetables and sauce on individual plates. Place cod in the centre of each plate; top with a large dollop of garlic-walnut sauce.
7. Garnish with parsley and serve immediately.

SERVES 4

STEWS AND RAGOUTS

Brazilian Fish Stew (Moqueca de Peixe)

Brazil

Moqueca, sometimes spelled *muqueca*, is a Brazilian seafood stew. Brazilians enjoy many versions of moquecas, originating from all regions of the country and using a variety of fish and shellfish (shrimp, crab, lobster, clams, crawfish tails, mussels, grouper, mahi mahi, salmon, monkfish, and squid). These three recipes use only salt cod but are distinctly Brazilian, thanks to the particular heartiness of thick coconut milk and the authentic flavour of *dende* or palm oil, a staple in Brazilian cuisine.

1 1/2 lb (675 g) salt cod steaks

2 tbsp (30 ml) olive oil

1 large onion, sliced

1 red bell pepper, sliced

1 green bell pepper, sliced

2 medium tomatoes, sliced

4 green onions, finely chopped

1 bunch fresh coriander, chopped, divided

2 tsp (30 ml) sweet paprika

1/2 tsp (2.5 ml) dried chili pepper flakes or
　　1 malagueta pepper, finely chopped

2 cups (500 ml) coconut milk

3 tbsp (45 ml) palm, annatto, or peanut oil

MARINADE

2 limes, juiced

1/2 tsp (2.5 ml) freshly ground black pepper

2 tsp (10 ml) garlic cloves, chopped

1. Use watered salt cod (page 80). Drain and remove any skin and bones. Break into chunks or bite-sized pieces. Set aside.
2. Prepare marinade by mixing lime juice, pepper, and garlic. Pour marinade over cod and refrigerate 1-2 hours.
3. Heat olive oil in a large saucepan. Layer half the onions, peppers, and tomatoes in the saucepan.
4. Cover vegetables with cod and marinade.
5. Layer remaining onions, peppers, and tomatoes on top. Sprinkle with green onions and half of the coriander.
6. Whisk paprika and chili pepper into the coconut milk; pour over vegetables and cod.
7. Drizzle entire mixture with palm oil.
8. Bring to a boil and simmer gently, covered, for 15 minutes. Uncover and simmer 25 minutes more, until vegetables are well cooked and tender.
9. Sprinkle remaining coriander over the hot stew. Serve in bowls alone or over rice.

SERVES 6

Salt Cod with Coconut Milk (Bacalhau com Leite de Coco)

Brazil

This basic recipe from Rio de Janeiro uses local fresh coconut and palm oil in the preparation of the salt cod.

- 1 lb (450 g) salt cod, steaks
- 1 fresh coconut
- 4 tbsp (60 ml) butter or oil
- 2 onions, chopped
- 2 tomatoes, chopped
- 2-3 drops hot pepper sauce
- 1 tbsp (15 ml) palm, annatto, or peanut oil

1. Use watered salt cod (page 80). Drain.
2. Prepare coconut milk. Pierce the three black eyes at the top of the coconut and drain out the watery juice. Crack coconut and remove coconut meat. Place half the coconut meat in a blender with 1 cup (250 ml) hot water and process 30 seconds. Repeat with remaining meat. Strain and squeeze milk through cheesecloth.
3. Fry cod in butter or oil with onions and tomatoes. Cook over low heat, occasionally stirring.
4. Shake pepper sauce on the cod. Add palm oil and stir in 1 cup (250 ml) coconut milk; heat through without letting the mixture boil.

SERVES 4

Salt Cod Bahia Style (Bacalhau a Baiana)

Brazil

This is an easy, yet tasty, salt cod stew from the Bahia state of the northeast region of Brazil.

- 1 lb (450 g) salt cod
- 3 tbsp (45 ml) vegetable oil
- 1 medium onion, chopped
- 1 garlic clove, crushed
- 1 red bell pepper, chopped
- 1 green bell pepper, chopped
- 3 medium tomatoes, peeled, chopped
- 1 cup (250 ml) hot water
- Salt and freshly ground black pepper
- 1 tbsp (15 ml) palm, annatto, or peanut oil
- 1 cup (250 ml) thick coconut milk
- 1 cup (250 ml) green onions, white and green parts, chopped

1. Use watered salt cod (page 80). Drain and remove any skin and bones. Pat dry and cut into 2-inch (5 cm) pieces. Set aside.
2. Heat oil in a large saucepan and sauté onion, garlic, and peppers until soft, about 5 minutes. Add tomatoes, cod, and hot water. Cover and simmer 15 minutes or until cod flakes easily with a fork.
3. Season to taste with salt, if necessary. Season with pepper and palm oil.
4. Stir in coconut milk and green onions; heat through without letting the mixture boil.

SERVES 4

STEWS AND RAGOUTS

Stewed Saltfish

Jamaica

In Jamaica, as in other parts of the Caribbean, the word "saltfish" is used more often than "salt cod." Jamaicans hardly think of saltfish as seafood, perhaps because cod is not caught in the Caribbean. It is, however, an essential item in the country's diet—to accompany ackee and to use for fritters and saltfish balls. It goes well with callaloo (a vegetable closely resembling spinach) and as a *ceviche* (raw with vinegar, onions, and pepper).

This is one of many versions of Jamaican saltfish stew. Lovers of the food still find creative ways to whip up their own variations, no doubt inspired by the calypso king Mighty Sparrow, who sings "Saltfish stew is what I like" in his song "Saltfish."

1 lb (450 g) salt cod

2 tbsp (30 ml) vegetable oil

2 tbsp (30 ml) butter

3 tomatoes, chopped

3 green onions, chopped

2 onions, chopped

Freshly ground black pepper

2 tbsp (30 ml) all-purpose flour

1 1/2 cups (375 ml) water

1/2 tsp (2.5 ml) curry powder

1. Use watered salt cod (page 80). Scald with boiling water, remove skin and bones; cut into small pieces.
2. Heat oil and butter and lightly fry tomatoes, green onions, onions, and pepper.
3. Stir in flour; add cod and enough water to make a medium-thick sauce. Stir in curry powder.
4. Cover, and stew over medium heat until cod is tender, about 20 minutes.

Adapted from Wenton O. Spence, *Jamaican Cookery*

SERVES 4

Baked Breadfruit and Saltfish Stew

St. Vincent and the Grenadines

Breadfruit is a large oblong or round fruit with thin bumpy skin that turns green-brown to yellow as the fruit ripens. The flesh is cream-coloured, mealy, and starchy. Like squash or potatoes, breadfruit can be roasted, baked, fried, or boiled before being eaten. If you don't have access to fresh breadfruit, substitute canned breadfruit, fresh plantains, or potatoes.

1 lb (450 g) salt cod

2 lb (900 g) breadfruit

1/4 cup (60 ml) vegetable oil

1 onion, chopped

1 tomato, chopped

1 small cucumber, sliced

Salt and freshly ground black pepper

Fresh thyme, chopped

Fresh parsley, chopped

1 tsp (5 ml) butter

1/4 cup (60 ml) water

1. Use watered salt cod (page 80). Simmer 5 minutes, drain, and remove any skin and bones. Cut cod into small pieces.
2. Bake breadfruit: Cut breadfruit in half and place, cut side down, on an oiled baking sheet or in a shallow pan with 0.5 inches (1-2 cm) or so of water. Bake at 400°F (200°C) for 1 hour or until breadfruit is easily pierced with a fork. Remove skin.
3. Heat oil in a frying pan. Add cod, onion, tomato, cucumber, seasoning, butter, and water; simmer for 20 minutes. Serve hot.
4. Serve with prepared and seasoned breadfruit.

SERVES 4

Baked Breadfruit and Saltfish Stew (with Plantains)

STEWS AND RAGOUTS

Norwegian Salt Cod over Stew of Grapes (Bacalao Noruego Sobre Estofado de Uvas)

Dominican Republic

This recipe and the recipe for Salt Cod Fillets in Plantain Crust with Green Sauce (Lomo de Bacalao en Costra de Platano en Salsa Verde) were submitted by Regis Batista Lemaire, the Trade Commissioner at the Canadian Embassy in the Dominican Republic, in response to my request for a contribution to this project.

The recipes were winners of the 2009 Norwegian salt cod recipe contest held in the Dominican Republic, organized by the Norwegian marketing council for seafood and fish. This is my suggested translation from the Spanish recipe.

2 lb (900 g) Norwegian salt cod, previously desalinated (*Bacalao Noruego previamente desalado*)

1 onion, cut lengthwise (*cebolla*)

1 garlic clove, finely chopped (*diente de ajo*)

2 red tomatoes, peeled (*tomatesrojos*)

8 chive stems (*tallitos de cebollino*)

4 fresh basil leaves (*hojas de albahaca*)

1 sprig fresh parsley (*perejilpicado*)

1 cup (250 ml) green pigeon peas, or yellow peas, black-eyed peas, or green peas (*gandules*)

1 12 oz (340 ml) bottle beer (*cerveza*)

3 cups (750 ml) fish stock (page 296) (*caldo de pescado*)

1/3 cup (85 ml) olive oil (*aceite de oliva*)

4 oz (115 g) fresh mushrooms (*hongoschampinones frescos*)

8 oz (225 g) red grapes (*uvasrojas*)

2/3 cup (165 ml) red grape juice (*jugo de uvasrojas*)

1. Use watered salt cod (page 80).
2. Place onion, garlic, tomatoes, chives, basil, and parsley in a stockpot. Add green pigeon peas, beer, and stock; simmer until tender.
3. Sauté mushrooms and grapes in olive oil; add to the simmering stew. Add grape juice.
4. Simmer the salt cod in the stew until cooked.

SERVES 6

Saltfish Stew

Trinidad

1 lb (450 g) salt cod

3 tbsp (45 ml) vegetable oil

2 medium onions, chopped

1 garlic clove, thinly sliced

1 jalapeno pepper, finely chopped, or
　　1 tsp (5 ml) dried chili pepper flakes

2 green bell peppers, chopped

4 tomatoes, chopped

1/3 cup (85 ml) ketchup

1. Use watered salt cod (page 80). Simmer cod 15 minutes. Drain, remove skin and bones; break into small pieces. Set aside.
2. Sauté onions, garlic, and pepper in oil over medium heat for 7 minutes, or until onion begins to soften.
3. Stir in bell peppers, tomatoes, ketchup, and prepared cod. Add enough water to cover all ingredients. Cover and simmer until vegetables and cod are cooked.
4. Serve with rice or bread.

SERVES 4

Saltfish Stew

STEWS AND RAGOUTS

Saltfish Stew

Puerto Rico

Salt cod was the defining ingredient in many Puerto Rican fish stews. The colonial influences of Spain, as well as regional variations from the more humid areas in the northeast (San Juan) and the arid climate of the southwest (Ponce), are all evident in the salt cod cuisine of Puerto Rico.

This recipe from the San Juan area uses annatto seeds to give a deep rich golden colour to the stew. Annatto seeds come from the shrub achiote and have a slightly sweet, peppery flavour. They are sometimes known as the "poor man's saffron," as the colour is similar to the more expensive seasoning. You may substitute saffron, soaked in a small amount of hot water, if you do not have access to annatto seeds.

Plantain or Puerto Rico tubers such as yucca, yautia, and batata are used as alternatives to potatoes.

1 lb (450 g) salt cod
4 tbsp (60 ml) olive oil, divided
2 tbsp (30 ml) annatto seeds
1 large red onion, sliced
1 tsp (5 ml) ground cumin
Freshly ground black pepper
1 lb (450 g) yucca, peeled, boiled, cut in chunks
2 limes, juiced
2 limes, for garnish

1. Use watered salt cod (page 80). Drain. Cover with fresh water, bring to a boil, and simmer 15 minutes, until the cod is tender. Drain and flake into large chunks.
2. Heat 3 tbsp (45 ml) olive oil in a large frying pan. Add annatto seeds and sauté 3-4 minutes to colour and flavour the oil. Remove seeds with a slotted spoon.
3. Add onion to oil; cook over low heat until soft and slightly brown. Add cod, cumin, and black pepper. Combine well and continue to simmer until everything is heated and takes on a bright orange colour.
4. Toss boiled yucca with lime juice and the remaining olive oil. Serve cod over yucca and garnish with lime wedges.

SERVES 4

Annatto seeds.

Spinach and Chickpeas with Salt Cod Dumplings

Spain

In November 2006, Spanish food and wine experts, chefs, and authors gathered in the United States for the World of Flavor International Conference and Festival, sponsored by The Culinary Institute of America. Chef Kisko Garcia from Cordoba, Spain, presented his version of this recipe, simmering salt cod dumplings in a classic Spanish Lenten potage of chickpeas and spinach. It was adapted by Martha Rose Shulman in *Spain and the World Table* in a recipe called Flamenco Stew. It is adapted again here.

Try your favourite salt cod appetizer recipe as a substitute for salt cod dumplings. Cod cakes, patties, puffs, croquettes, fritters, and others will all work. Improvise with other green vegetables and beans.

12 oz (340 g) salt cod, divided

1 cup (250 ml) dried chickpeas, soaked at least 8 hours

1 tbsp (15 ml) extra-virgin olive oil

1 cup (250 ml) onions, chopped

1 tbsp (15 ml) garlic, finely chopped

1 tsp (5 ml) sweet paprika

Pinch saffron

1 bay leaf

4 potatoes, cut in 1-inch (2.5 cm) cubes

8 oz (225 g) baby spinach

1/4 tsp (1.2 ml) freshly ground black pepper

1 tsp (5 ml) salt

SALT COD DUMPLINGS

1 cup (250 ml) all-purpose flour

2 tsp (10 ml) baking powder

Pinch salt

1 tbsp (15 ml) butter

1/2 cup (125 ml) milk

1. Use watered salt cod (page 80). Drain well. Place cod in a medium saucepan, cover with 5 cups (1.2 L) water, and simmer 8-10 minutes. Remove cod; reserve water. Remove any skin and bones; shred cod.

2. Heat oil in a saucepan over medium heat and add onions. Sauté until tender, about 5 minutes. Add garlic and paprika; stir briefly.

3. Drain chickpeas. Add chickpeas and reserved salt cod water to the saucepan with onions and garlic. Bring to a boil; add saffron and bay leaf. Reduce heat to medium, cover and simmer 1-1 1/2 hours, until chickpeas are tender.

4. Add potatoes and simmer until tender.

5. Stir in spinach, pepper, and 8 oz (225 g) cod. Remove from heat. Let stand, covered, while you make the dumplings.

6. Combine flour, baking powder, and salt. Work in butter. Add remaining cod. Mix in milk. Shape into balls. Set aside.

7. Adjust seasoning, if necessary. Bring the stew back to a simmer over low heat. Add the salt cod dumplings and simmer gently for 10 minutes, or until cooked. Serve.

SERVES 4

STEWS AND RAGOUTS

Spinach and Chickpeas with Salt Cod Dumplings

Bacalao Stew

Norway

In *Kitchen of Light: New Scandinavian Cooking*, Andreas Viestad describes this recipe as the classic Western Norwegian interpretation of bacalao, adding that ingredients such as garlic, olives, bay leaves, and cloves make the bacalao more Portuguese or Spanish. Finding your own favourite interpretation is part of the bacalao love affair. This dish tastes even better on the second day.

- 1 lb (450 g) salt cod
- 4 russet potatoes, sliced
- 2 large yellow onions, sliced
- 2 1/2 cups (625 ml) canned tomatoes, chopped, with juice
- 1 1/2 cups (310 ml) canned pimentos, drained, or 2 roasted red bell peppers, peeled, sliced
- 3 garlic cloves, sliced
- 1 bay leaf
- 1 dried hot red chili, chopped, seeded
- 7 black peppercorns
- 1 cup (250 ml) olive oil
- 3 tbsp (45 ml) fresh parsley, chopped, divided

1. Use watered salt cod (page 80). Drain cod and cut into chunks.
2. Layer potatoes, onions, and cod in a large frying pan.
3. Add tomatoes, pimentos, garlic, bay leaf, chili, peppercorns, olive oil, and 2 tbsp (30 ml) parsley.
4. Simmer gently for 30 minutes. Reduce heat to low; cook 45 minutes. Shake frying pan several times, but do not stir.
5. Ladle stew into bowls and sprinkle with remaining parsley.

SERVES 6-8

Salt Cod and Squid Stew

Newfoundland and Labrador

- 1 lb (450 g) salt cod
- 1 tbsp (15 ml) olive oil or rendered fatback pork
- 4 garlic cloves, thinly sliced
- 1 onion, chopped
- 1 small turnip, chopped
- 2 ribs celery, thinly sliced
- 3 medium potatoes, peeled, chopped
- 2 cups (500 ml) vegetable stock or fish stock (page 296)
- 16 oz (475 ml) can whole tomatoes
- Freshly ground black pepper
- 2 squid bodies, thinly sliced

1. Use watered salt cod (page 80). Remove any skin and bones. Break into large chunks.
2. Heat oil in a stockpot over medium heat. Add garlic; sauté until soft. Add onion and sauté, stirring often, until soft. Add turnip, celery, and potatoes. Stir to coat vegetables in oil.
3. Add broth and bring to a boil; reduce heat and simmer 10 minutes.
4. Add tomatoes and their liquid; bring to a boil.
5. Reduce heat. Carefully stir in cod. Simmer 15 minutes, stirring gently once or twice. Season with black pepper.
6. Increase heat to medium and add squid. Cook only until the squid turn bright white, approximately 2 minutes.
7. Serve at once.

SERVES 4

BOILED SALT COD DINNERS

The basic ingredients for these recipes are salt cod and potatoes. Each is elevated by a variety of sauces which show how local ingredients and traditions make a simple meal a regional specialty. The word "boiled" in the section heading reflects the traditional Newfoundland and Labrador expression of a boiled salt cod dinner. Don't be misled, however—it is hardly ever appropriate to boil salt cod. It should be cooked gently in simmering liquid.

As part of a celebratory meal, you could invite guests to sample sauces from different countries as they enjoy the boiled salt cod dinner. I suggest trying no more than three sauces in one meal in order to properly savour each.

Boiled Salt Cod	*Newfoundland and Labrador*	Codfish Breakfast	*Bermuda*
Rounders	*Newfoundland and Labrador*	Dried Salt Cod (Klipfish)	*Denmark*
Salt Cod Dish (Sancocho)	*Canary Islands*	Dried Salt Cod (Stokvis)	*Netherlands*
Boiled Salt Cod	*Scotland*	Christmas Eve Cod (Bacalhauda Consoada)	*Portugal*
Cabbie-Claw	*Scotland*	Salt Cod and Potato with Garlic and Herbs	*Greece*
		Lyonnaise Salt Cod (Morue à la Lyonnaise)	*France*

Boiled Salt Cod

Newfoundland and Labrador

In Newfoundland and Labrador homes this is the most regularly served of all salt cod dishes.

2 lb (900 g) salt cod

6-8 potatoes, peeled

SAUCES

Drawn butter (page 300)

Scrunchions (page 300)

Garlic, onions, and olive oil (page 300)

Mustard sauce (page 300)

1. Use watered salt cod (page 80). Drain. Place in a saucepan; cover with cold water. Bring to a boil and simmer until tender, approximately 15-20 minutes.
2. Boil potatoes in another saucepan or cut in half and cook with cod.
3. Strain potatoes and cod and serve with sauce of choice.

SERVES 4

VARIATIONS

 Boil turnip and/or parsnip with the potatoes.

 Simmer a whole onion with the cod and potatoes.

Boiled Salt Cod Dinner (with Drawn Butter)

BOILED SALT COD DINNERS

Rounders

Newfoundland and Labrador

> There were three different ways to prepare those [rounders] for eating: roast them in the oven, roast them in the [wood] stove or cook them on the stove.
>
> —*DNE*, s.v. "rounders"

Rounders are small cod or tomcods that have been gutted, headed, salted, and dried without being split. They are heavily dry-salted whole for winter keeping, and since the soundbones (backbones) are not removed, they retain their round shape. They are also called "leggies."

3-4 rounders

Vegetables: potato, turnip, and parsnip, as desired

SAUCES

Drawn butter (page 300)

Scrunchions (page 300)

Garlic, onions, and olive oil (page 300)

Mustard sauce (page 300)

1. Soak rounders in cold water up to 2 days, changing water several times. Wash well, remove tails, and put in a saucepan of cold water. Bring to a boil; simmer 30-45 minutes.
2. Place vegetables in a separate saucepan of salted water. Cook until tender.
3. Remove skin and bones after rounders are cooked or serve whole.
4. Serve rounders and vegetables with sauce of choice.

SERVES 4

SALT COD CUISINE: THE INTERNATIONAL TABLE

Salt Cod Dish (Sancocho)

Canary Islands

Mojos (sauces) give the salt cod cuisine of the Canary Islands an unmistakably Canarian touch. As well as mojo colorado, garlic and cumin sauce and onion, garlic, and tomato sauce are often used with Sancocho.

2 lb (900 g) salt cod, large portions

6-8 potatoes, peeled, roughly chopped

3 sprigs fresh parsley or coriander

1 medium onion

SAUCE
Mojo colorado (page 298)

1. Use watered salt cod (page 80).
2. Put potatoes in a saucepan with cod, parsley or coriander, and whole onion. Bring to a boil; simmer until ingredients are tender.
3. Drain and arrange cod and potatoes on a serving dish. Serve with sauce of choice.

Adapted from Flora Lilia Barrera and Dolores Hernandez Barrera Alama, *The Best of Canarian Sauces*, and Felisa Vera, *The Best of Canary Islands Cookery*

SERVES 4

VARIATION
- Use food local to the Canary Islands such as pumpkin, yam, pear, sweet potato, and chickpeas instead of potatoes.

Boiled Salt Cod

Scotland

2 lb (900 g) salt cod

6-8 potatoes, peeled

SAUCES
Egg sauce (page 199)

Mustard sauce (page 300)

1. Use watered salt cod (page 80). Drain; remove any skin and bones. Cut into serving-sized portions. Cover with cold water in a saucepan and bring to a boil. Simmer until tender, about 20-25 minutes. Drain. Place in a heated serving dish.
2. Boil and mash potatoes until fluffy.
3. Serve cod and potatoes with sauce of choice.

Adapted from Elizabeth Craig, *The Scottish Cookery Book*

SERVES 4

BOILED SALT COD DINNERS

Cabbie-Claw

Scotland

This recipe, published in 1929, requires the home salting of a small fresh cod for one to two days and then drying it for 24-48 hours, hung in the open air. Cabbie-Claw is a traditional dish from northeastern Scotland and Orkney. The name is a derivative of *cabillaud*, a French word for cod.

Unlike the egg sauce listed with the next recipe, Codfish Breakfast, this one calls for equal amounts of milk and fish stock. The choice is yours.

> Take a freshly caught codling (freshness is essential) of about three and a half pounds in weight; clean and skin it, and wipe it dry. Rub the fish inside and out with salt, and let it lie for about twelve hours; then hang it up in the open air. If it is a windy day, so much the better; but the fish should be kept out of the direct rays of the sun. Leave for from twenty-four to forty-eight hours, according to the degree of 'highness' desired. Place in a saucepan with sufficient water, heated to boiling-point, to cover. Add three or four sprigs of parsley and a tablespoonful of grated horseradish. Simmer very gently until the fish is cooked, but do not over-cook. Remove the fish, skin, lift all the flesh from the bone, and divide neatly into small pieces. Arrange a border of hot mashed potato on a heated ashet [large shallow oval dish], place the fish in the center, and cover with egg sauce made with milk and fish stock in equal parts. Serve very hot.
>
> —F. Marian McNeill, *The Scots Kitchen*

Codfish Breakfast

198 SALT COD CUISINE: THE INTERNATIONAL TABLE

BOILED SALT COD DINNERS

Codfish Breakfast

Bermuda

Food and lifestyle journalist Edward Bottone, also known as The Curious Cook and the author of *Spirit of Bermuda: Cooking with Gosling's Black Seal Rum*, writes that sitting down for a Bermuda codfish breakfast on a Sunday morning is a delicious habit—but one the outsider might not appreciate.

This breakfast uses two sauces; you may choose one or serve with both. Both contain a small amount of sherry pepper sauce. Bermudan sherry pepper sauce is made from piquant peppers and 17 herbs and spices steeped in dry sherry for several months. It gives the salt cod dish flavour and fire, but it is the flavour that lingers, not the heat.

4 salt cod steaks

8 medium potatoes

2 ripe avocados

1 lemon, quartered

4 small ripe bananas

1/4 cup (60 ml) fresh parsley, chopped

TOMATO SAUCE

5 tsp (25 ml) extra-virgin olive oil

1/2 red onion, thinly sliced

2 cups (500 ml) canned whole plum tomatoes, seeded, chopped

2 tsp (10 ml) fresh thyme

Salt and freshly ground black pepper

1/4 tsp (1.2 ml) sherry pepper sauce or other hot pepper sauce

EGG SAUCE

2 tbsp (30 ml) butter

2 tbsp (30 ml) extra-virgin olive oil

1 hard-boiled egg, chopped or mashed

1/4 tsp (1.2 ml) sherry pepper sauce or other hot pepper sauce

1. Use watered salt cod (page 80). Drain. Cover with cold water and bring to a simmer for 8-10 minutes, until the flesh begins to separate. Remove skin and bones.
2. Boil potatoes in a separate saucepan.
3. Prepare tomato sauce: Sauté onion in olive oil. Add tomatoes, thyme, salt, and pepper; simmer 10 minutes. Add pepper sauce.
4. Prepare egg sauce: Mix butter, oil, and egg in a small saucepan. Bring to a near boil; add pepper sauce. Remove from heat.
5. Peel and slice avocados and bananas. Rub both with lemon to prevent darkening. Arrange on 4 plates.
6. Add equal portions of cod and potatoes to each plate. Garnish with lemon slices and sprinkle with parsley.
7. Serve with either or both sauces.

Adapted from Edward Bottone, *Spirit of Bermuda*

SERVES 4

Dried Salt Cod (Klipfish)

Denmark

This is a multi-part recipe. First, prepare the salt cod and potatoes with a bowl of melted butter. Second, make the fish mustard (a variation of béchamel sauce), sometimes called *fiske sennep*. Third, prepare a variety tray of accompaniments.

2 lb (900 g) salt cod

6-8 potatoes, peeled

1/4 cup (60 ml) butter

FISH MUSTARD

Béchamel sauce (page 297), substituting fish stock (page 296) for half the milk

1 tsp (5 ml) yellow and brown mustard seeds, coarsely ground

1 tsp (5 ml) vinegar

Salt

GARNISH

4 hard-boiled eggs, sliced

Strips of horseradish, grated horseradish, or prepared horseradish

Sliced beetroot

1. Use watered salt cod (page 80). Cover with cold water in a saucepan. Bring to a boil and simmer until tender. Drain; remove any skin and bones.
2. Boil potatoes.
3. Melt butter.
4. Make fish mustard: Mix mustard seeds with vinegar and a pinch of salt; add to béchamel sauce.
5. Serve fish mustard, hard-boiled eggs, sliced beets, and horseradish on a tray.
6. Serve salt cod, potatoes, and a serving of melted butter to each person.

Adapted from Alan Davidson, *North Atlantic Seafood*

SERVES 4

VARIATION

- Use a traditional *suppevisk* (fresh parsley, celery, and leek tied together) when simmering the cod.

Dried Salt Cod (with garnishes)

BOILED SALT COD DINNERS

Dried Salt Cod (Stokvis)

Netherlands

In *North Atlantic Seafood*, Alan Davidson describes the origins of this recipe, a staple food in the Royal Netherlands Navy. It is customary to set a Rhine wineglass containing a raw egg by each plate; each diner mixes the egg on his plate and helps himself to the seven components of the meal.

The ingredients for this meal are numbered, as the pageantry requires they be brought to the table separately and in this order.

1. About 3 1/2 oz (100 g) salt cod per person, watered (page 80). The cod is tied in little rolls, simmered 45 minutes, untied, and served.
2. Boiled rice, "nice and dry."
3. Boiled potatoes.
4. Butter sauce made from 1/4 cup (60 ml) butter and 1 tsp (5 ml) lemon juice.
5. Fried onions.
6. Gherkins.
7. Mustard sauce made from 1 cup (250 ml) fish stock (page 296), 1/4 cup (60 ml) all-purpose flour, 2 tbsp (30 ml) water, and 2 tsp (10 ml) prepared mustard.
8. Sweet mango chutney, piccalilli, and spicy Indonesian sambal (chili sauce) are the usual condiments.

Christmas Eve Cod (Bacalhauda Consoada)

Portugal

Christmas Eve Cod brings many Portuguese families together for an evening of celebration and conversation, ending with the distribution of gifts. It is sometimes called "Cod's Eve."

4 salt cod steaks

1 medium cabbage, cut in large chunks

6 potatoes

4 hard-boiled eggs (1 or more per person)

SAUCE

1 cup (250 ml) extra-virgin olive oil

3 garlic cloves, halved

Wine vinegar or cider vinegar

2 tbsp (30 ml) fresh parsley, finely chopped, for garnish

1. Use watered salt cod (page 80). Drain.
2. Place cabbage in a large saucepan and cover with water. Bring to a boil; simmer until partially cooked, then add cod. Remove cod and cabbage when cooked to your preference.
3. Boil potatoes in their skins in a separate saucepan. Peel potatoes and arrange on a serving platter with cod, cabbage, and eggs.
4. Make sauce: Heat olive oil and garlic. Add a little vinegar when the sauce begins to simmer. Serve in a sauce dish.
5. Sprinkle parsley over platter of food. Serve.

Adapted from Ana Patuleia Ortins, *Portuguese Homestyle Cooking*

SERVES 4

VARIATION

 Use kale, spinach, or mustard greens instead of cabbage; boil whole carrots with the greens.

Christmas Eve Cod

BOILED SALT COD DINNERS

Salt Cod and Potato with Garlic and Herbs

Greece

This recipe starts with a broth, used for both simmering the fish and making a sauce. The broth ingredients below are suggestions. Feel free to experiment with others.

1 1/2 lb (675 g) salt cod, with skin and bones

3-4 medium potatoes, scrubbed

2 tbsp (30 ml) olive oil, divided

4 garlic cloves, chopped

1 cup (250 ml) fresh parsley, chopped

1/2 cup (125 ml) fresh dill, chopped

BROTH

1 medium onion, stuck with a clove

1 small leek

2 carrots, peeled

1 celery stalk, tops and leaves, chopped

2 garlic cloves

2 bay leaves

2 sprigs fresh parsley

8 black peppercorns

1 lemon, quartered

SAUCE

1 cup (250 ml) thick plain yogourt

5 saffron strands, soaked in 2 tbsp (30 ml) boiling water

1. Use watered salt cod (page 80). Drain. Remove skin and bones from cod; break into small slivers or flakes.
2. Place broth ingredients and potatoes into a large saucepan. Add enough water to cover ingredients (including cod, but do not add cod yet). Bring to a boil; simmer 15 minutes.
3. Add cod; simmer 10-15 minutes. Remove cod.
4. Remove potatoes when done; peel and quarter.
5. Strain broth. Reserve.
6. Place cod in a serving dish. Add potatoes, olive oil, garlic, parsley, and dill. Toss gently to mix. Taste and adjust for salt.
7. Make sauce: Beat together yogourt, soaked saffron strands and their liquid, and 1/2 cup (125 ml) reserved broth. Add more broth if needed.
8. Pour sauce over cod and potatoes. Serve.

VARIATION

- Prepare the dish *au gratin*. Slice potatoes and layer with salt cod and herbs. Sauté 1 cup (250 ml) dry whole wheat bread crumbs in olive oil until golden, then sprinkle over the top. Bake at 350°F (180°C) for about 30 minutes.

Adapted from Susie Jacobs, *Recipes from a Greek Island*

SERVES 4

Lyonnaise Salt Cod (Morue à la Lyonnaise)

France

Lyonnais (and its capital city, Lyon) is south of Burgundy in France. The former capital of Gaul, Lyon has many gourmet clubs and legendary chefs, but it also offers true bourgeois regional cooking.

This dish offers salt cod "boiled," then sautéed with onions and potatoes and seasoned with warm red wine vinegar.

- 1 lb (450 g) salt cod
- 1/2 tsp (2.5 ml) fresh thyme
- 1 bay leaf
- 3 medium onions, thinly sliced
- 1/4 cup (60 ml) vegetable oil
- 4 medium potatoes, peeled, boiled, sliced
- 1/4 cup (60 ml) unsalted butter
- 1 garlic clove, grated
- 1/4 cup (60 ml) fresh parsley, chopped
- 3 tbsp (45 ml) red wine vinegar
- 1 tsp (5 ml) coriander seeds, freshly crushed
- Freshly ground black pepper

1. Use watered salt cod (page 80). Drain. Place in a medium saucepan with the thyme and bay leaf and cover with cold water. Bring to a boil; poach 5 minutes. Drain. Remove any skin and bones; flake.
2. Sauté onions in oil until golden. Add potatoes; cook 5 minutes. Add cod; cook another 5 minutes.
3. Add butter, garlic, and parsley. Sauté until butter is melted.
4. Pour mixture into a serving dish. Keep warm.
5. Heat red wine vinegar briefly in the hot frying pan and drizzle it over cod, potatoes, and onions.
6. Sprinkle with pepper and coriander.

Adapted from Henri-Paul Pellaprat, *Modern French Culinary Art*, and Mireille Johnston, *The Cuisine of the Rose*

SERVES 4

Coriander seed and red wine vinegar.

SIMMERED DISHES

To simmer salt cod properly, cook it slowly and steadily in a sauce or other liquid over a gentle heat. Hold it just below the boiling point, so the surface of the liquid bubbles occasionally.

You'll usually need to simmer salt cod for 10-20 minutes, depending on its thickness, until it flakes easily when tested with a fork.

Salt Cod and Leeks (La Quinquebine Camarguaise)	*France*
Salt Cod Provençale	*France*
Salt Cod with White Wine and Olives (Morue à la Niçoise)	*France*
Salt Cod Bordelaise	*France*
Curried Salt Cod and Dumplings	*Antigua*
Salt Cod Sauce and Ducana	*Antigua*
Salt Cod and Cabbage (Couves do Lagar)	*Portugal*
Whipped Creamy Salt Cod with Soft Polenta	*Italy*
Pan-Simmered Salt Cod with Fried Polenta	*Italy*
Salt Cod with Red Pepper Sauce (Bacalao à la Vizcaina)	*Basque Country*
Salt Cod Club Ranero (Bacalao al Club Ranero)	*Basque Country*
Salt Cod with Turnip and Mace Purée	*Spain*
Salt Cod with Olives and Capers (Baccala con Olive e Capperi)	*Italy*

Persillade.

Leeks.

SIMMERED DISHES

Salt Cod and Leeks (La Quinquebine Camarguaise)

France

Persillade is a combination of finely chopped parsley and garlic. The flavour of the persillade is strong, although if added while the dish is cooking and allowed to cool slightly, as in this recipe, it will mellow. Persillade can also be added toward the end of the cooking or served as a garnish to provide a garlicky jolt.

Two variations of this recipe are in *Vieilles Recettes de Cuisine Provençale* by Calixtine Chanot-Bullier and *Provence the Beautiful Cookbook: Original Recipes from the Regions of Provence* by Richard Olney. Provence is a region of southeastern France on the Mediterranean adjacent to Italy. Camargue is a large river delta area at the mouth of the Rhone. I was directed to this recipe by Randy Bell, whom I met at a meeting of The 12,000 Stages Society to celebrate salt cod.

1 1/2 lb (675 g) salt cod

3 tbsp (45 ml) olive oil

2 lb (900 g) leeks, including tender green parts, thinly sliced

1/2 cup (125 ml) boiling water

Salt

2 tbsp (30 ml) all-purpose flour

2 cups (500 ml) milk

5 salted anchovy fillets, rinsed, chopped

Freshly ground black pepper

Whole nutmeg, grated

3/4 cup (185 ml) Gruyère, Parmesan, or Swiss cheese, grated

PERSILLADE

2 or more garlic cloves, finely chopped

3 tbsp (45 ml) fresh parsley, chopped

SERVES 4-6

1. Use watered salt cod (page 80). Simmer 10 minutes. Remove skin and bones; flake.
2. Warm olive oil in a heavy saucepan over medium-low heat. Add leeks and cook, stirring, 20 minutes or until softened.
3. Add boiling water. Salt lightly; simmer 8-10 minutes, until water evaporates completely.
4. Sprinkle flour evenly over the top, stir well, and slowly add milk, stirring continuously.
5. Combine persillade ingredients; add to saucepan. Simmer gently 15 minutes.
6. Stir in anchovies and cod; simmer 10 minutes. Add pepper and nutmeg to taste.
7. Stir in cheese and adjust for salt. Simmer 3-4 minutes; serve.

VARIATION

- Persillade invites variations, by adding and/or substituting other herbs such as oregano, tarragon, or basil in place of parsley. A little lemon zest can be added; a small amount of olive oil can make the persillade easier to work with.

Salt Cod Provençale

France

Provence encompasses highly fertile agricultural areas with a sun-blessed climate and an abundance of tomatoes, onions, garlic, parsley, and olives—all key ingredients in this dish.

1 1/2 lb (675 g) salt cod

1/4 cup (60 ml) olive oil

1 onion, coarsely chopped

2 tomatoes, skinned, chopped

1 garlic clove, crushed

16 black olives

Freshly ground black pepper

1 sprig fresh parsley, chopped

1. Use watered salt cod (page 80). Simmer 10 minutes. Drain, remove skin and bones, and break into large chunks.
2. Simmer onion in olive oil. Add tomatoes, garlic, and olives. Season with pepper.
3. Add cod; simmer 10 minutes.
4. Garnish with parsley.

SERVES 4

SIMMERED DISHES

Salt Cod with White Wine and Olives (Morue à la Niçoise)

France

À la Niçoise is a French phrase that means, literally, "as prepared in Nice," typifying the cuisine found in and around that French Riviera city. Tomatoes, black olives, garlic, and anchovies are integral to this cooking style.

1 1/2 lb (675 g) salt cod

1 medium onion, finely chopped

2 garlic cloves, chopped

2 tbsp (30 ml) olive oil

4 tomatoes, peeled, seeded, chopped

1/2 cup (125 ml) dry white wine, warmed

Salt and freshly ground black pepper

1/2 tsp (2.5 ml) dried chili pepper flakes

1/2 red bell pepper, sliced

3 medium potatoes, peeled, chopped

2 tbsp (30 ml) cognac

3 canned salted anchovy fillets, soaked in water 10 minutes, drained

16 black olives, pitted

SERVES 4

1. Use watered salt cod (page 80). Drain; remove any skin and bones. Flake.
2. Sauté onion and garlic in olive oil in a large saucepan until golden. Add cod. Simmer gently.
3. Add tomatoes, warmed wine, salt and pepper, chilies, and peppers. Simmer gently, covered, 15 minutes.
4. Add potatoes. Add a little hot water if necessary; simmer 20 minutes. Add cognac, anchovies, and black olives.
5. Stir briefly and serve hot.

Adapted from Time-Life Books, *Fish*

Salt Cod Bordelaise

France

Bordeaux, a port city on the Garonne River in southwest France, was once the principal port of entry for salt cod from Newfoundland. The recipe recommends Graves white wine, Graves being a sub-region of the Bordeaux wine region in France.

- 1 lb (450 g) salt cod fillets
- 4 tbsp (60 ml) olive oil
- 2 large onions, chopped
- 4 garlic cloves, crushed
- 4 medium tomatoes, peeled, seeded
- 2 green bell peppers, sliced in thin strips
- Bouquet garni of fresh thyme, bay leaf, and parsley
- 1 1/4 cups (310 ml) Graves or other white wine
- 1 tbsp (15 ml) tomato purée
- 1 tsp (5 ml) white sugar
- Toasted bread crumbs

1. Use watered salt cod (page 80). Poach cod 10-15 minutes, depending on the thickness of the fillets. Drain; reserve poaching water. Remove any skin and bones.
2. Heat olive oil and lightly fry onions, garlic, tomatoes, and peppers; add bouquet garni. Simmer several minutes over low heat.
3. Add wine and 1 1/4 cups (310 ml) simmering water. Add tomato purée and sugar. Cook gently for another 10 minutes.
4. Pour some of the sauce into a baking dish and place cod fillets on top. Pour remaining sauce over cod. Sprinkle bread crumbs on top; brown in a 400°F (200°C) oven for 10-15 minutes.

Adapted from Alan Davidson, *North Atlantic Seafood*

SERVES 4

Bouquet garni.

SIMMERED DISHES

Curried Salt Cod and Dumplings

Antigua

In this Caribbean recipe from my friend Rose Samson dumplings are covered or filled with curried salt cod. This provides a connection between Antigua and the ever-popular dumplings of Newfoundland and Labrador.

2 lb (900 g) salt cod

3 tbsp (45 ml) vegetable oil

2 tbsp (30 ml) unsalted butter

2 large tomatoes, peeled, chopped

3 fresh chives, chopped

3 medium onions, finely chopped

2 garlic cloves, finely chopped

3 tbsp (45 ml) curry powder, dissolved in 1 cup water

1/4 tsp (1.2 ml) dried chili pepper flakes

1/2 tsp (2.5 ml) ground cloves

1/2 tsp (2.5 ml) chili powder

3 medium potatoes, peeled, chopped

2 cups (500 ml) water

6-8 dumplings (use recipe below or your own)

DUMPLINGS

1 cup (250 ml) all-purpose flour

1 tbsp (15 ml) baking powder

1/2 tsp (2.5 ml) salt

2 tbsp (30 ml) unsalted butter

Cold milk, water, plain yogourt, or sour cream

1. Use watered salt cod (page 80). Drain. Remove any skin and bones. Break into fairly big pieces.
2. Place oil and butter in a frying pan over moderate heat. Add tomatoes, chives, onions, garlic, curry powder, chili flakes, cloves, and chili powder. Cook 1 minute.
3. Add potatoes; stir well. Add water. Cover and simmer until potatoes are almost tender, about 10 minutes.
4. Add cod and simmer until heated through and tender, about 10-15 minutes. Adjust seasoning.
5. Cook dumplings in a separate pot as described below. When ready, break open the dumplings.
6. Serve dumplings on dinner plates or in large soup bowls. Cover with curried cod and juices.

DUMPLINGS

1. Sift flour, salt, and baking powder into a bowl.
2. Rub in butter until the mixture is crumbly.
3. Add enough cold milk, water, yogourt, or sour cream to make a fairly stiff dough.
4. Shape into balls approximately 1-1.5 inches (2.5-4 cm) in diameter.
5. Drop into boiling water; cook 10 minutes.

SERVES 6

Salt Cod Sauce and Ducana

Antigua

The saltiness of the salt cod sauce balances the sweetness of the *ducana*, the sweet potato dumpling. Ducana are traditionally cooked in banana or grape leaves. Tinfoil offers an easy alternative and does not significantly affect the taste. If using banana or grape leaves, pass them through hot water before using to soften for easy folding.

SALT COD SAUCE

- 6 oz (170 g) salt cod
- 2 tbsp (30 ml) vegetable oil
- 1 small onion, chopped
- 1 green onion, chopped
- 2 garlic cloves, chopped
- 1/4 each red, green, and yellow bell pepper, chopped
- 2 tsp (10 ml) fresh parsley, chopped
- 1 sprig fresh thyme, or pinch of dried thyme
- 4 oz (115 g) tomato sauce
- Freshly ground black pepper

1. Use watered salt cod (page 80). Drain, cover with fresh water; simmer 10 minutes. Drain, remove skin and bones. Shred. Set aside.
2. Heat oil in a large frying pan over medium heat. Add onion, garlic, and bell peppers; sauté until onion is soft, about 5 minutes.
3. Add parsley, thyme, tomato sauce, cod, and pepper; simmer 15 minutes.

DUCANA

- 1 1/2 cups (375 ml) all-purpose flour
- 1/4 tsp (1.2 ml) salt
- 1/4 tsp (1.2 ml) nutmeg, ground or freshly grated
- 1/4 tsp (1.2 ml) ground cinnamon
- 2 cups (500 ml) sweet potato, grated
- 2 cups (500 ml) fresh coconut, grated
- 1 tbsp (15 ml) brown sugar
- 1 cup (250 ml) coconut water or milk
- 24 x 5-inch (12 cm) squares tinfoil

1. Mix flour, salt, nutmeg, and cinnamon in a mixing bowl.
2. Add sweet potato, coconut, and sugar; mix well.
3. Add enough coconut water or milk to dry ingredients to form a soft dough.
4. Place 2 tbsp (30 ml) dough on each tinfoil piece. Fold; roll and seal the ends.
5. Place sealed ducana in a large stockpot, cover with water, and bring to a boil. Cook until firm, about 15 minutes.
6. Unwrap and serve hot with cod sauce.

Adapted from Pamela Lalbachan, *The Complete Caribbean Cookbook*

SERVES 6

SIMMERED DISHES

Salt Cod and Cabbage (Couves do Lagar)

Portugal

This dish is often eaten at Christmas in parts of the Beira Baixa region of Portugal.

1 lb (450 g) salt cod steaks

1 medium white cabbage, quartered

6 medium potatoes

1 cup (250 ml) olive oil, divided

2 garlic cloves, crushed

1 bay leaf

1 hot chili pepper, malagueta if possible

1. Use watered salt cod (page 80).
2. Cook cod, cabbage, and potatoes, covered with water, in a stockpot. Remove cod after 15 minutes. Remove any skin and bones; flake.
3. Remove cabbage and potatoes when cooked. Reserve liquid. Quarter potatoes.
4. Pour just enough olive oil into a large saucepan to coat the bottom. Arrange ingredients in layers, beginning with half the cod, half the cabbage, and half the potatoes.
5. Heat the rest of the oil with the garlic, bay leaf, and hot peppers; pour half over the cod, cabbage, and potatoes.
6. Repeat with a second layer of cod, cabbage, and potatoes; add remaining olive oil. Add some reserved cooking liquid, if needed, to partially cover the ingredients and provide enough liquid for simmering.
7. Cover saucepan and bring to a boil. Simmer for a few minutes. Serve hot.

Adapted from Maria de Lourdes Modesto, *Traditional Portuguese Cooking*

SERVES 4

Whipped Creamy Salt Cod with Soft Polenta

Italy

Polenta is a Northern Italian staple of boiled cornmeal. It may be served in its creamy form, or allowed to solidify, after which it can be sliced and sautéed, grilled, or fried prior to serving. It is used in this and the next recipe, first as a side dish and then as a base for a salt cod topping.

- 1 lb (450 g) salt cod
- 5 cups (1.2 L) milk, divided
- 1 cup (250 ml) extra-virgin olive oil, divided
- 2 garlic cloves, finely chopped
- 1/4 cup (60 ml) fresh parsley, chopped
- 1 tsp (5 ml) freshly ground black pepper
- Basic polenta

1. Use watered salt cod (page 80). Drain. Place in a large saucepan. Add 4 cups (1 L) milk and just enough water to cover. Bring to a simmer; cook gently until cod is tender and flakes when pierced with a fork, about 15-20 minutes.
2. Drain cod; pat dry. Remove any skin and bones; use fingers to break and mash cod while warm.
3. Transfer cod to a large mixing bowl (use a blender or food processor if preferred). Stirring continuously with a wooden spoon or hands, gradually add alternating amounts of oil and remaining milk. Go slowly—it may not all be needed. Continue to mix 3-4 minutes, until cod is creamy and well emulsified. Mix in garlic. Cover and keep at room temperature.
4. Gently reheat a little olive oil in a frying pan before serving. Season with pepper and parsley.
5. Serve cod drizzled with heated olive oil next to a mound of soft, buttery polenta.

BASIC POLENTA

- 3 cups (750 ml) water
- 1 cup (250 ml) cornmeal
- 1/2 tsp (2.5 ml) salt
- 2 tbsp + 2 tsp (40 ml) butter (optional)

1. Pour cornmeal and 1 1/2 cups (375 ml) cold water into a large bowl. Whisk to eliminate lumps.
2. Bring remaining water and salt to a boil in a medium saucepan.
3. Stir in cornmeal and cold water gradually; simmer gently for about 30 minutes, until polenta is very thick. Stir frequently to avoid sticking.
4. Mix in butter.

TO SOLIDIFY POLENTA

5. Pour polenta into a greased bowl and leave for 10 minutes. It will take the shape of the bowl.
6. Invert bowl onto a flat plate. Let sit a few minutes. Lift bowl. Cut polenta into thick slices.

SERVES 4

SIMMERED DISHES

Pan-Simmered Salt Cod with Fried Polenta

Italy

Prepare the basic polenta (previous page) and let it solidify before you simmer the salt cod.

1 1/2 lb (675 g) salt cod

2/3 cup (165 ml) extra-virgin olive oil, divided

1 cup (250 ml) all-purpose flour

1 tbsp (15 ml) unsalted butter

1 garlic clove, finely chopped

2 tbsp (30 ml) fresh parsley, chopped, divided

1 cup (250 ml) dry white wine

Salt and freshly ground black pepper

1/2 fresh lemon, juiced

Basic polenta, solidified, sliced

1. Use watered salt cod (page 80). Drain, pat dry, and cut into 2-3-inch (5-7 cm) pieces. Remove skin and bones.
2. Heat 1/3 cup (85 ml) olive oil in a large frying pan over medium-high heat. Dust cod pieces with flour on both sides. Place in the pan without crowding and sauté, turning once, until lightly golden on both sides, about 5 minutes. Transfer to a plate.
3. Discard half the oil if necessary, and put the frying pan back over medium-high heat. Add butter, garlic, and 1 tbsp (15 ml) parsley; stir once or twice quickly. Add wine and stir, scraping the bottom of the pan to pick up the browned bits. Reduce wine to approximately one-half.
4. Turn heat to low, return cod, and cook at low simmer, stirring from time to time, until cooked through, about 10 minutes. Add a little water if cod sticks to pan. Taste and adjust seasoning.
5. Heat remaining olive oil over medium-high heat.
6. Fry 4 slices polenta, turning once, until golden. Place polenta on a plate; top with cod.
7. Add remaining parsley and lemon juice to the frying pan containing the cod, and stir quickly. Pour pan juices over cod; serve.

SERVES 4

Salt Cod with Red Pepper Sauce (Bacalao à la Vizcaina)

Basque Country

The Basque have applied imagination and dedication to the culinary use of salt cod. Classic dishes include salt cod with tomatoes and parsley, fried and coated with egg, served in an emulsion of garlic, olive oil, and the gelatin from the skin of the fish (Salt Cod with Pil Pil Sauce, page 222), and this dish (with a rich sauce of choricero peppers and ham), a favourite of the people of Vizcaya.

1 1/2 lb (675 g) salt cod, skin on

VIZCAINA SAUCE

- 1/3 cup (85 ml) olive oil
- 1 oz (30 g) salt pork belly
- 2 oz (60 g) cured ham, chopped
- 2 medium onions, finely chopped
- 1 garlic clove, chopped (optional)
- 2 tbsp (30 ml) fresh parsley leaves
- 4 dried choricero mild red peppers, soaked overnight, or roasted red bell peppers
- 2 hard-boiled egg yolks, crushed

1. Use watered salt cod (page 80). Cut into rectangular chunks 1.5-2 inches (4-5 cm) or larger. Keep skin on. Place cod in a large saucepan with plenty of cold water and heat very slowly for 20-25 minutes. Drain. Place cod, skin side up, back in saucepan.
2. Drain peppers, if necessary; remove flesh by peeling or scraping.
3. Place olive oil, salt pork, ham, onion, and parsley in a small saucepan. Cook very slowly for about 45 minutes; avoid caramelizing the onions. Add a little water and cook 15 minutes more.
4. Strain sauce through a sieve or colander. Add red peppers and egg yolks.
5. Pour sauce over cod and heat very slowly for a few minutes. Serve.

Adapted from Maria Jose Sevilla, *Life and Food in the Basque Country*

SERVES 4

Salt Cod with Red Pepper Sauce

SIMMERED DISHES

Salt Cod Club Ranero (Bacalao al Club Ranero)

Basque Country

It is not a new dish; in cooking it is practically impossible to invent or discover anything new. This dish is simply the combination of codfish, together with a fried mixture, which occurred to a French chef named Alejandro Caveriviere.
—Jose Maria Busca Isusi, *Traditional Basque Cooking*

While he was working at Bilbao in the 1930s, Alejandro Caveriviere reportedly combined two classic Basque recipes (Bacalao al Pil Pil and a vegetable stew) to create this dish. I have added chili pepper for heat and roasted red peppers and zucchini for additional flavour.

1 lb (450 g) salt cod, cut in strips

3 choricero dried red peppers, soaked 90 minutes, chopped, or 2 tbsp (30 ml) bottled red pepper paste

1 chili pepper, finely chopped

3 medium tomatoes, peeled, seeded, chopped

2 Spanish yellow onions, chopped

2 garlic cloves, finely chopped

1 sprig fresh parsley, chopped

2 roasted red bell peppers, cut in squares

1 small zucchini, finely chopped

1/3 cup (85 ml) olive oil

1. Use watered salt cod (page 80). Drain and dry. Remove any skin and bones. Cut into strips.
2. Combine choricero peppers, chili pepper, tomatoes, onions, garlic, and parsley; fry slowly in olive oil. Add roasted red peppers and zucchini. Drain liquid; reserve.
3. Place cod strips on fried mixture. Beat reserved liquid until creamy and oil is completely blended.
4. Pour sauce over cod; place over low heat. Gently move pan around so the sauce covers the cod. Cook slowly 20-25 minutes, until cod is done.

Adapted from Jose Maria Busca Isusi, *Traditional Basque Cooking*

SERVES 4

Salt Cod with Turnip and Mace Purée

Spain

Chef Francis Paniego presented his version of a modest family dish at the World of Flavor International Conference and Festival in 2006. He poached salt cod in oil, served it over a purée of potatoes and garlic, and finished it with strips of roasted red peppers. It is adapted here using turnip and mace purée; the variation uses a potato and parsnip purée.

The turnip has had a longer tradition in Europe than the potato. It was a popular pot vegetable in Britain and France. Chefs are now rediscovering its virtues and are preparing stuffed turnips, braised turnips in cider, turnip mousse, and sautéed turnips.

4 x 4 oz (115 g) salt cod fillets

2/3 cup (165 ml) extra-virgin olive oil, divided

1 cup (250 ml) unsweetened coconut, grated

6 tbsp (90 ml) butter

4 red bell peppers, roasted, for garnish

TURNIP AND MACE PURÉE

1 medium yellow-fleshed turnip, peeled, sliced

Pinch mace

2 tbsp (30 ml) butter

Salt

1. Use watered salt cod (page 80). Drain. Heat a frying pan over medium-high heat, adding just enough oil to cover the bottom. Sear cod about 2 minutes each side, until lightly browned, turning carefully to avoid breaking.
2. Combine remaining oil, coconut, and butter in a large saucepan over very low heat. Transfer salt cod to this mixture; poach 5 minutes. Remove from heat.
3. Prepare turnip purée: Cover turnip slices with water. Add mace and boil over medium heat until cooked. Drain; reserve cooking liquid. Mash turnip, add butter, and mix until smooth. Add just enough cooking liquid to create a thin purée. Season with salt if needed.
4. Divide purée onto 4 plates and arrange cod on top. Garnish with slices of roasted red peppers. Serve.

Adapted from Martha Rose Shulman, *Spain and the World Table*

SERVES 4

SIMMERED DISHES

Salt Cod with Turnip and Mace Purée

Salt Cod with Parsnip and Potato Purée

VARIATION

Potato and parsnip purée (use in step 4 above): I always grow lots of parsnip in my back garden and leave about half covered with green spruce boughs to overwinter in the ground. The starches turn to sugar, and the parsnips are much sweeter in the spring. Use about twice the weight of potato as that of parsnip.

8 oz (225 g) parsnips, peeled, cut in chunks

1 lb (450 g) potatoes, peeled, cut in chunks

Salt

3 medium garlic cloves, peeled, mashed

3/4 cup (185 ml) water

5 tsp (25 ml) olive oil

1/3 tsp (2 ml) cumin

1/3 tsp (2 ml) curry powder

Milk or cream

Bring parsnips, potatoes, garlic, salt, and water to a boil; simmer until tender. Do not drain—there should be very little liquid left in the saucepan. Mash. Add olive oil, cumin, and curry powder. Mash until smooth. Add milk or cream if purée is too thick.

Adapted from Kitty Drake and Ned Pratt, *Rabbit Ravioli*

Salt Cod with Olives and Capers (Baccala con Olive e Capperi)

Italy

This easy-to-prepare salt cod dish uses nine ingredients. In addition to capers and black olives, the dish, in Italian fashion, uses anchovies, plum tomatoes, and dry white wine to mix with salt cod, chopped onion, and olive oil.

4 x 6 oz (170 g) salt cod steaks

2 tbsp (30 ml) olive oil

1 medium onion, chopped

2 shallots, chopped

3 salted anchovy fillets, soaked a few minutes

2 plum tomatoes, chopped

1/2 cup (125 ml) dry white wine

2 tbsp (30 ml) capers, drained, rinsed

1 cup (250 ml) black olives, pitted, sliced

1. Use watered salt cod (page 80). Drain.
2. Heat oil in a large frying pan. Add onion and shallots. Cook for a few minutes, stirring occasionally.
3. Add anchovies and cook over low heat, stirring with a wooden spoon.
4. Add tomatoes; simmer 5 minutes.
5. Add white wine; heat.
6. Add fish, capers, and black olives. Simmer 10 minutes.

Adapted from Editoriale Domus, *The Silver Spoon*

SERVES 4

Salt Cod with Olives and Capers

FRIED DISHES

For these recipes, the salt cod is kept in fairly large pieces and is better suited for a main dish than an appetizer. The recipes require that the salt cod be fried in one of three ways: sautéed, battered and pan-fried, or deep-fried.

SAUTÉED

Salt Cod with Pil Pil Sauce (Bacalao al Pil Pil) *Basque Country*
Salt Cod Fisherman's Style
    (Baccala all'Usanzadei Pescatori) *Italy*
Braised Cod and Potatoes in Tomato Sauce
    (Baccala con le Patate Nel Sugo) *Campania, Italy*
Fried Salt Cod on a Bed of Onions
    (Baccala alla Trasteverina) *Italy*
Salt Cod Fillets in Plantain Crust with Green Sauce
    (Lomo de Bacalao en Costra de Platano en
    Salsa Verde) *Dominican Republic*
Kippered Salt Cod Benedict *Newfoundland and Labrador*
Salt Cod with Spinach (Morue à la Lessiveuse) *France*

BATTERED

Fried Salt Cod (Baccala Fritto) *Italy*
Batter-Fried Salt Cod with Skordalia
    (Bakaliaros Tighanitos me Skordalia) *Greece*

DEEP-FRIED

Deep-Fried Salt Cod *Newfoundland and Labrador*

sautéed

Salt Cod with Pil Pil Sauce (Bacalao al Pil Pil)

Basque Country

A Basque chef stands at the stove, creating alchemy. He is warming salt cod and olive oil in an earthenware cazuela over a low flame. As it starts to bubble, he takes the handles of the dish and begins to shake it gently. He shakes it slowly but continuously, the fish and the oil in constant motion. After about 20 minutes the olive oil and the protein- and gelatin-rich juices from the fish begin to emulsify, and soon the salt cod is coated in a thick, velvety sauce. This magical transformation of two ingredients is not a product of the "new" Spanish cooking, but a classic, much loved Basque dish called *bacalao al pil pil*.

—Martha Rose Shulman, *Spain and the World Table*

1 1/2 lb (675 g) salt cod steaks, skin on

3/4 cup (185 ml) extra-virgin olive oil

4 garlic cloves, sliced lengthwise

1 hot guindilla or other chili pepper

1. Use watered salt cod (page 80). Cover cod in a saucepan with cold water. Heat to warm but not to boil. After 5 minutes, or when froth begins to form on the surface, remove cod and drain on paper towels.
2. Heat oil in a stovetop earthenware dish (*cazuela*) or frying pan; add garlic slices and chili pepper, spicing to your taste. Stir occasionally for 2-3 minutes. Remove garlic and chili when garlic is deep golden brown and tender; put aside.
3. Put cod, skin side up, in the pan. Shake the mixture rhythmically.
4. Pass the oil over the cod in this manner for 20-25 minutes, on and off heat as necessary; gelatin will emerge from the skin and thicken to look like light mayonnaise.
5. Put garlic and red pepper on top of cod. Heat briefly. Swish pan gently so sauce does not lose consistency. When cod is warm, it is ready to serve.

SERVES 4

Salt Cod with Pil Pil Sauce

FRIED DISHES

Salt Cod Fisherman's Style (Baccala all'Usanzadei Pescatori)

Italy

Tradition holds that this salt cod be eaten cold.

4 x 6 oz (170 g) salt cod steaks	4 garlic cloves, finely chopped
All-purpose flour	1 sprig fresh rosemary leaves, crushed
Olive oil	1/2 cup (125 ml) white wine vinegar
Freshly ground black pepper	

1. Use watered salt cod (page 80). Drain.
2. Flour cod; fry in olive oil, turning once. Drain on paper towels.
3. Sauté garlic and rosemary in pan drippings left from frying the cod.
4. Stir in vinegar as soon as garlic begins to darken. Cook 5 minutes; pour over cod. Sprinkle with freshly ground black pepper.

SERVES 4

Braised Cod and Potatoes in Tomato Sauce (Baccala con le Patate Nel Sugo)

Campania, Italy

1 1/2 lb (675 g) salt cod	4 potatoes, peeled, thinly sliced
3/4 cup (185 ml) all-purpose flour	6 plum tomatoes, peeled, chopped
2 cups (500 ml) extra-virgin olive oil, divided	3 bay leaves
1 medium onion, thinly sliced	2 tbsp (30 ml) fresh parsley, chopped
3 garlic cloves, thinly sliced	Salt

1. Use watered salt cod (page 80). Drain. Remove any skin and bones.
2. Cut cod in 2-inch (5 cm) pieces; dust with flour.
3. Heat 1 1/2 cups (375 ml) olive oil in a frying pan; fry cod until golden. Remove and set aside on paper towels.
4. Heat remaining oil in the frying pan and sauté onion and garlic; when they have darkened, add potatoes. Cook 20 minutes, or until ready. Adjust salt; add tomatoes and bay leaves.
5. Cook about 10 minutes to blend flavours. Place cod in the mixture and simmer a few minutes to warm through. Sprinkle with parsley. Serve.

SERVES 4

Fried Salt Cod on a Bed of Onions (Baccala alla Trasteverina)

Italy

This popular and easy Roman recipe for fried salt cod served on a bed of onions could also be known as Salted Cod with Anchovies, Capers, and Pine Nuts. To the version below, recorded by Kyle Phillips, a food, wine, and travel writer from Tuscany, I have added chopped plum tomatoes.

Trastevere ("across the Tiber") is one of the many distinct neighbourhoods of Rome. The area is home to the John Cabot University, a private American liberal arts university founded in 1972 to honour Italian explorer John Cabot.

1 3/4 lb (790 g) salt cod

1/2 cup (125 ml) all-purpose flour

3 tbsp (45 ml) olive oil, divided

1 garlic clove, crushed

4 medium onions, finely sliced

3 plum tomatoes, finely chopped

Salt

1 tbsp (15 ml) capers

1 tbsp (15 ml) raisins, soaked

1 tbsp (15 ml) pine nuts

1 anchovy fillet, rinsed

1 lemon, juiced

1 tbsp (15 ml) fresh parsley, chopped

1. Use watered salt cod (page 80). Drain. Remove skin and bones.
2. Cut cod into 2-inch (5 cm) pieces. Flour and fry in half the oil until golden, carefully turning once. Drain on paper towels. Set aside.
3. Preheat oven to 400°F (200°C).
4. Heat remaining olive oil in frying pan and sauté garlic until golden; add onions and tomatoes. Season with salt to taste; add capers, raisins, and pine nuts. Add anchovy and stir until it dissolves.
5. Place onion mixture in a baking dish; arrange cod on top. Pour pan drippings over top. Bake 5 minutes.
6. Remove cod from oven, sprinkle with lemon juice and parsley. Serve hot.

SERVES 4

FRIED DISHES

Salt Cod Fillets in Plantain Crust with Green Sauce (Lomo de Bacalao en Costra de Platano en Salsa Verde)

Dominican Republic

This recipe, as well as the one for Norwegian Salt Cod over Stew of Grapes (Bacalao Noruego Sobre Estofado de Uvas), were submitted by Regis Batista Lemaire, the Trade Commissioner at the Canadian Embassy in Dominican Republic. The recipes were given to me in Spanish, which I have preserved in the list of ingredients.

6 salt cod fillets (*lomos de bacalao*)

Whole wheat flour, to coat (*harina de trigo para rebozar*)

6 eggs, rapidly stirred (*huevos ligeramente batidos*)

4 plantains, cut in fine pieces (*platanos fritos en hojas muy finas libres de grasa*)

Olive oil, for frying (*el aceite de oliva para freir*)

Salt and freshly ground black pepper (*sal y pimiento al gusto*)

GREEN SAUCE

4 oz (115 g) smoked cod (*fume de pescado*)

3 fresh basil leaves (*paquetes de albahaca*)

1/4 tsp (1.2 ml) salt (*sel*)

2 tbsp (30 ml) milk (*leche*)

1. Use watered salt cod (page 80). Drain and pat dry.
2. Fry plantain slices; mix in a blender. Remove to a separate container.
3. Prepare green sauce: Combine smoked cod, basil, and a pinch of salt in a blender. Transfer sauce to a small saucepan, heat gently, and add milk. Stir to mix.
4. Coat salt cod fillets with flour. Dip pieces into the egg mixture and into the blended pieces of plantains.
5. Fry in hot olive oil until golden.
6. Serve hot, accompanied by the sauce.

SERVES 6

Kippered Salt Cod Benedict

Newfoundland and Labrador

This recipe was prepared for this book by chef Stephen Vardy. Vardy is the recipient of the Ottawa Epicurean Chef of the Year Award 2006-2007, five CAA/AAA 4 Diamond Awards; four Where to Eat in Canada 2-Star Awards; and a Bronze Medal Winner Gold Medal Plates, 2004. He submitted this recipe when he was executive chef at Atlantica Restaurant in Portugal Cove-St. Philips, Newfoundland.

6 x 1 3/4 oz (50 g) salt cod

3 lemon poppy seed scones, halved (next page)

Hollandaise sauce (next page)

6 slices smoked ham

6 poached eggs

Fresh dill, for garnish

1. Use watered salt cod (page 80). Drain. Check for obvious bones but do not break pieces of cod. Air dry in the refrigerator at least 12 hours.
2. Place cod in a smoker (preferably cold smoke) and smoke at least 2 hours, depending on the strength of your smoker. Use sweet wood such as apple, cherry, or maple.
3. Remove cod and chill.
4. Coat cod with a light dusting of flour and, just before serving, pan-fry until warmed through. Season with fresh cracked pepper.

Kippered Salt Cod Benedict

Lemon Poppy Seed Scones

226 SALT COD CUISINE: THE INTERNATIONAL TABLE

LEMON POPPY SEED SCONES

1/2 cup (125 ml) unsalted butter
2 cups + 2 tbsp (530 ml) all-purpose flour
1/4 cup (60 ml) sugar
1 tsp (5 ml) baking powder
1/4 tsp (1.2 ml) baking soda
Pinch salt
1 cup (250 ml) 35% cream
1 1/2 tbsp (22.5 ml) poppy seeds
1 tbsp (15 ml) lemon zest

1. Preheat oven to 400°F (200°C).
2. Cut butter into 1-inch (2.5 cm) cubes and chill.
3. Mix flour, sugar, baking powder, baking soda, and salt in a large bowl. Add butter with fingertips; press cubes into large flakes. Stir in cream just until the flour is moistened and dough starts to come together in large clumps. Mix in poppy seeds and lemon; knead dough in the bowl just until it holds together. Turn onto a floured board.
4. Lightly flour the top of the dough and roll into a rectangle 1 inch (2.5 cm) thick and about 4 inches by 6 inches (10 cm by 15 cm) in size. Keep edges even as best you can. Fold dough into thirds. Lightly flour the board again and rotate dough so the closed side faces the left. Roll out into a rectangle again, fold, and rotate. Repeat two more times.
5. Roll dough out once more into a rectangle and trim edges so it will rise evenly. Cut dough in half lengthwise; you'll have 2 pieces, each about 2 inches by 6 inches (5 cm by 15 cm). Cut each piece of dough into triangles with a 2-3-inch (5-7.5 cm) base and space apart on a baking sheet. Cover with plastic wrap and refrigerate 1 hour.
6. Bake scones 15-20 minutes, rotating halfway through. Do not overcook; they will continue to bake slightly after removal from the oven.
7. Cool scones on cooking racks lined with linens; fold linens over loosely and allow to cool at room temperature.

HOLLANDAISE SAUCE

2/3 cup (165 ml) unsalted butter, divided
3 egg yolks
4 tsp (20 ml) cold water
2 tsp (10 ml) lemon juice
Pinch salt
Pinch freshly ground black pepper
Pinch cayenne pepper

1. Cut 2 tbsp (30 ml) butter into cubes and refrigerate. Melt remaining butter in a saucepan over medium heat; skim off foam. Keep warm over low heat.
2. Whisk egg yolks with cold water in a heatproof bowl until light. Place over saucepan of barely simmering water; continue to whisk until eggs are thickened, about 3 minutes. Remove from heat.
3. Whisk cool butter cubes into egg yolks. Slowly whisk in warm butter, then lemon juice, salt, pepper, and cayenne pepper. Whisk in a few more drops of water if sauce is too thick. Keep warm over a pan of hot water (off heat).

To plate: Cut 3 scones in half and divide among 6 plates. On each scone, place a slice of smoked ham, the warmed kippered salt cod, and a poached egg. Top with a generous spoonful of hollandaise sauce. Garnish with fresh dill.

Salt Cod with Spinach (Morue à la Lessiveuse)

France

This recipe, originally published by Charles Durand (Le Cuisinier Durand) in 1843, is an example of salt cod's popularity in France in the early 1800s. The recipe was recorded in *Fish*, part of "The Good Cook" series of cookbooks published by Time-Life Books.

1 1/2 lb (675 g) salt cod

1/2 cup (125 ml) all-purpose flour, divided

1/4 cup (60 ml) olive oil

1 lb (450 g) spinach, chopped

1/2 cup (125 ml) boiling water

2 tbsp (30 ml) fresh parsley, finely chopped

1 garlic clove, finely chopped

1 tsp (5 ml) orange peel, finely chopped

2 anchovy fillets, soaked 10 minutes, finely chopped

1. Use watered salt cod (page 80). Drain and cut into 2-inch (5 cm) squares.
2. Coat cod with flour; cook lightly in oil over low heat, approximately 3 minutes per side.
3. Rinse spinach; squeeze dry. Remove cod from pan; replace with spinach. Cook over high heat 2 minutes, tossing frequently.
4. Add 1 tsp (5 ml) flour, boiling water, parsley, garlic, orange peel, and anchovy fillets.
5. Bring to a boil; reduce heat to medium. Cook 5 minutes, until spinach is wilted.
6. Mix in cod and cook 3-4 minutes, until cod is ready. Shake pan during cooking. Serve.

Adapted from Time-Life Books, *Fish*

SERVES 4

FRIED DISHES

Fried Salt Cod (Baccala Fritto)

Italy

Grappa is an Italian alcoholic drink, traditionally made from pomace, the discarded grape seeds, stalks, and stems that are a by-product of the winemaking process. Since the Middle Ages Italians have sipped this firewater after meals and even add a little to their morning espresso to "correct" it. Here, grappa is used in the batter for fried salt cod.

4 x 6 oz (170 g) salt cod steaks

1 1/4 cups (310 ml) all-purpose flour

1 tbsp (15 ml) butter, melted

4 tbsp (60 ml) white wine

2 tbsp (30 ml) grappa

Salt

1 egg, separated

Olive oil, for frying

1. Use watered salt cod (page 80). Drain and pat dry.
2. Combine flour, butter, wine, grappa, and a pinch of salt in a large bowl; mix well. Stir in egg yolk. Let stand 30 minutes. Whisk egg white in a separate bowl; fold into flour mixture.
3. Heat at least 0.5 inches (1.5 cm) oil in a large frying pan.
4. Dip cod in the batter and fry 5-7 minutes on each side. Remove with a slotted spatula, drain, and serve.

Adapted from Editoriale Domus, *The Silver Spoon*

SERVES 4

Batter-Fried Salt Cod with Skordalia (Bakaliaros Tighanitos me Skordalia)

Greece

Many Greeks celebrate March 25 as a "double holiday" with parades and *bakaliaros* (crispy fried salt cod with garlic sauce). The parades mark the successful War of Independence waged by Greek revolutionaries between 1821 and 1830 against the Ottoman Empire; bakaliaros is often the dish of choice when the Greek Orthodox Church celebrates the Annunciation.

This is a very popular salt cod dish in Greece. For this version, I have included a basic batter recipe, but you may use your own.

1 1/2 lb (675 g) salt cod

Olive or vegetable oil, for frying

Fresh parsley sprigs, for garnish

1 lemon, sliced, for garnish

Skordalia (page 299)

BATTER

1 egg

1/4 cup (60 ml) water

2 tsp (10 ml) baking powder

1/4 tsp (1.2 ml) salt

1 cup (250 ml) all-purpose flour

Salt and freshly ground black pepper

1. Use watered salt cod (page 80). Drain well; remove skin and bones. Cut into 3-4-inch (7-10 cm) pieces.
2. Simmer cod for a few minutes in water. Drain.
3. Prepare batter: Mix egg and water and beat lightly until fluffy. Add baking powder, salt, and enough flour to make a medium-thin batter. Adjust seasoning.
4. Heat 0.5 inches (1.5 cm) oil in a deep frying pan. Dip cod in batter and fry until both sides are golden brown, about 4 minutes per side.
5. Garnish with sprigs of parsley and lemon slices; serve with skordalia.

SERVES 4

FRIED DISHES

Batter-Fried Salt Cod with Skordalia

deep-fried

Deep-Fried Salt Cod

Newfoundland and Labrador

Refer to the Methods of Cooking section (pages 82-85) for detailed information on deep-frying cod. Use the batter recipe below or your own.

2 lb (900 g) salt cod

All-purpose flour

Vegetable oil, for deep-frying

BATTER

1 cup (250 ml) all-purpose flour

1 1/4 cups (310 ml) lukewarm water

1/2 tsp (2.5 ml) salt

2 tsp (10 ml) baking soda

SALAD

Lettuce leaves, loosely arranged

1 small red onion, thinly sliced

3 tomatoes, coarsely chopped

2 tsp (10 ml) extra-virgin olive oil

1/2 lemon, juiced

Salt and freshly ground black pepper

Tartar sauce (page 302)

1. Use watered salt cod (page 80). Drain. Cut into 3-inch (7 cm) pieces.
2. Mix batter: 1 cup (250 ml) flour, water, salt, and baking soda in a large bowl. Set aside to rest for 1 hour.
3. Dry cod completely; dip pieces, one at a time, into remaining flour.
4. Pour oil into a deep fryer to 3 inches (7.5 cm) deep and heat to 375°F (190°C).
5. Dip cod into batter. When completely coated, drop several pieces into the hot oil. Fry 5 minutes, turning frequently with a slotted spoon, until crisp and golden brown. Keep cooked pieces warm in the oven while remaining cod is cooking.
6. Combine lettuce, onion, and tomatoes in a salad bowl; toss with olive oil, lemon juice, and salt and pepper to taste.
7. Divide cod and salad among 4 plates. Serve with tartar sauce.

Adapted from Joan McConnell-Over, *For the Love of Cod*

SERVES 4

BAKED DISHES

SOUFFLÉS
Salt Cod Soufflé (Soufflé de Bacalhau) — *Portugal*
Salt Cod Soufflé — *Newfoundland and Labrador*

AU GRATIN STYLE
Salt Cod au Gratin with Anchovy Sauce
  (Baccala alla Vicentina) — *Italy*
Salt Cod au Gratin — *Newfoundland and Labrador*
Salt Cod Gratin (Gratin de Morue) — *France*
Salt Cod in Casserole with Béchamel
  (Bakaliaros me Béchamel) — *Greece*
Salt Cod, Onions, and Potatoes
  (Bacalhau à Gomes de Sa) — *Portugal*
Salt Cod with Cream (Bacalhau com Natas) — *Portugal*
Salt Cod with Eggs (Pudim de Bacalhau com Ovos) — *Brazil*
Cod à Ze do Pipo — *Portugal*
Spiritual Cod (Bacalhau Espiritual) — *Portugal*

BAKED IN OTHER SAUCES
Salt Cod and Onion in Beer Sauce — *Portugal*
Cod with Bread Slices in Lafoes Style
  (Migas Lagareiras à Lafoes) — *Portugal*
Baked Whole Salt Cod — *Newfoundland and Labrador*
Salt Cod Plaki with Raisins — *Greece*
Baked Salt Cod Cakes (Bakaliaros Tou Fournou) — *Greece*
Casserole of Salt Cod Graciosa — *Spain*

VOL-AU-VENTS, PIES, TARTLETS
Green Fig and Saltfish Pie — *St. Lucia*
Salt Codfish Pie — *Newfoundland and Labrador*
Salt Cod Pie — *Newfoundland and Labrador*
Salt Cod Tartlets with Coconut — *Guadeloupe*
Salt Cod Tartlet (Tartaleta de Bacalao) — *Spain*
Salt Cod Pie (Bakaliaro Pitta) — *Greece*

OVEN ROASTED
Salt Cod in Viana Style (Bacalhau a Moda de Viana) — *Portugal*
Oven-Roasted Salt Cod — *Newfoundland and Labrador*
Salt Cod Baked in the Oven — *Newfoundland and Labrador*
Roasted/Baked Salt Cod and Potatoes — *Portugal*

soufflés

The basis of a soufflé is a firm foam made from egg whites. The bubbles in beaten egg whites expand with the steam generated while cooking, helping the soufflé to rise. The trapped air also makes the soufflé light. The more the egg whites are beaten, the whiter they get, and the smaller the bubbles become—and the smaller the bubbles, the better the soufflé. Very small bubbles create a uniform, smooth texture. As the egg whites cook, the foam sets.

TIPS FOR A SUCCESSFUL SOUFFLÉ

- Grease the baking dish with hard fat (butter or lard) to allow the soufflé to rise properly.
- Bake soufflé in a preheated oven so it starts cooking quickly.
- Use a dish with smooth vertical sides so the soufflé does not change its shape as it rises.
- A smaller soufflé dish makes it easier to cook the soufflé uniformly, without burning the outside.
- If a larger dish is used, cook the soufflé longer at a lower temperature.

Salt Cod Soufflé

BAKED DISHES

Salt Cod Soufflé (Soufflé de Bacalhau)

Portugal

Remember to reserve the water used to simmer the cod to use in the white sauce with onion and garlic that is part of this dish.

I was first introduced to this soufflé by Judy Dwyer, whose friend in Portugal prepared it regularly and described it as "like the clouds." This dish was served with a mixed salad of lettuce, tomatoes, onions, salt, olive oil, and coriander "for the real Portuguese final touch."

10 oz (280 g) salt cod

2 tbsp + 2 tsp (40 ml) butter

1 small onion, grated

2 garlic cloves, finely chopped

1/3 cup + 1 tbsp (100 ml) whole wheat flour

1 1/4 cups (310 ml) milk

1 1/4 cups (310 ml) fish stock (page 296) or reserved simmering liquid

Salt and freshly ground black pepper

Lemon juice

3 eggs, separated

Butter, softened

Bread crumbs

Grated cheese

SERVES 4

1. Use watered salt cod (page 80). Simmer 10 minutes in just enough water to cover. Remove cod; reserve liquid. Remove skin and bones; shred cod as finely as possible.
2. Preheat oven to 400°F (200°C).
3. Heat butter, onion, and garlic in a medium saucepan; stir until slightly browned. Add flour; stir. Continue to stir while slowly pouring milk and 1 1/4 cups (310 ml) stock or reserved simmering liquid.
4. Add cod; stir until mixture begins to bubble. Remove saucepan from heat and season mixture with salt, pepper, and lemon juice.
5. Add egg yolks one at a time in small amounts, whisking continuously.
6. Put egg whites and a pinch of salt into a mixing bowl; beat into soft peaks.
7. Stir a small amount of beaten egg white into cod mixture to lighten. Carefully fold in remaining egg whites, using a rubber spatula and an over-and-under cutting motion.
8. Butter 4 small soufflé dishes; sprinkle with bread crumbs.
9. Fill dishes with the mixture; sprinkle with grated cheese. Turn oven down to 325°F (160°C) and bake for about 25 minutes.
10. The soufflé will be puffed and golden when ready. Serve immediately.

Adapted from Chefe Silva, *Bacalhau a Portuguesa*

Salt Cod Soufflé

Newfoundland and Labrador

This recipe requires care, skill, and experience. The fat in the egg yolks and butter in the roux will begin to burst some of the bubbles in the egg-white foam as soon as they are folded in.

1 lb (450 g) salt cod

1 cup (250 ml) béchamel sauce (page 297)

1 tbsp (15 ml) fresh parsley, chopped

1 tsp (5 ml) onion, grated

3 eggs, separated

Butter, softened

Salt and freshly ground black pepper

1. Use watered salt cod (page 80). Bring just to a boil and simmer 10-15 minutes. Drain. Remove any skin and bones; shred finely.
2. Preheat oven to 400°F (200°C).
3. Add parsley and onion to prepared béchamel sauce in a medium saucepan. Simmer until thickened.
4. Add cod; stir in well-beaten egg yolks. Season to taste.
5. Beat egg whites until stiff; fold into the cod mixture, using an over-and-under cutting motion with a rubber spatula.
6. Pour into a buttered soufflé dish.
7. Turn oven down to 325°F (160°C). Place dish in a pan of warm water and bake 40 minutes or until firm. Serve.

SERVES 4

BAKED DISHES

Au gratin generally refers to a dish topped with a browned crust, often using bread crumbs, grated cheese, egg, butter, or béchamel sauce. A gratin is usually prepared in a shallow dish and baked in the oven or cooked under an overhead grill or broiler for a golden crust.

Salt Cod au Gratin with Anchovy Sauce (Baccala alla Vicentina)

Italy

Il Cucchiaio d'argento is an important Italian cookbook originally published in 1950—it has since gone through eight editions—by the design and architecture magazine *Domus*. It contains about 2,000 recipes from all over Italy. An English version, *The Silver Spoon*, was published in 2005. A distinguishing characteristic of this version of Baccala alla Vicentina is the use of anchovy sauce. The version below uses layers of salt cod and fillets of anchovies.

1 1/2 lb (675 g) salt cod

6 tbsp (90 ml) olive oil, divided

1 medium onion, chopped

6 anchovy fillets, canned in oil, drained, chopped

1/4 cup (60 ml) fresh parsley, chopped

2/3 cup (165 ml) Parmesan cheese, grated, divided

3 cups (750 ml) milk

2 tbsp (30 ml) dry white wine

Salt and freshly ground black pepper

1. Use watered salt cod (page 80). Drain, remove any skin and bones; cut into fairly large pieces.
2. Preheat oven to 350°F (180°C).
3. Combine onion, anchovies, parsley, and 1/2 cup (125 ml) cheese. Set aside.
4. Heat 3 tbsp (45 ml) olive oil in frying pan; sauté cod until golden.
5. Heat 3 tbsp (45 ml) olive oil in baking dish. Add layers of fish, onion, cheese, and anchovy mixture.
6. Repeat layers, ending with onion and anchovy mixture. Top with remaining cheese.
7. Cover with milk and wine.
8. Bake 1 1/2 hours, until milk is absorbed.

Adapted from Domus Editoriale, *The Silver Spoon*

SERVES 4

Salt Cod au Gratin

Newfoundland and Labrador

1 lb (450 g) salt cod
2 bay leaves
6 whole cloves
2 sprigs fresh parsley
1 tsp (5 ml) fresh or dried thyme
2 cups (500 ml) milk
1/2 cup (125 ml) water
2 garlic cloves, finely chopped
2-3 potatoes
1/3 cup (85 ml) olive oil
2 tbsp (30 ml) cream (optional)
Salt and freshly ground black pepper
Pinch nutmeg
2/3 cup (165 ml) white cheddar cheese, grated

1. Use watered salt cod (page 80).
2. Tie bay leaves, cloves, parsley, and thyme in a cheesecloth. Place cod in a medium saucepan with herbs. Cover with milk and water; add garlic. Soak 45 minutes. Remove cod; reserve liquid but discard herbs. Remove any skin and bones; flake cod.
3. Preheat oven to 350°F (180°C).
4. Boil and mash potatoes.
5. Mix together cod, potatoes, olive oil, and 1/2 cup (125 ml) liquid used to soak the cod. Blend in a small amount of cream. Season to taste with salt, pepper, and nutmeg.
6. Place mixture in a lightly greased baking dish. Drizzle with olive oil. Bake for 25 minutes.
7. Sprinkle cheese on top. Bake 10 more minutes.

SERVES 4

Salt Cod Gratin (Gratin de Morue)

France

In this recipe the potatoes—not the salt cod—are simmered in milk.

1 lb (450 g) salt cod
4 potatoes, peeled, thinly sliced
Salt
Freshly ground white pepper
Freshly grated nutmeg
3 cups (750 ml) milk
1 egg yolk
1/4 cup (60 ml) cream
1/2 garlic clove, peeled
2 tbsp (30 ml) unsalted butter, divided

1. Use watered salt cod (page 80). Place cod in a pot of cold water, bring to a boil, simmer 2 minutes. Drain. Remove any skin and bones and finely shred cod. Set aside.
2. Preheat oven to 350°F (180°C).
3. Place sliced potatoes in a medium saucepan. Season with salt, pepper, and nutmeg and cover with milk. Bring to a boil and simmer 10 minutes.
4. Mix egg yolk and cream in a bowl.
5. Remove potatoes from heat. Add egg mixture, stirring constantly. Adjust seasoning.
6. Rub baking dish with garlic and grease with butter.
7. Pour half the potatoes into the baking dish. Cover with cod and add remaining potatoes. Dot with remaining butter. Bake 30 minutes until the top is crispy.

Adapted from Mireille Johnston, *The Cuisine of the Rose*

SERVES 4

BAKED DISHES

Salt Cod in Casserole with Béchamel (Bakaliaros me Béchamel)

Greece

- 2 lb (900 g) salt cod
- 1 bay leaf
- 1 medium onion, quartered
- 4 medium potatoes, sliced
- Salt and freshly ground black pepper
- 1 tbsp (15 ml) butter
- 3 tbsp (45 ml) fresh parsley, finely chopped
- 1 tsp (5 ml) dried oregano
- 1/2 cup (125 ml) white wine
- 2 cups (500 ml) béchamel sauce (page 297)
- 2 garlic cloves, crushed
- 1/2 cup (125 ml) Greek graviera (Gruyère) cheese

1. Use watered salt cod (page 80). Place cod, bay leaf, and onion in a large saucepan. Cover with water and bring to a boil; simmer 15 minutes. Drain. Remove any skin and bones; break into flakes or slivers. Slice potatoes.
2. Preheat oven to 300°F (150°C).
3. Place half the cod in an oiled baking dish and cover with potatoes. Sprinkle lightly with salt and pepper and dot with butter. Top with remaining cod; sprinkle with parsley, oregano, and white wine.
4. Add garlic to the béchamel sauce. Pour over the cod mixture; sprinkle with grated cheese.
5. Bake for 30-40 minutes.

Adapted from Eva Zane, *Greek Cooking for the Gods*

SERVES 6

Salt Cod in Casserole with Béchamel

Salt Cod, Onions, and Potatoes (Bacalhau à Gomes de Sa)

Portugal

I have brought this to many dinner parties.

1 lb (450 g) salt cod

2 cups (500 ml) milk

4 potatoes

1/2 cup (125 ml) olive oil

2 large onions, thinly sliced

1 garlic clove, sliced

Freshly ground black pepper

2 hard-boiled eggs, for garnish

10 black olives, for garnish

2 tbsp (30 ml) fresh parsley, chopped, for garnish

1. Use watered salt cod (page 80). Cover with fresh water; bring to a boil. Simmer 15 minutes, until tender. Drain. Remove any skin and bones; flake cod into large pieces and place in a pan.
2. Preheat oven to 425°F (220°C).
3. Bring milk to a boil and pour over cod. Let stand 1 hour. Drain.
4. Boil potatoes in their skins just until tender. When cool enough to handle, peel and cut into slices, half moons, or quarters.
5. Heat oil in a frying pan over medium-low temperature. Sauté onions and garlic until tender and just barely browned.
6. Increase heat to medium-high and add potatoes, cod, and pepper to taste. Stir gently and cook 1-2 minutes.
7. Spoon cod and potato mixture into a baking dish. Bake for 15 minutes, until heated through and the top is slightly golden.
8. Sprinkle with parsley and garnish the middle of the dish with slices of hard-boiled eggs. Place black olives along the edges. Serve immediately.

SERVES 4

BAKED DISHES

Salt Cod with Cream (Bacalhau com Natas)

Portugal

A popular way of cooking salt cod in Portugal, Bacalhau com Natas consists of layers of cod, onion, fried potato slices, and cream and has dozens of variations. In this recipe, cod is poached in water, then in milk to make it milder and whiter, and then combined with sautéed vegetables and a rich cream sauce.

1 lb (450 g) salt cod

3 cups (750 ml) milk, heated

1 1/2 cups (375 ml) olive oil, divided

1 large onion, thinly sliced

1 bay leaf

1 carrot, shredded or julienned

1 garlic clove, finely chopped

Pinch coarse salt

Freshly ground black pepper

1 tbsp (15 ml) fresh parsley, chopped

3 medium potatoes, peeled, julienned

1 1/2 cups (375 ml) molho branco (page 298)

1/2 cup (125 ml) fresh bread crumbs

1. Use watered salt cod (page 80). Drain. Bring enough water to cover cod to a boil in a large saucepan. Turn off heat; add cod. Cover and poach for 15 minutes. Drain, reserving some of the broth for the sauce. Remove any skin and bones; shred cod.
2. Pour hot milk over cod, cover, and let stand 45 minutes.
3. Preheat oven to 350°F (180°C).
4. Sauté onion and bay leaf in 3 tbsp (45 ml) olive oil until onion is soft. Stir in carrot and garlic; sauté 1 minute. Season with salt and pepper; add parsley.
5. Fry potatoes in remaining oil. Drain on paper towels. Set aside.
6. Drain cod. Put cod, onion mixture, and potatoes in a large bowl; toss lightly. Fold half of the white sauce into the mixture. Transfer to a baking dish and pour remaining sauce over top. Sprinkle with bread crumbs.
7. Bake for about 20 minutes, or until top is lightly golden and bubbly.

Adapted from Ana Patuleia Ortins, *Portuguese Homestyle Cooking*

SERVES 4

Salt Cod with Eggs (Pudim de Bacalhau com Ovos)

Brazil

12 oz (340 g) salt cod fillets

2 tbsp (30 ml) cornstarch

2 cups (500 ml) milk

5 tbsp (75 ml) butter, divided

1 medium onion, chopped

2 medium tomatoes, peeled, seeded, chopped

2 tbsp (30 ml) capers, drained

Salt and freshly ground black pepper

6 eggs

4 tbsp (60 ml) Parmesan cheese, grated

Butter

1. Use watered salt cod (page 80). Drain and rinse; remove bones. Cover with water and simmer gently 15-20 minutes, or until cod flakes easily. Drain. Flake and set aside.
2. Preheat oven to 400°F (200°C).
3. Dissolve cornstarch in a little milk. Add remaining milk; pour into a small saucepan. Add 1 tbsp (15 ml) butter and cook, stirring, over medium heat until mixture is smooth and slightly thickened. Set aside.
4. Heat 4 tbsp (60 ml) butter in another saucepan. Add onion and cook for a few minutes, stirring. Add tomatoes; cook until mixture is thick and well blended.
5. Stir in sauce and capers. Fold in cod; add a little salt if necessary. Season generously with pepper. Cool slightly.
6. Butter 6 1-cup (250 ml) ramekins or other small ovenproof serving bowls. Break an egg into each. Pour cod mixture over each egg; sprinkle with cheese.
7. Bake for 8 minutes.

Adapted from Elisabeth Lambert Ortiz,
The Book of Latin and American Cooking

SERVES 6

BAKED DISHES

Cod à Ze do Pipo

Portugal

Ze do Pipo was the nickname for the owner of a once-famous eating house in Oporto, the second largest city in Portugal. This recipe belongs to the traditional cuisine of this seaside city.

1 lb (450 g) salt cod

2 cups (500 ml) milk

2 medium onions, chopped

4 tbsp (60 ml) olive oil

1 bay leaf

Salt and freshly ground black pepper

1 cup (250 ml) mayonnaise (page 302)

2 egg yolks

4 medium potatoes, boiled, mashed

2 tbsp (30 ml) butter

Black olives, for garnish

1. Use watered salt cod (page 80). Remove any skin and bones; break into large pieces. Simmer in milk for 10-15 minutes. Drain, reserving milk.
2. Preheat oven to 325°F (160°C).
3. Grease a large (or 4 small) baking dish with mayonnaise; place cod into the dish.
4. Fry onions with olive oil, bay leaf, salt, pepper, and 2 tbsp (30 ml) poaching milk. Do not allow onions to brown.
5. Place onions on the cod.
6. Add butter to mashed potatoes; add reserved milk to reach desired consistency.
7. Arrange a border of mashed potatoes around the inside of the dish. Lightly brush with egg yolk.
8. Cover cod with mayonnaise and bake for 15 minutes, until browned.
9. Garnish with black olives.

SERVES 4

Cod à Ze do Pipo

Spiritual Cod (Bacalhau Espiritual)

Portugal

Onions, carrots, garlic, bread, and béchamel sauce are common ingredients in the many rich and flavourful Bacalhau Espiritual dishes.

1 1/4 lb (570 g) salt cod

Milk or water, for simmering cod

4 slices whole wheat bread

Milk, for soaking the bread

1/3 cup (85 ml) olive oil

2 onions, finely grated

3 medium carrots, peeled, finely grated

2 garlic cloves, finely grated

2 cups (500 ml) béchamel sauce (page 297)

Salt and freshly ground black pepper

Butter

2 eggs, separated

2 tbsp (30 ml) Parmesan cheese, grated

1. Use watered salt cod (page 80). Drain. Cover with milk or water; simmer for about 10 minutes. Drain. Remove any skin and bones; shred into very small pieces.
2. Preheat oven to 350°F (180°C).
3. Soak bread in milk until milk is absorbed. Squeeze milk out; break the bread.
4. Heat olive oil and add onions, carrots, garlic, cod, and bread. Stir until mixture is dry and almost browned.
5. Pour half the prepared béchamel sauce over cod mixture and stir well. Season with salt and pepper. Grease a baking dish or individual gratin dishes with butter; add mixture and spread evenly.
6. Beat egg whites until stiff.
7. Add 2 yolks to remaining sauce, followed by beaten egg whites. Mix well.
8. Pour sauce over cod, sprinkle with cheese and bake until browned, approximately 20-25 minutes.

SERVES 4

baked in other sauces

BAKED DISHES

Salt Cod and Onion in Beer Sauce

Portugal

Hot pepper sauce with onions and beer give this battered cod a flavour to remember.

1 1/2 lb (675 g) salt cod

3 eggs

3 tbsp (45 ml) fresh parsley, chopped

Vegetable oil, for frying

1/2 cup (125 ml) all-purpose flour

3/4 cup (185 ml) cornmeal

3 onions, thinly sliced

2 hard-boiled eggs, sliced, for garnish

20 black olives, for garnish

BEER AND TOMATO SAUCE

3 tbsp (45 ml) olive oil

3 garlic cloves, chopped

3/4 cup (185 ml) beer

1 tbsp (15 ml) tomato paste

3 medium tomatoes, chopped

1 tbsp (15 ml) hot pepper sauce

Salt

1/4 cup (60 ml) fresh parsley, chopped

Freshly ground black pepper

1. Use watered salt cod (page 80). Drain; pat dry. Without shredding the cod, carefully remove any skin and bones; cut lengthwise into fillets 2 inches (5 cm) wide.
2. Preheat oven to 350°F (180°C).
3. Whisk together eggs and parsley. Heat vegetable oil in a large frying pan. Dip cod into flour, then into egg mixture, and finally into cornmeal. Cook in batches, about 2 minutes per side, or until golden brown. Remove with a slotted spoon; drain.
4. Sauté onions until tender, not browned.
5. Grease baking dish. Arrange onions on bottom with cod on top.
6. Prepare beer and tomato sauce: Heat oil in a frying pan over medium-low heat. Add garlic and cook for 2 minutes. Stir in beer, tomato paste, tomatoes, and hot pepper sauce. Cook, stirring, for 8 minutes, until thickened. Season with salt if necessary; add parsley and pepper.
7. Pour sauce over cod. Bake uncovered, for 20 minutes or until cod is heated through. Cover and let stand 20 minutes for stronger taste.
8. Garnish with olives and egg slices.

Adapted from Carla Azevedo, *Uma Casa Portuguesa*

SERVES 4

Cod with Bread Slices in Lafoes Style (Migas Lagareiras à Lafoes)

Portugal

This dish is often served on Christmas Eve.

1 1/2 lb (675 g) salt cod

1 small cabbage, shredded

6 slices whole wheat bread, thinly cut

1/2 cup (125 ml) olive oil, divided

3 garlic cloves, crushed

1. Use watered salt cod (page 80).
2. Preheat oven to 350°F (180°C).
3. Boil cabbage in a medium saucepan. After 20 minutes, add cod; simmer until tender. Remove cod and cabbage; reserve cooking water.
4. Drain and flake cod. Remove any skin and bones.
5. Place a layer of cod in a baking dish, followed by layers of cabbage and thinly sliced bread. Add half the olive oil and 1/2 cup (125 ml) reserved cooking liquid. Sprinkle with crushed garlic.
6. Repeat layers until all ingredients have been used. Ensure top pieces of bread are moist.
7. Bake for 10-15 minutes or until heated through.

Adapted from Maria de Lourdes Modesto, *Traditional Portuguese Cooking*

SERVES 6

Baked Whole Salt Cod

Newfoundland and Labrador

The idea for this recipe is from Eleanor Bennett, St. John's, who enjoyed a similar dish in a restaurant on the Douro River in Porto, Portugal.

Whole salt cod (except rounders) are difficult to find. It would be best to clean a whole fresh cod and salt it yourself.

2 lb (900 g) whole salt cod, not split, soundbone left in, skin on

All-purpose flour, for coating cod

5 tbsp (75 ml) olive oil, divided

3 medium tomatoes, sliced

2 medium onions, finely sliced

3 garlic cloves, finely chopped

3 carrots, sliced diagonally

1/2 red pepper, finely sliced

20 black olives, not pitted

3 sprigs fresh parsley

4 potatoes, peeled, sliced

1. Use watered salt cod (page 80). Drain; dry. Remove all fins.
2. Preheat oven to 375°F (190°C).
3. Dust the whole cod with flour. Heat 3 tbsp (45 ml) olive oil in large frying pan. Sear cod on both sides.
4. Transfer cod to roasting pan. Add tomatoes, onions, garlic, carrots, pepper, olives, parsley, and 2 tbsp (30 ml) olive oil.
5. Cover and bake for 30 minutes.
6. Fry potatoes.
7. Cut cod in large chunks and serve with potatoes. Cover with vegetables and any sauce from roasting.

SERVES 6

BAKED DISHES

Salt Cod Plaki with Raisins

Greece

The Greek term *plaki* is frequently used to describe a dish cooked with olive oil, tomatoes, and vegetables in the oven. In this recipe, the salt cod is cooked in plaki style with raisins. Sometimes it is cooked with lemon and white wine.

- 1 lb (450 g) salt cod fillets
- 1/2 cup (125 ml) dark seedless raisins
- 9 tbsp (135 ml) olive oil, divided
- 2 red onions, coarsely chopped
- 2 garlic cloves, coarsely chopped
- 2 tsp (10 ml) tomato paste, diluted in 2 tbsp (30 ml) water
- 1 cup (250 ml) canned plum tomatoes, chopped
- 3 potatoes, peeled and sliced
- Salt and freshly ground black pepper
- 1 bay leaf
- 1 small cinnamon stick

1. Use watered salt cod (page 80). Drain and cut into 2-inch (5 cm) squares. Remove any bones.
2. Preheat oven to 375°F (190°C).
3. Place raisins in a small bowl and cover with warm water to plump.
4. Heat 3 tbsp (45 ml) olive oil in a frying pan and sauté onions and garlic for 5 minutes. Add tomato paste and tomatoes and sauté another 5 minutes. Remove from heat.
5. Grease a baking dish. Place potatoes in the dish; season with salt and pepper. Place onions around the potatoes. Pour raisins and their liquid over potatoes and onions. Add bay leaf and cinnamon; toss lightly. Drizzle another 3 tbsp (45 ml) olive oil over the top; add enough water to come about halfway up the potatoes. Bake for 45 minutes.
6. Dredge cod lightly in flour. Heat remaining olive oil in a frying pan and fry cod (in batches, if necessary) until lightly golden. Drain on paper towels.
7. Place cod on potato mixture and bake for 10 more minutes so the flavours meld. Serve warm or at room temperature.

SERVES 4

Salt Cod Plaki with Raisins

Baked Salt Cod Cakes (Bakaliaros Tou Fournou)

Greece

1 lb (450 g) salt cod

2 garlic cloves, finely chopped

4 green onions, finely chopped

3 tbsp (45 ml) fresh parsley, chopped

1 egg, lightly beaten

1 cup (250 ml) bread crumbs

Salt and freshly ground black pepper

All-purpose flour

2 tbsp (30 ml) butter

2 tbsp (30 ml) olive oil

SAUCE

1 medium onion, finely chopped

1/4 cup (60 ml) olive oil

3 tbsp (45 ml) fresh parsley, finely chopped

1 tsp (5 ml) fine herbs

16 oz (475 ml) can whole tomatoes

1/2 cup (125 ml) white wine

1. Use watered salt cod (page 80). Cover with water. Bring to a boil and simmer until tender. Drain, remove any skin and bones, and flake.
2. Preheat oven to 400°F (200°C).
3. Combine cod with garlic, green onions, parsley, egg, and bread crumbs; season with salt and pepper. Form mixture into 4 patties and dust lightly with flour.
4. Pan-fry cod cakes in a mixture of butter and olive oil until lightly browned.
5. Make sauce: Sauté onion in olive oil; add all other ingredients. Simmer 20 minutes.
6. Place cod cakes in an oiled baking dish. Cover with sauce and bake for 30 minutes.

Adapted from Eva Zane, *Greek Cooking for the Gods*

SERVES 4

BAKED DISHES

Casserole of Salt Cod Graciosa

Spain

1 lb (450 g) salt cod

2 tbsp (30 ml) olive oil

3 cups (750 ml) canned tomatoes with juice

2 onions, sliced in rounds

2 green peppers, sliced in rounds

2 sprigs fresh parsley, chopped

2 potatoes, sliced

12 oil-cured black olives

1. Use watered salt cod (page 80). Remove any skin and bones; cut into cubes.
2. Preheat oven to 325°F (160°C).
3. Cover bottom of baking dish with 1 tbsp (5 ml) olive oil. Layer about one-third of the tomatoes, cod, onions, peppers, parsley, and potatoes. Repeat until all ingredients are used, ending with a layer of potatoes. Drizzle remaining olive oil over the top.
4. Cover and bake for 45 minutes, or until potatoes are tender.
5. Add olives to the top of the casserole for the last 20 minutes.

Adapted from David Gray and Yoka Gray, *The Newfoundland Gourmet*

SERVES 4

vol-au-vents, pies, tartlets

Green Fig and Saltfish Pie

St. Lucia

This national dish of St. Lucia was first brought to my attention by Annie Brown, a graduate of Naparima Girls' High School, Trinidad and Tobago. It was published in *The Multi-Cultural Cuisine of Trinidad & Tobago & the Caribbean*, a project by the school to commemorate the school's Diamond Jubilee in 1987.

The cuisine of St. Lucia is influenced by West Indian, Creole, and French food. Salt cod often appears with vegetables like cassava (yucca), dasheen (taro), and sweet potato. Green bananas (referred to as "green figs" in the Caribbean), boiled or stewed, are often served with salt cod as a breakfast food. Marinated salt cod and green bananas is a favourite entrée in Martinique.

1 lb (450 g) salt cod

2 lb (900 g) green bananas

1/2 cup (125 ml) evaporated milk, divided

1 tbsp (15 ml) lime juice

2 green bell peppers, cut in strips

1 onion, chopped

2 tomatoes, thinly sliced

2 cups (500 ml) grated cheese

1/2 tsp (2.5 ml) freshly ground black pepper or hot pepper

1 tbsp (15 ml) bread crumbs

1. Use watered salt cod (page 80). Drain. Break cod in pieces and simmer in water for 10 minutes. Drain, remove skin and bones, and flake.
2. Preheat oven to 350°F (180°C).
3. Boil bananas in their peels until tender. Peel while still hot and crush with 1/4 cup (60 ml) milk and a little salt; sprinkle with lime juice to prevent discoloration.
4. Press half the bananas in a greased pie plate. Add half the cod, bell pepper, onion, tomatoes, cheese, and pepper.
5. Repeat layers, ending with cheese and pepper. Top with remaining 1/4 cup (60 ml) milk and sprinkle with bread crumbs.
6. Bake for 25-30 minutes.

SERVES 6

BAKED DISHES

Salt Codfish Pie

Newfoundland and Labrador

This recipe is from the *The Treasury of Newfoundland Dishes*, originally published in 1958 as a joint project of the Newfoundland Home Economics Association and Maple Leaf Milling Company.

>Line a 1 1/2-quart baking dish with mashed potatoes, well covering the bottom. Nearly fill the dish with boiled salt cod which has been minced or finely shredded. Add about 1 cup drawn butter sauce [page 300] made with a little chopped onion. Spread a thick layer of mashed potatoes over the fish. Bake at 350°F. [180°C] for 30 to 40 minutes.

Salt Cod Pie

Newfoundland and Labrador

8 oz (225 g) salt cod	1 tbsp (15 ml) all-purpose flour
4 slices bacon	1 1/4 cups (310 ml) milk, divided
2/3 cup (165 ml) onion, chopped	1/4 tsp (1.2 ml) dried thyme
1/4 cup (60 ml) green bell pepper, chopped	1/4 tsp (1.2 ml) freshly ground black pepper
1/4 cup (60 ml) pimento or red bell pepper, chopped	2 eggs, separated
	1 baked 9-inch (23 cm) pie shell

1. Use watered salt cod (page 80). Simmer until tender, remove skin and bones, and flake. Set aside.
2. Preheat oven to 350°F (180°C).
3. Fry bacon in a large frying pan until crisp; remove, break into pieces.
4. Cook onion, green pepper, and red pepper in the bacon fat until tender. Sprinkle with flour and gradually stir in 1 cup (250 ml) milk. Cook, stirring, until thickened.
5. Add cod, bacon, thyme, and pepper. Beat egg yolks with remaining 1/4 cup (60 ml) milk; add to frying pan and cook 3 minutes. Beat egg whites until stiff but not dry, and fold into cod mixture.
6. Fill pie shell and bake for 20 minutes, or until lightly browned.

Adapted from St. Mary's Beaver, Cub & Scout Ladies Auxiliary, Our Favourite Recipes

SERVES 4

Salt Cod Tartlets with Coconut

BAKED DISHES

Salt Cod Tartlets with Coconut

Guadeloupe

In this recipe, tartlet pans are layered with a pastry bottom, filled with salt cod, and then baked. In the next recipe, Salt Cod Tartlet, pastry is cut into equal shapes and baked before being layered with salt cod and toppings.

1 lb (450 g) salt cod

1 sprig fresh thyme, leaves only, chopped

1 tbsp (15 ml) olive oil

2 shallots, chopped

2 garlic cloves, finely chopped

3/4 cup (185 ml) coconut milk

1 tbsp (15 ml) crème fraîche or sour cream

Salt and freshly ground black pepper

1 egg

Butter

All-purpose flour

1/2 lb (225 g) prepared puff pastry

2 tbsp (30 ml) bread crumbs

1. Use watered salt cod (page 80). Drain; cover with water and add thyme. Bring to a boil; simmer until tender. Drain; remove any skin and bones; shred and mash.
2. Preheat oven to 400°F (200°C).
3. Heat oil in large saucepan over medium heat and sauté shallots and garlic. Add cod and cook 3 minutes, stirring frequently.
4. Warm coconut milk and crème fraîche in a small saucepan. Add gradually to cod mixture. Season with salt and pepper. Simmer 4 minutes, or until liquid is absorbed. Add egg and stir vigorously. Remove from heat.
5. Butter and lightly flour 6 2-3-inch tartlet pans. Cover with pastry and prick the bottoms. Fill pastry with cod mixture and sprinkle with bread crumbs.
6. Bake 25 minutes. Reduce heat to 300°F (150°C). Bake 10 minutes more. Serve hot.

Adapted from Babette de Rozieres, *Creole*

SERVES 6

Salt Cod Tartlet (Tartaleta de Bacalao)

Spain

1 lb (450 g) salt cod, skin on
1/2 lb (225 g) prepared puff pastry
All-purpose flour, for dusting
2/3 cup (165 ml) olive oil, divided
2 garlic cloves, crushed
1 green bell pepper, cut in strips
1 red bell pepper, cut in strips
Freshly ground black pepper
1 lemon, quartered

1. Use watered salt cod (page 80). Drain; keep skin on.
2. Preheat oven to 375°F (190°C).
3. Roll out pastry on a floured board. Cut into 12 pieces; place on baking sheets and bake 10 minutes, or until pastry turns golden and starts to puff. Cool.
4. Heat 2 tbsp (30 ml) olive oil in a frying pan. Add garlic and pepper strips and gently cook about 10-12 minutes. Remove pepper and allow to cool. Peel skin from peppers.
5. Add remaining oil to frying pan. Place cod, skin side down, and fry 10-12 minutes. After a few minutes, shake pan every 30 seconds to release gelatin from under the skin.
6. Lift cod out of pan. Remove skin and bones; flake. Reserve gelatin-thickened sauce.
7. Cover tartlets with cod. Garnish with pepper strips. Season with pepper; spoon on small amount of sauce. Sprinkle with lemon juice.

SERVES 4

Salt Cod Tartlet

BAKED DISHES

Salt Cod Pie (Bakaliaro Pitta)

Greece

1 3/4 lb (790 g) salt cod

1 cup (250 ml) olive oil, divided

2 onions, finely chopped

3 small ripe tomatoes, peeled, seeded, chopped

2 garlic cloves, finely chopped

2 sprigs fresh parsley, finely chopped

Freshly ground black pepper

1 cup (250 ml) brown rice, cooked

Pastry for 2 pie crusts

VARIATIONS

- Use 5-7 sheets of phyllo pastry for each crust. Follow directions for the prepared phyllo; brush each layer with a little olive oil and melted butter. Leave 1 inch (2.5 cm) hanging over the rim. Pinch and roll top and bottom layers together.
- Use phyllo pastry as above. At step 3, add 1 egg, 1 tsp (5 ml) dried mint, dash of allspice, and 1/4 cup (60 ml) grated Parmesan cheese.
- Use saffron-flavoured fried rice instead of brown rice.

1. Use watered salt cod (page 80). Drain. Remove any skin and bones; cut into small pieces.
2. Preheat oven to 350°F (180°C).
3. Heat 3/4 cup (185 ml) olive oil in a saucepan. Brown onions; add cod, tomatoes, garlic, parsley, and pepper. Stir for a few minutes over medium heat.
4. Add rice and cook 1-2 minutes longer.
5. Oil pie dish with olive oil. Line with first pie crust; fill with cod mixture.
6. Cover with second crust and brush the top with remaining oil.
7. Bake for 1 hour or until top crust is golden brown.

SERVES 4

oven roasted

Salt Cod in Viana Style (Bacalhau a Moda de Viana)

Portugal

Viana do Castelo is the most northerly city on the Atlantic coast in Portugal. Founded by King Afonso III of Portugal and located at the mouth of the Lima River, Viana was one of the main ports from which Portuguese explorers set sail in the sixteenth century.

This is one of many Bacalhau a Moda de Viana recipes. Thick pieces of salt cod are wrapped in cabbage leaves, baked in the oven, and served with boiled potatoes and onions.

4 x 6 oz (170 g) cod steaks

1 large cabbage

8 medium potatoes

3 tbsp (45 ml) olive oil

4 medium onions, sliced

Salt and freshly ground black pepper

1. Use watered salt cod (page 80). Drain but do not wipe or dry the cod.
2. Wrap each steak in one or more cabbage leaves. Tie with kitchen twine.
3. Bake at 375°F (190°C) for about 40 minutes, until cod is tender and cabbage leaves have turned brownish and dry.
4. Boil potatoes.
5. Heat oil in a frying pan. Add onions and cook gently until soft and golden. Season with salt and pepper.
6. Carefully remove and discard twine and cabbage leaves. Place a steak and 2 potatoes on each of 4 plates.
7. Cover cod and potatoes with onions; serve immediately.

Salt Cod in Viana Style

SERVES 4

BAKED DISHES

Oven-Roasted Salt Cod

Newfoundland and Labrador

This is probably the easiest Sunday morning salt cod breakfast to make.

4 salt cod pieces, skin on

Butter

1. Use watered salt cod (page 80). Drain. Place pieces of cod, skin side down, on a shallow baking sheet on the middle rack of a preheated 350°F (180°C) oven.
2. Bake 15-20 minutes until cod turns a little brown on top. Serve with butter.

SERVES 4

VARIATION

- Dollop butter on top of watered salt cod; wrap in parchment paper, seal, and bake approximately 20 minutes.

Courtesy of Everett Fancy

Salt Cod Baked in the Oven

Newfoundland and Labrador

4 x 6 oz (170 g) salt cod steaks, skin removed

1 lemon, sliced

2 cups (500 ml) milk

4 garlic cloves, sliced

3 medium onions, sliced

1 sprig fresh parsley, coarsely chopped

Freshly ground black pepper

1 cup (250 ml) olive oil, divided

5 medium potatoes, peeled, sliced

1. Add lemon slices to water when watering the salt cod (page 80), changing water and lemon slices until cod has been completely soaked. Drain.
2. Preheat oven to 350°F (180°C).
3. Bring watered cod and milk to a boil. Drain and wash cod in cold running water.
4. Place cod in a baking dish. Add garlic, onions, and parsley. Season with pepper and drizzle with 1/2 cup (125 ml) olive oil.
5. Surround cod with sliced potatoes and sprinkle with remaining olive oil.
6. Bake until potatoes are cooked, approximately 30 minutes.

SERVES 4

Roasted/Baked Salt Cod and Potatoes

Portugal

Elements of this recipe are similar to dishes from other countries, including Salt Cod with Sour Cherries from Italy, and Norwegian Salt Cod over Stew of Grapes (Bacalao Noruego Sobre Estofado de Uvas) from the Dominican Republic. Here the salt cod is dipped into flour, egg, and cornmeal, placed on a bed of onions and garlic, and roasted in the oven.

4 x 6 oz (170 g) salt cod steaks, skin on

All-purpose flour

1 egg, beaten

Cornmeal or bread crumbs

1/2 cup (125 ml) olive oil

4 garlic cloves, thinly sliced, divided

2 medium onions, thinly sliced, divided

8 small potatoes, peeled, parboiled

4 hard-boiled eggs, for garnish

16 black olives, pitted, for garnish

1. Use watered salt cod (page 80). Drain. Place cod into boiling water for 2 minutes to blanch or scald. Remove any obvious bones but do not break the steaks.
2. Preheat oven to 350°F (180°C).
3. Dry steaks. Dip into flour, egg, and then cornmeal or bread crumbs.
4. Pour 1/4 cup (60 ml) olive oil into a baking dish. Spread 2 sliced garlic cloves and 1 sliced onion evenly in the bottom of the dish. Place steaks on top.
5. Place parboiled potatoes around cod. Spread remaining onion and garlic on top of cod.
6. Drizzle potatoes and cod with remaining olive oil. Bake for 20-25 minutes, drizzling occasionally with olive oil until the mixture browns.
7. Serve garnished with black olives and hard-boiled eggs.

Adapted from Chefe Silva, *Bacalhau a Portuguesa*

SERVES 4

Roasted/Baked Salt Cod and Potatoes

PUDDINGS

These puddings are not desserts—they are main-course dishes of salt cod mixed with rolled oats, rice, potatoes, or another binder such as butter, flour, cereal, eggs, or suet. Puddings can be baked, steamed, or boiled and served either hot or cold. There is no special topping applied during cooking; the pudding is most often served with a sauce on the side.

SALT COD PUDDINGS

Salt Cod Puddings	*Newfoundland and Labrador*
Salt Cod Pudding	*Iceland*
Salt Cod Pudding	*Scotland*
Salt Cod and Vegetable Pudding (Pudim de Bacalhau)	*Portugal*

SALT COD LOAVES

Salt Cod Loaf	*Newfoundland and Labrador*
Individual Salt Cod Loaves	*Newfoundland and Labrador*

BURIAL OF THE COD — *Portugal*

Salt cod pudding links.

Single salt cod pudding.

Sliced, fried salt cod pudding.

Salt Cod Puddings

Newfoundland and Labrador

Pepper and savoury are musts for a tasty pudding. Of course, the spices and herbs should be added to suit your taste. Consider using garlic salt or powder, white pepper, nutmeg, sage, thyme, paprika, coriander, or marjoram.

In this recipe, contributed by Margie Nurse of Porter's Puddings and Sausages in Conception Bay South, Newfoundland and Labrador, the pudding is enclosed in a linked-sausage-style synthetic sleeve. You will need an extruder to do this. Be sure to use a thermometer for accuracy.

5 lb (2.25 kg) salt cod
1 lb (450 g) beef fat (suet), coarsely chopped
1 1/2 lb (675 g) onions, coarsely chopped
1 lb (450 g) finely ground bread crumbs
3 tbsp (45 ml) dried savoury
1 tbsp (15 ml) freshly ground black pepper
4 cups (1 L) water
Sausage casings

1. Use watered salt cod (page 80). Drain; remove skin and bones. Break into small pieces.
2. Grind together cod, suet, and onions.
3. Mix together crumbs, savoury, and pepper. Add water and stir.
4. Mix all ingredients thoroughly in a large pan.
5. Slip a casing on the horn or neck of the extruder.
6. Start stuffing the mixture into the casings. Tie off the end after you have stuffed the first 6 inches, then continue, allowing the casing to slip off the horn when it is moderately packed. Tie off the last end.
7. Loop and twist the long stuffed casing into links approximately 5-6 inches (12.5-15 cm) long.
8. Place the whole string of linked puddings into a stockpot of water to cook 15-17 minutes. Do not let cooking water exceed 190°F (90°C) or the puddings will burst.
9. Hang puddings to cool at room temperature for 45-60 minutes. Package and refrigerate or freeze until ready to use.
10. Slice puddings into thin pieces to fry. Serve with eggs and beans for breakfast.

Salt Cod Pudding

Iceland

1 lb (450 g) salt cod

1/4 cup (60 ml) uncooked rice

Butter

1 1/4 cups (310 ml) milk

3 eggs, beaten

1. Use watered salt cod (page 80). Simmer 15 minutes or until tender. Drain, remove any skin and bones, and shred.
2. Cook rice and mix well with cod. Place in a buttered baking dish.
3. Mix beaten eggs with milk. Pour over cod and rice. Bake for 40 minutes.
4. Serve with boiled potatoes and turnips.

SERVES 4

Salt Cod Pudding

Scotland

1 lb (450 g) salt cod

4 medium potatoes, boiled, mashed

1 cup (250 ml) milk, heated

Butter

Freshly ground black pepper

2 hard-boiled eggs, sliced, for garnish

Fresh parsley, chopped, for garnish

1. Use watered salt cod (page 80). Simmer 15 minutes or until tender and cooked. Remove any skin and bones; flake or shred.
2. Pound cod in a mortar with a pestle. Measure volume of pounded cod.
3. Mash boiled potatoes and measure a quantity equal to the cod. Season with pepper; moisten with hot milk and butter to taste. Blend well.
4. Add cod to seasoned potatoes. Whisk until blended.
5. Place mixture in buttered baking dish. Dot with butter. Bake until lightly browned.
6. Garnish with hard-boiled eggs and/or parsley.

SERVES 4

PUDDINGS

Salt Cod and Vegetable Pudding (Pudim de Bacalhau)

Portugal

This pudding can be served hot or cold. Portuguese molho branco sauce adds an elegant touch.

1 lb (450 g) salt cod

2 potatoes

2 carrots, divided

6 oz (170 g) day-old French or Italian bread, cut in 1-inch (2.5 cm) cubes

1 cup (250 ml) milk

2 tbsp (30 ml) olive oil

1 1/2 cups (375 ml) onions, chopped

2 garlic cloves, finely chopped

10 black olives, pitted, chopped

2 eggs, lightly beaten

1/4 cup (60 ml) fresh parsley, chopped

1/4 tsp (1.2 ml) piri piri or other hot pepper sauce

Freshly ground black pepper

2 tbsp (30 ml) fresh bread crumbs

1 cup (250 ml) molho branco (page 298)

1 hard-boiled egg, chopped, for garnish

Shredded lettuce, for garnish

12 black olives, whole, for garnish

1. Use watered salt cod (page 80). Simmer 10-15 minutes or until tender. Drain, remove any skin and bones, shred coarsely.
2. Preheat oven to 350°F (180°C).
3. Steam or boil potatoes and 1 carrot until almost tender, about 15-20 minutes. Drain and dice finely.
4. Place bread in bowl, cover with milk, and set aside for 10 minutes.
5. Heat olive oil in a large frying pan and sauté onions and garlic for a few minutes. Add olives, cod, and bread. Cook 2 minutes until heated through, stirring occasionally.
6. Remove from heat and whisk eggs in slowly, until combined. Stir in potatoes and carrots, parsley, piri piri sauce, and pepper.
7. Grease baking dish and sprinkle with bread crumbs. Pour mixture into dish. Bake 35 minutes, or until pudding is set. Let cool in dish for 10 minutes.
8. Remove pudding from the dish and invert onto a serving plate lined with shredded lettuce. Julienne remaining carrot. If serving pudding warm, cover with molho branco and decorate with chopped hard-boiled eggs, whole olives, and julienned carrot.

Adapted from Carla Azevedo, *Uma Casa Portuguesa*

SERVES 4

salt cod loaves

Salt Cod Loaf

Newfoundland and Labrador

- 1 lb (450 g) salt cod
- 1/2 cup (125 ml) rolled oats
- 1/2 cup (125 ml) milk
- 2 tbsp (30 ml) mayonnaise (page 302)
- 2 tbsp (30 ml) fresh parsley, chopped, or 2 tsp (10 ml) dried parsley flakes
- 2 tsp (10 ml) onion, chopped
- Salt and freshly ground black pepper
- 2 tbsp (30 ml) lemon juice
- 2 eggs, beaten
- Drawn butter (page 300) or garlic, onions, and olive oil (page 300)

1. Use watered salt cod (page 80). Simmer 10-15 minutes or until tender. Drain, remove any skin and bones; shred finely.
2. Preheat oven to 375°F (190°C).
3. Combine rolled oats and milk. Add mayonnaise, parsley, onion, salt, pepper, and lemon juice; mix well.
4. Blend in beaten eggs and cod.
5. Grease a loaf pan or mould with butter; press in cod mixture.
6. Bake for 50-55 minutes.
7. Turn onto a warmed platter and serve with sauce of choice.

SERVES 4

Individual Salt Cod Loaves

Newfoundland and Labrador

- 1 lb (450 g) salt cod
- 6 medium potatoes, peeled, chopped
- 1 tbsp (15 ml) onion, finely chopped
- 1 tbsp (15 ml) fresh parsley, finely chopped
- 1 tbsp (15 ml) butter
- Freshly ground black pepper
- Pinch ground nutmeg
- Milk, heated
- Cornflakes, crushed
- Molho branco (page 298) or tomato sauce

1. Use watered salt cod (page 80). Drain, remove skin and bones; break into small pieces.
2. Preheat oven to 350°F (180°C).
3. Place cod and potatoes in a large saucepan. Cover with water and simmer until potatoes are tender, about 15 minutes. Drain well and mash.
4. Add onion, parsley, butter, pepper, and nutmeg, and blend in enough hot milk to make the mixture creamy. Add salt if needed. Beat until very light.
5. Grease 12 muffin cups with butter and coat with cornflakes. Fill with mixture. Bake for 20 minutes.
6. Turn out and serve with molho branco or tomato sauce.

SERVES 4

PUDDINGS

Salt Cod Loaf

SALT COD CUISINE: THE INTERNATIONAL TABLE

Burial of the Cod

Portugal

Also known as *Enterro do Bacalhau* and *Bacalhau Escondido* (Hidden Bacalhau), this event traditionally took place in some communities in Portugal on Saturday Alleluia (Easter Saturday) to celebrate the end of deprivation during Lent. It is not widespread today.

The burial of the cod is a theatrical event, with a funeral as its central theme. The public play marks the end of abstinence from meat, condemning and symbolically burying the cod as a protest against eating so much cod during Lent. As the actors walk along the streets, they form a kind of court that has the power to condemn the cod. The characters include the doctor's funeral judge, the lawyers, the bailiff, the defendant, and witnesses—cod, parsley, garlic, onion, and various seasonings.

A meal of salt cod often followed the theatre. The ingredients—such as precooked salt cod, onions, heavy cream, and diced, frozen potatoes—were combined into a rather uninviting protest dish.

STOVETOP VARIATIONS

HASH

Seamen's Salt Cod Hash (Fischlabskaus)	*Germany*
Salt Cod on Toasted Homemade Bread	*Newfoundland and Labrador*
Salt Cod Hash	*Newfoundland and Labrador*
Salt Cod Hash	*Newfoundland and Labrador*
Salt Cod with Red Capsicum (Bacalad al Ajo Arriero)	*Spain*

FISH AND BREWIS

Fish and Brewis	*Newfoundland and Labrador*
Homemade Hard Bread	*Newfoundland and Labrador*

SCRAMBLED

Salt Cod Scrambled with Eggs and Potatoes (Bacalhau a Bras)	*Portugal*
Saltfish and Ackee	*Jamaica*

hash

Seamen's Salt Cod Hash (Fischlabskaus)

Germany

This recipe is a variation of *lapskaus*, a culinary specialty from Northern Germany designed to make preserved meat and salted fish tasty. Traditionally, ships' crews used to eat it on their voyages. Today, people still enjoy the hearty flavour of this dish.

Lapskaus can be made with meat (corned or salted or similarly preserved), salted fish, or both. This recipe uses salt cod. To use both cod and meat, simply reduce the amount of salt cod and add that amount of preserved meat.

1 lb (450 g) salt cod

4 potatoes

3 onions, finely chopped

6 tbsp (90 ml) butter

1 tbsp (15 ml) prepared mustard

1 tbsp (15 ml) juice from a jar of sliced beets

3 tbsp (45 ml) juice from a jar of gherkins

Salt

Ground nutmeg

Beets, sliced, for garnish

Gherkins, for garnish

Hard-boiled or fried eggs, for garnish

1. Use watered salt cod (page 80). Cover with water; simmer until cooked. Drain, remove any skin and bones, and flake.
2. Peel, boil, and coarsely mash potatoes.
3. Fry onions in butter in a heavy frying pan. Stir in mustard, juices, salt, and nutmeg to taste.
4. Add cod and potatoes. Stir just enough to mix ingredients and cook until heated through.
5. Arrange the mixture on a heated platter.
6. Garnish with sliced beets, gherkins, and eggs.

Adapted from Alan Davidson, *North Atlantic Seafood*

SERVES 4

Salt Cod on Toasted Homemade Bread

Newfoundland and Labrador

This is an ideal way to use leftovers from a boiled salt cod dinner. Even if there are no leftovers, the meal is well worth making.

1. Use watered salt cod (page 80). Simmer cod for 20 minutes, remove any skin and bones, and coarsely flake.
2. Prepare a basic white sauce (page 298). Add cod to the sauce and stir to heat through.
3. Butter slices of homemade bread. Toast in the oven until the butter melts and bread browns. Pour cod and sauce over the toast and serve.

A loaf of homemade bread.

Salt Cod Hash

Newfoundland and Labrador

Another great way to use leftover salt cod.

1/2 lb (225 g) salt cod

3 potatoes

1/4 lb (115 g) fatback pork (scrunchions, page 300)

1 onion, chopped

1. Use watered salt cod (page 80). Simmer 15 minutes. Drain, remove any skin and bones, and flake the cod.
2. Boil and mash potatoes. Use twice the amount of potatoes as cod.
3. Prepare scrunchions in a large frying pan. Place scrunchions and some of the liquid fat in a side dish; sauté onions in remaining fat.
4. Place cod and potatoes in the frying pan with onions; mix thoroughly to warm.
5. Serve with hot fat and scrunchions.

SERVES 4

VARIATIONS

- Fry or poach 4 eggs. Mound salt cod hash in the centres of 4 plates and top each with an egg.
- Replace fatback pork with olive oil and garlic.

Salt Cod Hash

Newfoundland and Labrador

This hash is served upside down with the brown crust from the bottom of the frying pan on top.

1 lb (450 g) salt cod

2 dried hot peppers, finely chopped

1/2 cup (125 ml) boiling water

4 potatoes, peeled, cooked, chopped

1 small yellow onion, chopped

2 tbsp (30 ml) cold water

2 tbsp (30 ml) all-purpose flour

2 oz (60 g) fatback pork, chopped

4 tbsp (60 ml) butter

Sliced beets, for garnish

Sliced hard-boiled eggs, for garnish

1. Use watered salt cod (page 80). Drain. Simmer cod 10 minutes, drain. Shred and remove any skin and bones.
2. Place peppers and boiling water in a bowl for 30 minutes to plump.
3. Combine cod, potatoes, onion, and peppers (with soaking liquid) in a bowl. Mix cold water and flour; add to mixture and toss.
4. Fry chopped fatback pork. Remove scrunchions and reserve. Add butter to melted fat.
5. Spread cod evenly in the bottom of a frying pan. Reduce heat and continue cooking until the bottom of the cod is brown and crusty.
6. Turn cooked hash onto a serving platter so that the bottom crust is on top.

SERVES 4

Salt Cod Hash

STOVETOP VARIATIONS

Salt Cod with Red Capsicum (Bacalad al Ajo Arriero)

Spain

This recipe is more elaborate than the Salt Cod Hash from Newfoundland and Labrador. Practically all regions of Spain have a variation of this dish, with local ingredients.

This is one of many recipes that teams salt cod with red peppers and tomatoes. The sweetness of the peppers and the acidity of the tomatoes are balanced by the texture and saltiness of the cod.

- 8 oz (225 g) salt cod
- 4 tbsp (60 ml) olive oil
- 1 onion, chopped
- 4 garlic cloves, finely chopped
- 1/2 red bell pepper, julienned
- 1 medium turnip, chopped, boiled
- 3 whole tomatoes, finely chopped
- 1/2 tsp (2.5 ml) sweet paprika
- 2 tbsp (30 ml) fresh parsley, chopped
- 1 tbsp (15 ml) fresh rosemary, chopped
- 1 tbsp red wine
- Coarse salt and freshly ground black pepper
- Sliced baguette or other crusty bread

1. Use watered salt cod (page 80). Simmer gently until tender. Remove any skin and bones; flake.
2. Heat olive oil in a large saucepan over medium-low heat. Add onion and garlic and sauté 5 minutes. Add red pepper and cook another 5 minutes, until pepper and onions are soft, but not browned.
3. Stir in cod, turnip, and tomatoes; mix well. Cook for 5 minutes, stirring lightly.
4. Add paprika, parsley, rosemary, and wine; cover and simmer over low heat for 10 minutes.
5. Stir in parsley, adjust seasoning, and serve with bread.

Adapted from Michael F. Nenes, *International Cuisine*

SERVES 4

fish and brewis

Fish and Brewis

Newfoundland and Labrador

Brewis, also known as hard bread or hard tack, is readily available through Purity Factories Ltd. in Newfoundland and Labrador and beyond. Hard bread was developed from the ancient sea biscuit which formed the basis of meals on fishing vessels and cargo ships prior to the 1840s. Brewis (pronounced "bruise") probably refers to the breaking up or bruising of the bread prior to being soaked for 10-12 hours.

1 1/2 lb (675 g) salt cod

4 cakes hard bread

1/4 lb (115 g) fatback pork (scrunchions, page 300)

VARIATIONS
- Combine some of the fat and scrunchions with the cod and brewis. Leave the remainder for individual garnishes.
- Add a chopped onion to the fat and scrunchions during the latter stages of frying.
- If fatback pork is not to your taste, consider topping fish and brewis with a good grade of molasses (hot or cold), drawn butter (page 300), or extra-virgin olive oil.

1. Use watered salt cod (page 80). Put cod in fresh water. Bring to a boil, reduce heat and simmer until tender, about 15-20 minutes. Drain; remove any skin and bones. Break into small pieces or coarse flakes. Set aside and keep warm.
2. Break or split cakes of hard bread into quarters (or smaller), place in a large saucepan, and cover with water. There should be at least 2 inches (5 cm) water over the bread. Let it soak overnight, until it swells to approximately twice its original size.
3. Bring hard bread and soaking water to a near boil over high heat. Remove from heat; drain thoroughly. Break bread into smaller pieces.
4. Prepare fatback pork as scrunchions to serve as a garnish.
5. Mix cod and hard bread in a large bowl. Combined in this manner, the dish is traditionally called Fisherman's Brewis. Serve separate portions of cod and the cooked hard bread on the same plate and the dish is known as Fish and Brewis.

SERVES 4

Cakes of hard bread.

STOVETOP VARIATIONS

Fisherman's Brewis (with molasses)

SALT COD CUISINE: THE INTERNATIONAL TABLE

Homemade Hard Bread

According to Bob Hardy of Hardy Fish Co. Ltd., in Conception Bay South, Newfoundlanders and Labradorians cannot take the chance of missing out on traditional Fish and Brewis should there be a shortage of commercial hard bread. This is his recipe, printed here with permission, to produce a replicate product.

2 cups (500 ml) all-purpose flour

1 cup (250 ml) water

1 tsp (5 ml) salt

1. Preheat oven to 375°F (190°C).
2. Add the salt to the water. Mixing slowly and thoroughly, add flour to salted water. Mix until smooth; generally, the more mixing, the better the results. Roll the thick flour dough into a thin sheet and prepare squares or cakes.
3. Place cakes onto a glass or non-stick baking pan. Keep dough 1-1.5 inches (2.5-4 cm) thick and cut into 2-3-inch (5-7.5 cm) strips, to allow thorough heating. Pierce both the top and the bottom of the strips to further allow inner layers to cook and dry evenly.
4. Bake strips 35-40 minutes.
5. Rotate and flip solidified hard bread pieces; bake an additional 25 minutes.
6. Allow oven to cool with the bread inside to ensure more complete drying.
7. Place on counter or shelf, wrap in paper towels, and allow the baked bread to further dehydrate for 24-48 hours.

scrambled

Salt Cod Scrambled with Eggs and Potatoes (Bacalhau a Bras)

Portugal

1 lb (450 g) salt cod

4 potatoes, peeled, cut in matchstick-sized pieces

Vegetable oil, for frying

3 tbsp (45 ml) olive oil

2 onions, coarsely chopped

1 garlic clove, finely chopped

1 bay leaf

15 black olives, pitted, sliced

4 eggs

Salt and freshly ground black pepper

1 sprig fresh parsley, chopped

1. Use watered salt cod (page 80). Simmer until tender in just enough water to cover. Remove any skin and bones; flake.
2. Fry potatoes in hot vegetable oil over medium-high heat until lightly browned. Drain on paper towels.
3. Heat olive oil, onions, garlic, and bay leaf in a large frying pan. Cook, stirring occasionally and gently, for 4-5 minutes, or until onions are golden.
4. Remove bay leaf. Add cod to onion, olive oil, and garlic so the cod soaks up some of the olive oil. Add potatoes and stir carefully (do not mash cod) until cod and potatoes are blended and heated through. Stir in olives.
5. Whisk eggs, season with salt, if necessary, and pepper; add to cod and potato mixture. Simmer until eggs are cooked.
6. Serve immediately topped with pepper and parsley.

SERVES 4

VARIATION

- For Bacalhau a Bras (Lisboa), boil 2 oz (60 g) spicy meat sausage (*chourico de carne*) for 5 minutes; cut in small pieces. Add to the mixture at step 4.

Saltfish and Ackee

Jamaica

Ackee is the national fruit of Jamaica; ackee and salt cod is a national dish.

As the pear-shaped ackee ripens on the tree, it splits opens naturally to show its soft white to yellow flesh surrounding three black seeds. This flesh is the only edible part of the fruit. For safety, only canned ackee is available for purchase; it is a major export product from Jamaica. The ackee tree came to Jamaica from West Africa with the transatlantic trade during the eighteenth century.

- 1 lb (450 g) salt cod
- 4 oz (115 g) fatback pork, chopped
- 5 tbsp (75 ml) vegetable or coconut oil
- 2 onions, chopped
- 3 green onions or leeks, chopped
- 2 tomatoes, chopped
- 1 small hot pepper, chopped
- 2 cups (500 ml) canned ackee
- Freshly ground black pepper
- 1/3 tsp (2 ml) dried thyme
- 6 slices bacon, fried crisp

1. Use watered salt cod (page 80). Simmer 15 minutes, or until tender. Remove any skin and bones; flake.
2. Fry fatback pork until all fat is rendered and only crisp pork remains. Remove pork from the fat; set aside.
3. Add oil to rendered pork fat. Fry onions, green onions, tomatoes, and hot pepper for 5 minutes.
4. Drain ackee and rinse with warm water. Add ackee and cod to onion mixture and heat through.
5. Transfer to a warm serving dish. Season with pepper.
6. Garnish with crisp chopped pork. Try other garnishes: fresh parsley, radish roses, bell pepper rings, johnnycakes (fried dumplings), or boiled green bananas.

SERVES 4

Canned ackee.

OTHER SALT COD PARTS

There is almost no waste to a cod. The head is more flavorful than the body, especially the throat, called a tongue, and the small disks of flesh on either side, called cheeks. The air bladder, or sound, a long tube against the backbone that can fill or release gas to adjust swimming depth, is rendered to make isinglass, which is used industrially as a clarifying agent in some glues. But sounds are also fried by codfishing peoples, or cooked in chowders or stews. The roe is eaten, fresh or smoked. Newfoundland fishermen also prize the female gonads, a two-pronged organ they call the britches, because its shape resembles a pair of pants. Britches are fried like sounds. Icelanders used to eat the milt, the sperm, in whey. The Japanese still eat cod milt. Stomachs, tripe, and livers are all eaten, and the liver oil is highly valued for its vitamins.

—Mark Kurlansky, *Cod*

With the exception of salt cod roe and liver, all salt cod parts including heads, tongues, cheeks, sounds, vens, bellies, and tails were provided for recipe development by Taylor's Fish, Fruit, and Vegetable Market in Conception Bay South, Newfoundland and Labrador.

HEADS
Fried Salt Cod Heads	*Newfoundland and Labrador*
Fried Salt Cod Heads (Caras de Bacalhau Fritas)	*Portugal*
Boiled Salt Cod Heads	*Newfoundland and Labrador*
Salt Cod Heads Chowder	*Newfoundland and Labrador*

TONGUES, CHEEKS
Fried Salt Cod Tongues	*Newfoundland and Labrador*
Fried Salt Cod Cheeks	*Newfoundland and Labrador*
Cod Tongues (Linguas de Bacalhau)	*Portugal*
Salt Cod Tongue Stew (Caldeirada de Linguas de Bacalhau com Ovos)	*Portugal*
Baked Salt Cod Tongues and Cheeks	*Newfoundland and Labrador*

SOUNDS
Fried Salt Cod Sounds	*Newfoundland and Labrador*
Salt Cod Sounds Stew	*Newfoundland and Labrador*
Salt Cod Sounds Pie	*Newfoundland and Labrador*
Salt Cod Sounds (Samos de Bacalhau)	*Portugal*

ROE, LIVER
Preserving Cod Roe	
A Pocketful of Roe (Kuit in een Zak)	*Belgium*
Cod-Liver Bannock	*Scotland*
Fried Salt Cod Roe	*Newfoundland and Labrador*
Boiled Cod Roe	*Scotland*

VENS, BELLIES, TAILS
Salt Cod Vens Omelette	*Newfoundland and Labrador*
Salt Cod Vens and Bellies	*Newfoundland and Labrador*
Salt Cod Skin	*Spain*
Salt Cod Tails	*Portugal*

heads

In the old days Icelanders not only ate cods' heads fresh, a common practice in communities where people are really knowledgeable about fish, but also dried them for later consumption. Ponies would carry the cods' heads inland [to a farmhouse], often taking several days for the round trip. Each carried 120; 60 on each side, sticking out into the air like the wings of a small Icelandic Pegasus. The custom gradually died out …

—Alan Davidson, *North Atlantic Seafood*

By and large, when people speak of [cod] heads they are actually referring to 'skulps' [sculps]. These are the two side flaps cut from the sides of the head proper and joined by the bottom jaw … Skulps provide hours of sticky pleasure for those who enjoy picking [cod] bones.

—*DNE*, s.v. "sculp"

278   SALT COD CUISINE: THE INTERNATIONAL TABLE

OTHER SALT COD PARTS

Fried Salt Cod Heads

Newfoundland and Labrador

This recipe is based on the most basic recipe for fried fresh cod heads. It is used as well with thoroughly watered salt cod heads. The texture will not be the same as when the cod is fresh, but it tastes good.

8 salt cod heads

3 fatback pork strips

All-purpose flour

Salt and freshly ground black pepper

1. Water salt cod heads as you would pieces of salt cod (page 80).
2. Cut each head in two. Clean and skin as necessary, using cold water. (Skinning is optional and a matter of taste and aesthetics.) Dry heads with paper towels.
3. Fry strips of salt pork.
4. Dip cod in flour seasoned with salt and pepper. Fry in the rendered fat until cooked and browned on both sides.
5. Serve with accompaniments of your choice or with boiled potatoes and mashed turnips.

SERVES 4

Fried Salt Cod Heads (Caras de Bacalhau Fritas)

Portugal

8 small salt cod heads

Pepper

Lemon juice

3 garlic cloves, crushed

Olive oil, for frying

1. Water salt cod heads as you would pieces of salt cod (page 80).
2. Cut each head in two. Clean and skin as necessary, using cold water. Dry with paper towels.
3. Season heads with pepper, a little lemon juice, and garlic. Let stand for 1 hour.
4. Shake off garlic and fry heads in a little olive oil.

SERVES 4

VARIATION

- Breaded and fried salt cod heads (caras de bacalhau pandas): In step 4 above, coat heads in all-purpose flour, shaking off any excess. Dip in a beaten egg, followed by bread crumbs. Ensure heads are fully coated; fry in olive oil.

Salt cod head.

SALT COD CUISINE: THE INTERNATIONAL TABLE

Boiled Salt Cod Heads

Newfoundland and Labrador

Skinning cod heads is optional and a matter of taste and aesthetics, although for boiling most people prefer to keep the skin on.

8 salt cod heads
2 whole onions
6 potatoes
1 turnip, sliced
Freshly ground black pepper

1. Water salt cod heads as you would pieces of salt cod (page 80).
2. Cut each head in two. Clean and skin as necessary, using cold water.
3. Put heads and onions in a large saucepan and cover with cold water; simmer for 30 minutes.
4. Boil potatoes and turnip in another saucepan. Add salt if necessary.
5. Serve potatoes and turnip on one platter and heads and onions on another.

SERVES 4

VARIATION

- Boiled salt cod heads with chickpeas: In step 3 above, add 1 1/2 cups (375 ml) canned chickpeas to the heads after simmering 20 minutes. Continue to simmer heads and chickpeas for 15 minutes. Remove heads and strain chickpeas. Serve both on a platter. Serve with a dish of chopped onions and chopped parsley.

Adapted from Chefe Silva, *Bacalhau a Portuguesa*

Salt Cod Heads Chowder

Newfoundland and Labrador

8 salt cod heads
3 strips fatback pork
2 onions, sliced
6 potatoes, quartered
1 tbsp (15 ml) butter
Pepper

1. Water salt cod heads as you would pieces of salt cod (page 80).
2. Cut each head in two. Clean and skin as desired in cold water.
3. Fry salt pork. Add sliced onions; fry until golden. Transfer to a large saucepan.
4. Add heads and potatoes. Cover with cold water; cook until potatoes are done. Season with pepper. Add butter.

SERVES 4

tongues, cheeks

OTHER SALT COD PARTS

Fried Salt Cod Tongues

Newfoundland and Labrador

1 lb (450 g) salt cod tongues

1/4 lb (115 g) fatback pork, diced

All-purpose flour

Freshly ground black pepper

1. Water salt cod tongues as you would pieces of salt cod (page 80). Soak 6-10 hours or longer depending on saltiness. Rinse, drain, and completely dry tongues.
2. Mix flour and pepper in a bowl or brown paper bag. Roll or shake tongues in mixture until completely coated on both sides.
3. Fry diced fatback pork until pieces (scrunchions, page 300) are crisp and brown. Remove scrunchions.
4. Use enough fat to cover bottom of a frying pan. Fry tongues over medium heat until browned on both sides. Do not allow pan to go dry.
5. Remove tongues when crisp and nicely browned. Place, with scrunchions, on a warmed platter to serve.

SERVES 4

Salt cod tongues.

SALT COD CUISINE: THE INTERNATIONAL TABLE

Fried Salt Cod Cheeks

Newfoundland and Labrador

Cook salt cod cheeks in the same manner as Fried Salt Cod Tongues.

1 lb (450 g) salt cod cheeks
1/4 lb (115 g) fatback pork, diced
All-purpose flour
Freshly ground black pepper

SERVES 4

Cod Tongues (Linguas de Bacalhau)

Portugal

1 lb (450 g) salt cod tongues
All-purpose flour
Olive oil, for frying
2 eggs, beaten

SAUCE
1 small onion
1 sprig fresh parsley
1 hard-boiled egg
1 cup (250 ml) olive oil
1/4 cup (60 ml) white vinegar
Salt and freshly ground black pepper

1. Water salt cod tongues as you would pieces of salt cod (page 80). Soak 6-10 hours or longer depending on saltiness. Drain and pat dry.
2. Dip tongues in flour and then in beaten egg. Fry in hot oil.
3. Drain on paper towels.
4. Prepare sauce: Chop onion, parsley, and egg into small pieces. Mix with olive oil, vinegar, salt, and pepper.
5. Serve tongues with sauce.

SERVES 4

Salt cod cheeks.

OTHER SALT COD PARTS

Salt Cod Tongue Stew (Caldeirada de Linguas de Bacalhau com Ovos)

Portugal

Caldeirada is a Portuguese stew of fish (in this case, salt cod tongues) with a base of non-seafood ingredients including potatoes, onions, peppers, tomatoes, garlic, and parsley. White wine and olive oil supplement the flavours of the tongues and vegetables.

Chefe Silva in *Bacalhau a Portuguesa* serves this stew with poached eggs on top. I have enjoyed an adaptation of this salt cod tongue stew covered with a crust.

1 lb (450 g) salt cod tongues

1/3 cup (85 ml) olive oil

2 onions, sliced

1/2 red bell pepper, thinly sliced

3 garlic cloves, thinly sliced

1 bay leaf

2 sprigs fresh parsley

4 ripe medium tomatoes, halved

2 tbsp (30 ml) tomato paste

2 tbsp (30 ml) white wine

4 medium potatoes, peeled, sliced

Salt and freshly ground black pepper or hot pepper sauce to taste

CRUST

2 cups (500 ml) all-purpose flour

4 tsp (20 ml) baking powder

Pinch salt

2 tbsp butter

3/4 cup (185 ml) water

1. Water salt cod tongues as you would pieces of salt cod (page 80). Soak 6-10 hours (or longer), depending on saltiness.
2. Preheat oven to 400°F (200°C).
3. Heat olive oil in a medium saucepan with onions, red pepper, and garlic; cook, stirring frequently, until soft. Do not allow to brown.
4. Add bay leaf, parsley, tomatoes, tomato paste, and white wine.
5. Transfer tomato mixture to a baking dish. Add potatoes and tongues. Stir and cover everything with water. Season, if required, with salt and pepper or hot pepper sauce and bake for 10 minutes.
6. Make crust: Combine flour, baking powder, and salt. Work in butter with a fork. Add water slowly, mixing continuously, until a smooth paste forms. Drop mixture over the stew, using a teaspoon.
7. Cover and bake 30 minutes.

Adapted from Chefe Silva, *Bacalhau a Portuguesa*

SERVES 4

Baked Salt Cod Tongues and Cheeks

Newfoundland and Labrador

1/2 lb (225 g) salt cod tongues
1/2 lb (225 g) salt cod cheeks
5 tbsp (75 ml) butter, divided
Freshly ground black pepper
1 tsp (5 ml) dried savoury
1 cup (250 ml) bread or cracker crumbs
2 onions, sliced
1 cup (250 ml) milk

1. Water tongues and cheeks as you would pieces of salt cod (page 80). Soak 6-10 hours (or longer), depending on saltiness. Drain and dry. Clean if required. Cut any pieces larger than 2 inches (5 cm) into smaller pieces.
2. Preheat oven to 350°F (180°C).
3. Layer half of the tongues and cheeks in a buttered 8-inch (20 cm) baking dish. Sprinkle with pepper, savoury, and half the crumbs.
4. Melt 2 tbsp (30 ml) butter in a frying pan over moderate heat. Add onions and cook, stirring frequently, until soft. Pour half of this mixture over tongues, cheeks, and crumbs.
5. Repeat layers and seasoning; end with a layer of crumbs. Dot with remaining butter.
6. Cover with milk.
7. Bake for about 60 minutes, or until tongues and cheeks are firm. Serve.

SERVES 4

Baked Salt Cod Tongues and Cheeks

sounds

OTHER SALT COD PARTS

Fried Salt Cod Sounds

Newfoundland and Labrador

The sound is a strip of membrane lying along the inside of the backbone of the cod.

The *Dictionary of Newfoundland English* defines sound as the air bladder, or hydrostatic organ, of a cod, removed during splitting and salted as a delicacy. The sound controls the buoyancy of the fish.

Salted sounds, which bear a striking resemblance to tripe, must be soaked overnight in fresh water before use.

1 1/2 lb (675 g) salt cod sounds

1/4 lb (115 g) fatback pork, cut in strips

2 onions, sliced

1. Soak salt cod sounds in water for 10-12 hours. Drain water and clean sounds if necessary. Check for and remove any black lining. Cut into bite-sized pieces. Put into a saucepan of cold water and simmer until cooked. No need to be gentle; sounds can withstand a lot of cooking. Drain.
2. Fry salt pork. Add sliced onions and sounds and fry.

SERVES 4

Salt Cod Sounds Stew

Newfoundland and Labrador

1 1/2 lb (675 g) salt cod sounds

1/4 lb (115 g) fatback pork, cut in strips

2 onions, quartered

4-6 potatoes, boiled, coarsely chopped

1. Soak salt cod sounds in water for 10-12 hours. Drain water and clean sounds if necessary. Check for and remove any black lining. Cut into small bite-sized pieces. Put into a saucepan of cold water and simmer until cooked. Drain.
2. Fry fatback in a frying pan. Add onions, sounds, and potatoes. Mix well. Add a little water if necessary. Stew 30 minutes.

SERVES 4

Salt cod sounds.

SALT COD CUISINE: THE INTERNATIONAL TABLE

Salt Cod Sounds Pie

Newfoundland and Labrador

This was adapted from a recipe by Mrs. Stella Boyd of Summerford in Newfoundland and Labrador, which appeared in *Fat-back and Molasses* by Ivan Jesperson and in Alan Davidson's *North Atlantic Seafood*.

> This recipe came from Western Head, Notre Dame Bay, and may originally have come from our great great grandparents who came from England. It was always served for Christmas Eve Supper. The Sounds were brought from Labrador where our fathers fished in the summer months. The Sounds were salted down in wooden butter tubs ... Today, where Sounds are available, the fifth generation of our family still has "Cod Sound Pie" on Christmas Eve and it really is a delicacy.
>
> —Quoted in Alan Davidson, *North Atlantic Seafood*

1 1/2 lb (675 g) salt cod sounds

2-3 cakes hard bread, broken, soaked overnight

1/4 lb (115 g) fatback pork, diced

1/2 tsp (2.5 ml) ground cloves

1/2 tsp (2.5 ml) ground allspice

1 tsp (5 ml) ground cinnamon

1/2 cup (125 ml) molasses

1 cup (250 ml) raisins

1. Soak sounds in cold water for 10-12 hours. Drain and clean sounds if necessary. Check for and remove any black lining. Put sounds into a pot of cold water, heat, and simmer until tender, approximately 15-20 minutes. Drain; cut in small pieces.
2. Preheat oven to 350°F (180°C).
3. Drain hard bread; break into smaller pieces.
4. Mix bread and sounds in a baking dish.
5. Combine fatback pork with spices, molasses, and raisins. Pour over sounds and hard bread.
6. Bake for 2 hours.

SERVES 4

OTHER SALT COD PARTS

Salt Cod Sounds (Samos de Bacalhau)

Portugal

Sounds can be used in fish stews (*caldeiradas*), soups, fried dishes, pasta dishes, and stews with potatoes, beans, chickpeas, or rice. This basic recipe uses beans.

1 lb (450 g) salt cod sounds

1 1/4 cups (310 ml) dried white northern beans, soaked 12 hours

1/2 cup (125 ml) olive oil

2 garlic cloves, chopped

1 onion, chopped

1 bay leaf

1 tbsp (15 ml) tomato paste

2 tomatoes, chopped

Salt and freshly ground black pepper

Dash piri piri or other hot pepper sauce

2 sprigs fresh parsley, coarsely chopped, for garnish

1. Soak sounds in cold water for 10-12 hours. Drain water and clean sounds if necessary. Check for and remove any black lining. Put sounds into a pot of cold water, heat, and simmer until tender, approximately 15-20 minutes. Drain; cut in small pieces.
2. Simmer beans for 1 hour or until tender.
3. Add olive oil to saucepan and sauté onion and garlic until brown. Add bay leaf, tomato paste, and tomatoes, stirring occasionally. Simmer 10 minutes.
4. Mix in sounds and white beans. Simmer another 10 minutes, stirring occasionally. Season to taste with salt, pepper, and piri piri.
5. Sprinkle with parsley and serve.

Adapted from Chefe Silva, *Bacalhau a Portuguesa*

SERVES 4

roe, liver

Cod roe, or hard roe, is the mass of eggs, or spawn, within the ovarian membrane of the female cod; the sperm, or milt, of a male cod is called soft roe. The most prized of hard roe is that of the sturgeon, from which comes caviar.

DNE lists "breeches," also "britches," "britchet(s)," and "britchin'(s)," as terms for the cod roe and the ovarian membrane which contains it.

PRESERVING COD ROE

The best roe for cooking and salting is neither very immature nor fully ripe: immature eggs are small and hard and have little flavour; eggs ready for spawning are soft, easily crushed, and quick to develop unpleasant odours.

Use fresh and firm whole roe to preserve with salt. Wash in a light brine to remove any blood and pieces of intestines. Pour a layer of salt on the bottom of a closed tight container and add a layer of roe; alternate layers until the container is full. Use about 1 pound of salt to 3 pounds of roe. Leave roe in the closed container for about 10 days before draining. Discard any damaged roe and carefully wash again in brine. Repack using the same amount of salt. Keep contents chilled until you are ready to use them.

Whole salt cod roe.

Cooked sliced salt cod roe.

OTHER SALT COD PARTS

A Pocketful of Roe (Kuit in een Zak)

Belgium

Flemish fishermen had this simple method for preparing cod roe.

> Take a large cod's roe and wrap it carefully in muslin. Place it in salted water, bring it to the boil, then drain it and let it cool. Unwrap it, cut it into slices, fry these and serve them on toast or bread.
>
> —Alan Davidson, *North Atlantic Seafood*

Cod-Liver Bannock

Scotland

> Take the liver of a fair-sized cod, fresh from the sea, and let it lie overnight in salted water. Mince roughly or tear up with the fingers, removing all the stringy bits. Mix in a bowl with a tablespoonful of oatmeal, add a pinch of baking soda, and season with pepper and salt. Form into a bannock [a flat round], put it on a plate, and place in a pot of boiling water. Put the fish [watered salt cod] over it, and let it cook slowly till ready.
>
> —F. Marian McNeill, *The Scots Kitchen*

Fried Salt Cod Roe

Newfoundland and Labrador

This is a basic recipe from Newfoundland and Labrador.

1 lb (450 g) salt cod roe

1/4 lb (115 g) fatback pork, diced

Freshly ground black pepper

1/4 cup (60 ml) milk

1 egg, beaten

Bread crumbs or all-purpose flour

1. Water the roe for about 6 hours, depending on the amount of salt originally used. Simmer 30 minutes; drain and allow to cool.
2. Fry fatback pork until scrunchions (page 300) are crisp.
3. Cut roe in 0.5-inch (1.2 cm) slices. Combine pepper, milk, and egg. Dip roe into bread crumbs or flour, then into milk mixture.
4. Fry each slice in pork fat until browned on both sides; serve with hot scrunchions.

SERVES 4

Boiled Cod Roe

Scotland

1 lb (450 g) salt cod roe

2 tsp (10 ml) vinegar or lemon juice

All-purpose flour

Salt and freshly ground black pepper

Fat, for frying

1. Water cod roe for about 6 hours, depending on the amount of salt originally used. Add vinegar or lemon juice.
2. Tie roe in a piece of cheesecloth, nylon bag, or butter muslin, or securely wrap in foil to protect the roe and help prevent it from bursting. Simmer 15-20 minutes if thin; allow about 30 minutes if thick.
3. Remove roe from water and cool before further preparation.
4. Remove outer membrane of roe carefully; cut roe into 0.5-inch (1.24 cm) slices. Do not skin roe until you are ready to use it, as the skin keeps it moist.
5. Combine flour with salt and pepper to taste. Dip roe in flour. Fry in a little hot fat until crisp and golden brown on both sides.

SERVES 4

VARIATIONS

- Dip each piece in batter (see Fried Dishes section for recipes) flavoured with chopped parsley, and deep-fry until golden brown. Drain on paper towels.
- Salt cod roe fritters: Dip each piece in all-purpose flour seasoned with salt and pepper, then egg, then bread crumbs. Deep-fry.
- Cod roe Elizabeth: Dip roe in all-purpose flour seasoned with salt and pepper. Fry in a little hot onion butter, very slowly, until golden brown. Remove from pan. Add cream to butter, allowing 1/2 tbsp (7.5 ml) per slice of roe. Garnish with chopped fresh parsley. Serve with crisp hot toast and butter.
- Cover roe slices and sliced onions with béchamel sauce (page 297), or one of its variations, in a baking dish. Top with bread crumbs and bake at 425°F (220°C) for 10 minutes.
- Slice roe thinly and use as an omelette filling.

vens, bellies, tails

OTHER SALT COD PARTS

Salt Cod Vens Omelette

Newfoundland and Labrador

Three things contributed to the creation of this recipe. First, I read Mark Kurlansky's description of a salt cod omelette as a specialty item of the Basque cider mills. This recipe combined onions, parsley, olive oil, eggs and *lono* (top-quality salt cod steak). That same day, I bought a package of salt cod vens at Bidgood's market in Goulds, Newfoundland and Labrador. Third, I recalled the many times I enjoyed omelettes for breakfast in Mexico. These omelettes included hot red peppers, red bell peppers, mushrooms, and eggs.

After some experimenting, this dish was ready for a Sunday morning breakfast.

1 lb (450 g) salt cod vens

1/2 medium onion, finely chopped

4 fresh mushrooms, thinly sliced

1/2 tsp (2.5 ml) dried parsley flakes

1 tbsp (15 ml) hot red pepper, seeded, chopped

1 tbsp (15 ml) red bell pepper, chopped

Olive oil, for sautéing

4-6 eggs, beaten

Milk

Freshly ground black pepper

1. Water salt cod vens as you would other salt cod (page 80). Taste for the freshness/saltiness you desire. Simmer vens for about 10-15 minutes. Drain; remove skin, bones, and the black nape. Shred vens into small pieces. Drain and dry.
2. Sauté onion, mushrooms, parsley, and peppers in olive oil.
3. Add vens to the sautéed mixture.
4. Whisk eggs in a separate bowl, adding a small amount of water and milk.
5. Combine everything in a frying pan. Season to taste with ground black pepper. Cook over moderate heat, turning once. Cook omelette in two or more sections for ease of turning.

SERVES 4

Salt cod vens.

Salt cod bellies.

OTHER SALT COD PARTS

Salt Cod Vens and Bellies

Newfoundland and Labrador

Vens are cut off when the fresh cod is being filleted. The vens (and collars) are often salted. If the salt cod is cut primarily for thick steaks, then the thin pieces (bellies) between the vens and the solid tailpiece could be used. Vens and Bellies could be called Collars and Loins—but that's not a Newfoundland and Labrador expression.

8 oz (225 g) salt cod vens, cleaned

8 oz (225 g) salt cod, thin belly pieces, cleaned

1 cup (250 ml) cooked chickpeas or lima beans (optional)

1 cup (250 ml) mushrooms, ideally chanterelles or another seasonal wild mushroom

2 tbsp (30 ml) fresh parsley, chopped

SAUCE

1 onion, finely chopped

4 garlic cloves, crushed

2 tsp (10 ml) butter

2 tsp (10 ml) all-purpose flour

1/2 cup (125 ml) white wine

1 1/3 cups (335 ml) fish stock (page 296)

1. Use watered salt cod vens and bellies (page 80). Note: these thin pieces lose salt more quickly than other pieces of cod and will not take as long to water as other pieces of salt cod. Simmer vens and bellies for about 10 minutes. Clean off any skin and bones; flake into small pieces.
2. Prepare sauce: Cook onion and garlic gently in butter for 2-3 minutes, until soft. Add flour and mix well; gradually stir in wine and stock. Bring to a boil and simmer 5-6 minutes.
3. Add vens and bellies and simmer 10-15 minutes. Add chickpeas. Simmer another 10-15 minutes. Check seasoning, adding salt and pepper if necessary.
4. Add mushrooms and parsley; simmer 5 minutes.
5. Serve with crusty bread.

SERVES 4

Salt Cod Skin

Spain

Dry salt cod skin in the oven until crisp and use for garnish.

Salt Cod Tails

Portugal

Use salt cod tails to give a rice dish the flavour of the sea.

Salt Cod Tails

STOCK AND SAUCES

> I would know you, salt cod
> Even if you were wearing a disguise.
> —Cuban Proverb, quoted in Kurlansky, *Cod*

Sauces specific to one recipe in this book—such as yogourt and saffron, persillade, or garlic-walnut sauce—are described as part of that recipe. Fish stock, sauces, scrunchions, and other more versatile accompaniments are listed below.

Fish Stock
Béchamel Sauce (White Sauce)
Molho Branco (White Sauce)
Mojo Colorado (Red Sauce)
Skordalia
Drawn Butter
Scrunchions

Garlic, Onions, and Olive Oil
Mustard Sauce
Egg Sauce
Green Parsley Oil
Mayonnaise
Aioli (Garlic Mayonnaise)
Salsa Verde
Salsa Romesco

Fish Stock

The better the stock, the better the flavour of soups, chowders, and other recipes. The ingredients used to make stock, other than water, fall into three basic groups:

- Fish frames, fish heads, and bones, all fresh
- Aromatic vegetables, such as onions, leeks, carrots, and celery with their greens
- Herbs, such as thyme, bay leaf, parsley, ground pepper, and fennel

The key to making a flavourful stock is the fish head, as it contains a fine gelatin. Some species are superior to others for this purpose: the head of a cod, red snapper, trout, salmon, striped bass, or lake whitefish produces a rich stock.

Extra fish stock can be kept frozen in small portions in ice cube trays or 1-cup packages. Fish stock is also available as fish cubes and in bottles of concentrated fish sauce.

Here is a basic recipe; yours will depend on available ingredients.

2 lb (900 g) cod heads, bones, and trimmings

1/2 tsp (2.5 ml) salt

1 medium onion, chopped

1/2 cup (125 ml) leeks, chopped

1 celery stalk, including leaves, chopped

1 carrot, peeled, chopped

2-3 sprigs fresh parsley, roughly chopped

1 bay leaf

1 sprig fresh thyme

Pinch dried fennel (optional)

5 cups (1.2 L) cold water

1 cup (250 ml) dry white wine (optional)

1. Wash cod; remove gills from heads.
2. Place cod bones, heads, and trimmings into a large saucepan. Cover with water; add 1/2 tsp (2.5 ml) salt. Bring just to a boil, reduce heat, and simmer gently 25-30 minutes. Skim occasionally. Do not cook longer as a bitter taste or the taste of glue will result.
3. Strain, using a cheesecloth-lined sieve, into another pan. Add vegetables and herbs and bring back to a boil. Simmer 30-35 minutes. Some reduction will occur. Strain once more. Use or store as required.

MAKES 4-5 CUPS

STOCK AND SAUCES

Béchamel Sauce (White Sauce)

This basic sauce is used in its simplest form in many recipes in this book. It is also used as a base for other sauces and has a wide range of variations.

2 tbsp (30 ml) butter

2 tbsp (30 ml) all-purpose flour

1 cup (250 ml) room-temperature milk, or a combination of milk and fish stock (page 296), vegetable stock, cream, or dry white wine

1/4 tsp (1.2 ml) salt

Pinch white pepper

1. Melt butter in a small saucepan.
2. Remove saucepan from heat. Sprinkle in flour, stirring until blended. Slowly add milk, stirring constantly, as sauce becomes smooth and faintly yellow.
3. Return saucepan to heat; stir. As sauce begins to bubble, add salt and white pepper. Continue cooking over low heat, stirring constantly, until sauce is hot and thick.

MAKES ABOUT 1 CUP

VARIATIONS

- For a thicker (for binding) or thinner (for pouring) sauce, decrease or increase the volume of milk. Increasing the flour and butter will also result in a thicker sauce.
- For a richer sauce, add 2 tbsp (30 ml) milk or cream to the yolk of an egg, and whisk until blended. Add a ladleful of the hot sauce and continue whisking until blended. Add mixture to the rest of the sauce and heat, still over low heat and stirring constantly, until sauce is hot and thick.
- White wine sauce: Substitute white wine for milk.
- Mornay sauce: Generally used for gratins. Add 1/2 cup (125 ml) grated Parmesan cheese to finish the sauce above. Some classic recipes use a combination of grated Parmesan and full-flavoured, well-aged cheddar cheese (if the cheddar is too young, the sauce will not only lack flavour but will be stringy). Stir sauce just enough for cheese to melt; overcooking the cheese can cause it to turn stringy.

Béchamel Sauce

SALT COD CUISINE: THE INTERNATIONAL TABLE

Molho Branco (White Sauce)

The creamy and lemony molho branco adds elegance to baked or fried salt cod. The sauce is light yellow; for a whiter sauce, omit the egg yolk.

2 tbsp (30 ml) butter
2 tbsp (30 ml) all-purpose flour
1 cup (250 ml) milk, heated
1/4 tsp (1.2 ml) salt
1 tsp (5 ml) lemon rind, finely grated
4 tsp (20 ml) lemon juice
Pinch freshly grated nutmeg
Pinch white pepper
1 egg yolk, lightly beaten

1. In a small saucepan, melt butter over medium heat; whisk in flour and cook over medium-low heat for about 3 minutes, stirring constantly. Whisk in hot milk. Simmer.
2. Stir in salt, lemon rind, lemon juice, nutmeg, and pepper. Reduce heat and cook until slightly thickened. Remove from heat and whisk in egg yolk.
3. Return to heat and continue to whisk until sauce blends and becomes smooth and creamy.

Adapted from Carla Azevedo, *Uma Casa Portuguesa*

Mojo Colorado (Red Sauce)

1/2 tsp (2.5 ml) cumin seeds
3 hot red peppers
1 small head garlic, cloves separated and skinned
1/4 tsp (1.2 ml) sweet paprika
1/4 tsp (1.2 ml) salt
1/2 cup (125 ml) olive oil
White vinegar
Cold water

1. Lightly toast cumin and pound in a mortar. Soften peppers by soaking in hot water. Remove seeds. Pound peppers with the cumin.
2. Put garlic, paprika, and salt into the mortar and crush with the contents, adding oil and vinegar to taste and a little cold water. Blend well and serve.

VARIATION

- Mojo verde (green sauce): Substitute hot green peppers for hot red peppers; omit paprika and use 2 sprigs fresh parsley, chopped.

Skordalia

People of classical Greece concocted a favourite sauce of bread, oil, garlic, and a dash of vinegar they called *skorothalmi*. Skordalia is the modern Greek equivalent. It is a thick sauce made by combining crushed garlic with a purée of potatoes or soaked bread and then mixing in olive oil to make an emulsion.

- 2 cups (500 ml) mashed potatoes
- 1/4 tsp (1.2 ml) freshly ground black pepper
- 6-8 garlic cloves, chopped or grated
- 1/2 tsp (2.5 ml) salt
- 1 cup (250 ml) extra-virgin olive oil
- 1/4 cup (60 ml) red or white wine vinegar

Sprinkle potatoes with pepper. Place garlic, potatoes, and salt in a blender, cover and blend at high speed until smooth. While blending, slowly add olive oil and vinegar, alternating, testing as you go, until mixture is smooth. Skordalia should be creamy and thick; if it is too thick, it may be thinned with several tablespoons of cold water. Decrease or increase the amount of garlic to taste.

VARIATIONS

- Instead of mashed potatoes, use 5-6 slices day-old bread, broken, with crusts removed. Place broken bread in a large bowl, add 1 1/2 cups (375 ml) water, and soak until saturated, about 2 minutes. Drain bread; squeeze out all the liquid. Place bread in a food processor, add remaining ingredients, and blend until smooth. Use immediately, or cover and store in refrigerator for as long as overnight.
- In various regions of Greece, chopped walnuts, almonds (blanched or ground), or pine nuts are added. Lemon juice may be added as well.
- Soak bread in olive oil instead of in water.
- Use half bread and half potato.
- Instead of potato or bread, use chickpeas, lima beans, broad (fava) beans, or another mealy legume.
- Add a pinch of cayenne pepper.
- Add 8-10 pitted black olives and 1 tbsp capers.

Skordalia

Drawn Butter

2 cups (500 ml) water

1 medium onion, chopped

3 tbsp (45 ml) butter

Salt and freshly ground black pepper

2 tbsp (30 ml) all-purpose flour

1. Boil water, onion, and butter with salt and pepper to taste in a saucepan for approximately 20 minutes.
2. Make a paste with flour and just enough cold water.
3. Stirring constantly, slowly add paste to butter mixture until desired consistency is reached. Cook over low heat for 2-3 minutes. Keep warm.

VARIATION

- For a creamy sauce, replace 1/4 cup (60 ml) water with an equal amount of milk.

Scrunchions

Cut 1/4 lb (115 g) fatback pork into small cubes about 0.2 inches (0.5 cm) thick. Fry until rendered of fat and golden brown and crispy.

The fat and scrunchions can be served together or separately. If you wish, pour fat into a heated bowl or gravy boat; place scrunchions in a separate serving dish.

Garlic, Onions, and Olive Oil

2 medium onions, sliced or sectioned

3-4 garlic cloves, finely chopped

1/4 cup (60 ml) olive oil

Heat olive oil. Add onions and garlic and fry gently until lightly golden and soft, being careful not to burn the garlic.

Mustard Sauce

1 hard-boiled egg

1/4 cup (60 ml) white sugar

1 tbsp (15 ml) all-purpose flour

1 tsp (5 ml) mustard powder

Salt and freshly ground black pepper

1 cup (250 ml) beef, chicken, or fish stock (page 296)

1/4 cup (60 ml) white vinegar

1. Mash egg and sugar together. Add flour, mustard, salt, and pepper.
2. Stir in liquids gradually. Cook in a small saucepan over medium heat until mixture thickens.

Mustard Sauce

STOCK AND SAUCES

Egg Sauce

- 2 tbsp (30 ml) butter
- 2 tbsp (30 ml) all-purpose flour
- 1 1/4 cups (310 ml) milk
- 2 hard-boiled eggs, finely chopped
- 1 tbsp (15 ml) fresh chives, chopped
- Salt and freshly ground black pepper

1. Melt butter in a small saucepan but do not let it brown. Add flour gradually and stir until smooth. Cook over gentle heat for 2-3 minutes, stirring constantly.
2. Remove from heat and add milk gradually, stirring after each addition to prevent lumps.
3. Bring sauce to a boil, stirring continuously until thickened.
4. Add eggs, chives, salt, and pepper. Reheat for 2-3 minutes. Serve hot.

Green Parsley Oil

This method of infusing oil works with other leafy herbs such as basil, sage, thyme, and rosemary.

- 1/4 cup (60 ml) extra-virgin olive oil
- 1/4 cup (60 ml) fresh parsley leaves

1. Blanch parsley leaves in salted water for 10-15 seconds, then immerse in ice water. Drain.
2. Combine blanched parsley with half of the oil in a blender; purée until very fine. Add purée to remaining oil. Strain through a cheesecloth, if desired.
3. Transfer oil to a bottle or other storage container. Store in refrigerator or a cool, dark area. Use within 3-4 days.

Egg Sauce

Green Parsley Oil

SALT COD CUISINE: THE INTERNATIONAL TABLE

Mayonnaise

This traditional mayonnaise recipe uses a high proportion of oil to egg yolks, making it quite thick.

2 egg yolks

2 tsp (10 ml) prepared mustard (optional)

1/3 tsp (2 ml) fine salt

Pinch ground white pepper

1-2 tsp (5-10 ml) white wine vinegar or lemon juice

3/4 cup (185 ml) safflower oil

1. Combine egg yolks, mustard, salt, pepper, and half of the vinegar. Lightly stir or whisk until mixture is smooth.
2. Slowly beat in oil. When mixture begins to thicken, the emulsion has been established. Add remaining oil in a steady stream, continuing to whisk or beat. Adjust seasonings.

Try flavouring this basic mayonnaise sauce with fresh chopped mint and capers, anchovies and fresh parsley, garlic, or any of the variations at right.

VARIATIONS

- Tartar sauce: To 1 cup (250 ml) mayonnaise add 2 finely chopped shallots, 1 tbsp (15 ml) finely chopped chives, and 2 tsp (10 ml) mustard.
- Mustard-flavoured mayonnaise: Mustard, when used in small amounts, provides a subtle flavouring for mayonnaise. Almost any variety can be used. The amount depends on the strength of the mustard and the preference of the chef. Try 4 tsp (20 ml) mustard per 1 cup (250 ml) mayonnaise to start.
- Partridgeberry mayonnaise: Mix 2 tbsp (30 ml) partridgeberry jam into 1 cup (250 ml) mayonnaise.
- Curry garlic mayonnaise: Purée in a food processor or blender until smooth and creamy: 1 cup (250 ml) mayonnaise, 1/2 tsp (2.5 ml) cayenne pepper, 2 tsp (10 ml) curry powder, 2 tsp (10 ml) fresh lemon juice, and 6 finely chopped garlic cloves.

STOCK AND SAUCES

Aioli (Garlic Mayonnaise)

4 garlic cloves

Salt

2 egg yolks

1/3 cup (85 ml) extra-virgin olive oil

1/4 cup (60 ml) corn oil

1 tbsp (15 ml) lemon juice or white wine vinegar

1. Put garlic cloves in a bowl with a pinch of salt. Crush with the back of a spoon, or use a mortar and pestle.
2. Beat in 2 egg yolks. Begin adding olive and corn oil in drops, while continuing to beat. As aioli begins to thicken, add oil in a constant stream, until mixture is creamy.
3. Thin with lemon juice or vinegar; add additional salt to taste.

Salsa Verde

2 garlic cloves, chopped, crushed

3/4 cup (185 ml) fresh parsley leaves

3/4 cup (185 ml) fresh basil leaves

1/4 cup (60 ml) fresh mint leaves

1 cup (250 ml) extra-virgin olive oil

3 tbsp (45 ml) capers, drained

2 oz (60 g) sour gherkins

1 tbsp (15 ml) Dijon mustard

1/2 cup (125 ml) white wine vinegar

Salt and freshly ground black pepper

4-8 tbsp (60-120 ml) bread crumbs, for a thicker vinaigrette (optional)

1. Wash and dry parsley and basil. Sprinkle leaves with 2 tbsp (30 ml) olive oil to prevent basil from turning black during chopping.
2. Finely chop herbs, capers, and gherkins; combine with garlic in a bowl and add mustard and vinegar. Gently stir in remaining olive oil. Add salt and pepper to taste.

Adapted from James Peterson, *Sauces*

Salsa Verde

SALT COD CUISINE: THE INTERNATIONAL TABLE

Salsa Romesco

Spanish salsa romesco is a well-seasoned purée of almonds, hazelnuts, peppers, garlic, and bread crumbs, often flavoured with tomatoes. It originates from Tarragona, Catalonia, in northeastern Spain. In this book, salsa romesco accompanies tapas but it can also be used with salads, as a dip, or stirred into salt cod stews.

- 4 garlic cloves
- 2 medium ripe tomatoes, cored
- 1 red bell pepper
- 1/2 medium Spanish onion, quartered (optional)
- 2 tbsp (30 ml) extra-virgin olive oil, divided
- 4 tbsp (60 ml) whole blanched almonds or almond slivers
- 4 tbsp (60 ml) peeled hazelnuts
- Salt
- 2 tbsp (30 ml) sherry vinegar or red wine
- 1/2 tsp (2.5 ml) smoked sweet paprika
- 1 slice day-old bread, crustless, cubed

1. Rub excess dry skin from garlic cloves; place on baking sheet with tomatoes, onion, and red pepper; drizzle all with 1 tbsp (15 ml) olive oil. Roast 40-50 minutes at 400°F (200°C), until tomatoes and garlic are well caramelized but not burnt. Let cool. Discard skins from tomatoes, garlic, and peppers. Place pulp in a bowl.
2. Blanch and completely dry almonds. Process almonds and hazelnuts in a food processor until finely ground. Add garlic, onion, tomato, and pepper. Add salt to taste.
3. Pour in the remaining olive oil in a slow, steady stream, keeping the processor running. Continue by adding vinegar and paprika. Add more vinegar if desired for extra zing.
4. Process romesco until it comes together as a thick, creamy sauce, but does not lose its coarse, nutty texture. Add 1-2 tbsp (15-30 ml) red wine if sauce is too thick; add bread, and pulse, if it is too thin.

Salsa Romesco

Appendix 1

Methods

The information for kench curing and pickle salting is from Robert Hardy and Lana White, *Handling and Processing Salt Cod* (St. John's: Seafood Development Unit, Newfoundland and Labrador Institute of Fisheries and Marine Technology, 1990).

The brine salting information is from Kristin Lauritzsen, "Quality of salted cod (*Gadus morhua* L.) as influenced by raw material and salt consumption" (Dr. scient. thesis, University of Tromso, 2004).

The following methods (with inevitable variations) for salting cod were used:

1. Kench Curing
   - Heavy salted: 55 lb (25 kg) salt / 100 lb (45 kg) cod
     21 days or longer
   - Light salted: 12-15 lb (5-7 kg) salt / 100 lb (45 kg) cod
     5-9 days

2. Pickle Salting
   - Heavy salted: 40 lb (18 kg) salt / 100 lb (45 kg) cod
     usually 21 days or longer
   - Light salted: 10 lb (4 kg) salt / 100 lb (45 kg) cod
     4-6 days, depending on temperature

3. Corning: amount of salt to taste
   a few hours, more or less

4. Brine Salting: the mass of salt (sodium and chloride) is 18-25% of the total mass (w/w "by weight") of the solution

Appendix 2

Classifications

The information in this section is from Norman Macpherson, *The Dried Codfish Industry* (St. John's, NL: Department of Natural Resources, 1935), 11-14.

Light-Salted Shore Cod and Medium-Salted Bank Cod
The traditional shore-cured, air-dried, and light- to medium-salted dried cod (average salt content 19.9%).

- Choice (Number 1) Spanish: sound quality, extra thick, light amber colour, even surface, thoroughly clean on both back and face, no blood stains, clots, liver or gut; well split and no excessive salt on the face.
- Prime (Number 2) Spanish: same qualities as choice but of fair thickness.
- Merchantable: as choice and prime but not thick.
- Madeira: any cod not choice, prime, or merchantable; rough in appearance.
- West India: broken, sunburned, slimy, dun, oversalted, or otherwise defective cod.
- Damp fish: if shore or Bank cod not thoroughly hard dried, they were classified as damp (e.g., damp merchantable or damp West Indian).

Fish caught on the Labrador coast or in the Straits but light- or medium-salt cured as shore or Bank cod were described as Labrador Shore Cure or Straits Shore Cure and came under the same classifications.

Size classifications for all shore and Bank cod for sale: tomcods (8-11 inches [20-28 cm]); small (11-18 inches [28-46 cm]); medium (18-20 inches [46-51 cm]); and large (over 20 inches [over 51 cm]).

Genuine Labrador Soft Cure Cod (caught north of Blanc Sablon)
The heavier-salted cod from Labrador (average salt content 33.4%).

- Choice (Number 1): sound quality, well split, thoroughly clean; no excessive blood stains, clots, liver, or gut; thoroughly salted and firm; if not quite white on the face, must have a lean, clear surface.
- Prime (Number 2): poorly split, extremely thin, with excessive blood or liver clots; uneven surface, but in other respects similar to choice.
- Cullage: not up to the standard of prime.

Heavy-Salted Soft Cure Newfoundland Cod
Cod caught off the shores of Newfoundland or Labrador south of Blanc Sablon and cured in Labrador style were culled under the same standards as those applied to Genuine Labrador Soft Cure Cod.

Salt Bulk or Wet Salted Cod (from any location)
- Number 1: sound quality, well split, no excessive blood stains, clots, liver or gut; thoroughly salted and firm; a clear even surface.
- Number 2: similar to Number 1 but poorly split.
- Cullage: not up to the standard of Number 2.

Endnotes

1. Mark Kurlansky, *Cod: A Biography of the Fish that Changed the World* (New York: Penguin, 1997), 17. "Codlandia" is Kurlansky's term.
2. George Rose, *Cod: The Ecological History of the North Atlantic Fisheries* (St. John's: Breakwater, 2007), 18.
3. Rose, 18.
4. Mark Kurlansky, *Salt: A World History* (Alfred K. Knopf Canada, 2002), 113.
5. Kurlansky, *Salt*, 114.
6. Marguerite Ragnow, "Cod," http://www.lib.umn.edu/bell/tradeproducts/cod, accessed August 11, 2009.
7. Ragnow, "Cod."
8. Quoted in Rose, 81.
9. For example, see Salt Cod Plaki with Raisins, page 247.
10. From a permanent display, "Cod: A Fish that Meant Business," at The Rooms, St. John's, Newfoundland.
11. Peter Pope, *Fish into Wine: The Newfoundland Plantation in the Seventeenth Century* (Omohundro Institute of Early American History and Culture, Chapel Hill, NC: University of North Carolina Press, 2004), 91.
12. Pope, 95.
13. George M. Story, "'A tune beyond us as we are': Reflections on Newfoundland Community Song and Ballad," *Newfoundland Studies* 4.2 (1988), 129-144, quotation from 133.
14. Jenny Higgins, "19th Century Trade," http://www.heritage.nf.ca/society/fish_trade.html, accessed March 22, 2010. See Appendix 2 for grades of fish.
15. Higgins, "19th Century Trade."
16. Shannon Ryan, *Fish Out of Water: The Newfoundland Saltfish Trade: 1814-1914* (St. John's: Breakwater, 1986), 77.
17. Rose, 312.
18. *Dictionary of Newfoundland English* (DNE), s.v. "jigger."
19. *DNE*, s.v. "cod seine."
20. *DNE*, s.v. "bultow."
21. *DNE*, s.v. "cod trap."
22. Jenny Higgins, "Cod Moratorium," http://www.heritage.nf.ca/society/moratorium.html, accessed May 17, 2012.
23. J.P. Andrieux, *The Grand Banks: A Pictorial History* (St. John's: Flanker, 2011), 27-29, 87-152. This summary is based on Andrieux's 69-page description of the Portuguese White Fleet.
24. Andrieux, 27.

25 Andrieux, 92.
26 Andrieux, 29.
27 Andrieux, 100.
28 Andrieux, 51-61. The countries and dates mentioned in this paragraph are from Chapter 3.
29 Claude Emery, *The Northern Cod Crisis* (Political and Social Affairs Division, Government of Canada, 1992), 25.
30 Andrieux, 272.
31 D. Murdock Parsons and R. Stead, *Overview of Sentinel Surveys in NAFO Divisions 2J3KL and Subdivisions 3Ps 1995-2008*, DFO Can. Sci. Advis. Sec. Res. Doc. 2009/092.
32 Mark Bitterman, *Salted: A Manifesto on the World's Most Essential Mineral with Recipes* (Berkeley, CA: Ten Speed Press, 2010), 38.
33 Bitterman, 41.
34 Bitterman, 83.
35 Quoted in Helen Studley, "Salt Cod Almighty," *Food Arts Magazine*, New York, March 2007, http://www.foodarts.com/Foodarts/FAFeature/0.254,00.html, accessed March 25, 2010.
36 Norman L. Macpherson, *The Dried Codfish Industry* (Fisheries Services Bulletin Vol. II, No. 4, Department of Natural Resources, Newfoundland [1935]), 26.
37 F.W. Wheaton and T.B. Lawson, *Processing Aquatic Food Products* (New York: John Wiley and Sons, 1985), 273.
38 Kristin Lauritzsen, "Quality of salted cod (*Gadus morhua L.*) as influenced by raw material and salt composition" (Dr. scient. thesis, University of Tromso, 2004), 3.
39 Larry Small, "The Foundering Stage," *Around the Red Land* (St. John's: Breakwater, 2007), 23-24.
40 Roy Dwyer, *Old Harbours: A Strange Twilight: Tilting Harbour et al.: Essays and Short Stories* (Transcontinental Print, 2007), 26.
41 Dwyer, 24.
42 Robert Hardy and Lana White, *Handling and Processing Salt Cod* (St. John's: Seafood Development Unit, Newfoundland and Labrador Institute of Fisheries and Marine Technology, 1990), 4.
43 Macpherson, 25.
44 Macpherson, 24.
45 Hardy and White, 6.
46 Mark Ferguson, "Making Fish: Salt-Cod Processing on the East Coast of Newfoundland: A Study in Historic Occupational Folklife" (Master of Arts thesis, Memorial University of Newfoundland, 1996), 110.
47 See Appendix 1.
48 A.J. Walsh, *Newfoundland Fisheries Development Committee Report* (St. John's, Newfoundland), 153, n.14.

49 Small, "The Culler," *Around the Red Land*, 25.
50 Dwyer, 15.
51 Pamela J. Gray, "Traditional Newfoundland Foodways: Origin, Adaptation and Change" (Master of Arts thesis, Memorial University of Newfoundland, 1977). The listed factors are based on Gray's thesis.
52 C. Grant Head, *Eighteenth Century Newfoundland* (Toronto: McClelland and Stewart, 1976), 100-137. The ideas and the specific foods and export countries in this section are based on Chapter 6.
53 Kippered Salt Cod Benedict, developed by Steve Vardy. See page 226.
54 Elaine Sciolino, "A Portuguese tradition faces a frozen future," *New York Times*, December 16, 2008, http://www.nytimes.com/2008/12/16/world/europe/16ht-16cod.html, accessed April 10, 2010.
55 La Mancha is also associated with *The Ingenious Gentleman Don Quixote of La Mancha*, a novel written by Miguel de Cervantes in the early 1600s.
56 Robert Hayman, 1628 (*DNE*, s.v. "Poor John"). Also called "Poor Jack" in reference to salt cod.
57 See recipe for Salt Cod Vens and Salt Bellies, page 293.
58 Kurlansky, *Cod*, 237.
59 Harold McGee, *On Food and Cooking: The Science and Lure of the Kitchen* (1984; New York: Scribner, 2004), 191.
60 Peter Barham, *The Science of Cooking* (Germany: Springer-Verlag Berlin Heidelberg, 2001), 92.
61 Len Margaret, *Fish & Brewis: Toutens & Tales* (St. John's: Breakwater, 1980), 46.

Bibliography

The following books contributed to the recipes in this book.

Accademia Italiana della Cucina (The Italian Academy of Cuisine). *La Cucina: The Regional Cooking of Italy*. Translated by Jay Hyame. New York: Rizzoli International Publications, 2009.

Alexiadou, Vefa. *Greek Cuisine*. Greece: Thessaloniki, 1989.

Aris, Pepita. *Recipes from a Spanish Village*. New York: Simon and Schuster, 1990.

Azevedo, Carla. *Uma Casa Portuguesa: Portuguese Home Cooking*. Toronto, ON: Summerhill Press, 1990.

Barrera, Flora Lilia and Dolores Hernandez Barrera Alamo. *The Best of Canarian Sauces*. Gran Canaria: Centro De La Cultura Popular Canaria, 2000.

Bellefontaine, Jacqueline et al. *Tapas: Greatest Ever*. UK: Paragon, 2004.

Benghiat, Norma. *Traditional Jamaican Cookery*. London: Penguin, 1985.

Boni, Ada. *The Talisman Italian Cook Book*. New York: Crown Publishers, 1950.

Bottone, Edward. *Spirit of Bermuda: Cooking with Gosling's Black Seal Rum*. Bermuda: Bermudian Publishing Company, 1998.

Chanot-Bullier, Calixtine. *Vieilles Recettes de Cuisine Provençale*. Marseille: Tacussel, 2000.

Condaratos, Stelios, ed. *300 Traditional Recipes: Greek Cookery*. Athens: Summer Dream Editions, 2000.

Craig, Elizabeth. *The Scottish Cookery Book*. London: Andre Deutsch Limited, 1956.

Davidson, Alan. *North Atlantic Seafood*. New York: Viking, 1979.

Dettore, Mariapaola. *Flavours of Italy: Sicily*. Florence, Italy: McRae Books, 1999.

Drake, Kitty and Ned Pratt. *Rabbit Ravioli: Photographs, Recipes & Literary Vignettes of Newfoundland*. St. John's, NL: Breakwater, 1994.

Editoriale Domus. *The Silver Spoon*. New York: Phaidon, 2005.

Fish: The Good Cook Techniques and Recipes Series. Alexandria, VA: Time-Life Books, 1979.

Gray, David and Yoka Gray. *The Newfoundland Gourmet*. St. John's, NL: Jesperson, 1982.

Haro, Rafael de. *Classic Tapas: Authentic Spanish Recipes*. Cordoba, Spain: Edara Ediciones, S.L., 2002.

Isusi, Jose Maria Busca. *Traditional Basque Cooking*. Reno, NV: University of Nevada Press, 1987.

Jacobs, Susie. *Recipes from a Greek Island*. New York: Simon & Schuster, 1991.

Jenkins, Sara and Mindy Fox. *Olives & Oranges: Recipes and Flavor Secrets from Italy, Spain, Cyprus & Beyond*. New York: Houghton Mifflin, 2008.

Jessel, Camilla. *The Taste of Spain: Traditional Spanish Recipes and Their Origins*. New York: St. Martin's, 1991.

Johnston, Mireille. *The Cuisine of the Rose: Classical French Cooking from Burgundy and Lyonnais*. New York: Random House, 1982.

Kurlansky, Mark. *Cod: A Biography of the Fish that Changed the World*. New York: Penguin, 1997.

——. *Salt: A World History*. Alfred K. Knopf Canada, 2002.

Lalbachan, Pamela. *The Complete Caribbean Cookbook*. Vancouver, BC: Raincoast Books, 1994.

Leite, David. *The New Portuguese Table: Exciting Flavors from Europe's Western Coast*. New York: Clarkson Potter, 2009.

Llamas, Beatriz. *A Taste of Cuba*. New York: Interlink Books, 2005.

McConnell-Over, Joan. *For the Love of Cod*. St. John's, NL: Creative, 1989.

McNeill, F. Marian. *The Scots Kitchen: Its Traditions and Lore with Old-Time Recipes*. 1929. London: Blackie & Son Limited, 1963.

Modesto, Maria de Lourdes. *Traditional Portuguese Cooking*. Lisbon/Sao Paulo: Editorial Verbo, 1982.

The Multi-Cultural Cuisine of Trinidad & Tobago & the Caribbean: Naparima Girls' High School Cookbook. Trinidad, West Indies: Naparima Girls' High School, 1988.

Nenes, Michael F. *International Cuisine*. Hoboken, NJ: John Wiley & Sons, 2009.

Olney, Richard. *Provence the Beautiful Cookbook: Original Recipes from the Regions of Provence*. San Francisco: HarperCollins, 1999.

Ortega, Simone and Ines Ortega. *1080 Recipes*. New York: Phaidon, 2007.

——. *The Book of Tapas*. London: Phaidon, 2010.

Ortins, Ana Patuleia. *Portuguese Homestyle Cooking*. Northampton, MA: Interlink Books, 2008.

Ortiz, Elisabeth Lambert. *Caribbean Cooking*. Middlesex, England: Penguin, 1973.

——. *The Book of Latin and American Cooking*. London, UK: HarperCollins, 1994.

Pasparakis, Aristedes and Byron Ayanoglu. *New Greek Cuisine*. Toronto: HarperCollins, 2005.

Pellaprat, Henri-Paul. *Modern French Culinary Art*. London: Virtue & Company Limited, 1984.

Peterson, James. *Sauces: Classical and Contemporary Sauce Making*. Hoboken, NJ: John Wiley and Sons, 2008.

Recipe Club of Saint Paul's Greek Orthodox Cathedral. *The Complete Book of Greek Cooking*. New York: Harper & Row, 1996.

Rozieres, Babette de. *Creole*. New York: Phaidon, 2007.

Sevilla, Maria Jose. *Life and Food in the Basque Country*. London: Weidenfeld and Nicolson, 1989.

Sheasby, Anne. *The Ultimate Soup Bible*. New York: Barnes & Noble, 2006.

Shulman, Martha Rose. *Spain and the World Table*. New York: DK Publishing, 2008.

Silva, Chefe. *Bacalhau a Portuguesa: Codfish the Portuguese Way*. Lisboa: Texto Editores, 2004.

Spence, Wenton O., ed. *Jamaican Cookery: Recipes from Old Jamaican Grandmothers*. Kingston, Jamaica: Heritage Publishers, 1981.

St. Mary's Beaver, Cub & Scout Ladies Auxiliary (St. John's). *Our Favourite Recipes*. Lenexa, KS: Cookbook Publishers, 1978.

Tonks, Mitchell. *The Fishmonger's Cookbook*. London, England: Penguin, 2005.

The Treasury of Newfoundland Dishes. St. John's, NL: Maple Leaf Mills Limited, 1976.

Vera, Felisa et al. *The Best of Canary Islands Cookery*. Gran Canaria: Centre of Canarian Popular Culture, 1992.

Viestad, Andreas. *Kitchen of Light: New Scandinavian Cooking*. New York: Artisan, 2003.

Young, Ron, ed. *Downhome Household Almanac & Cookbook*. St. John's, NL: Downhome Publishing, 1996.

Zane, Eva. *Greek Cooking for the Gods*. San Francisco, CA: 101 Productions, 1978.

Zaldumbide, J.M. *El Bacalao: Recetario de la PYSBE*. Donostia, Spain: Ttarttalo, 1992.

Photo Credits

Part 2: Recipes

Thank you to those who helped prepare, sample, style and shoot the recipes in Salt Cod Cuisine. The food photographers, and the pages on which their photographs appear, are listed below.

Valerie Sooley: 88, 92, 93, 94, 99, 100, 112, 118, 122, 128, 129, 130, 131, 132, 135, 140, 141, 145, 146, 156, 159, 162, 168, 171, 174, 179, 189, 191, 194, 198, 200, 202, 206, 210, 216, 219, 222, 231, 252, 254, 256, 258, 260, 269, 272, 273, 276, 279, 281, 282, 285, 292, and 294.

Jason Kearley: 90, 93, 103, 104, 109, 113, 114, 117, 121, 138, 149, 160, 164, 165, 176, 180, 185, 188, 204, 220, 239, 243, 247, 265, 270, 284, 288, 297, 299, 300, 301, 303, and 304.

Phillip Cairns: 106, 144, 226, and 234.

Florence Donaway: 186.

Index of Recipes

ackee
    Saltfish and Ackee 276
Aioli 303
    Salt Cod Salad with Aioli 123
anchovies
    Fried Salt Cod on a Bed of Onions 224
    Salt Cod and Leeks 207
    Salt Cod au Gratin with Anchovy Sauce 237
    Salt Cod with Olive Salad 116
    Salt Cod with Olives and Capers 220
    Salt Cod with White Wine and Olives 209
    Salt Cod with Spinach 228
annatto seeds
    Saltfish Stew 189
artichoke hearts
    Salt Cod Stew 179
avocados
    Avocado with Tarama 138
    Codfish Breakfast 199
    Hot Avocado with Salt Cod 142
    Salt Cod and Avocado 130
    Salt Cod Salad with Olives and Avocado 121

Bacalao Stew 192
Baccala Soup 166
bacon
    Salt Cod over Embers 95
    Salt Cod Pie 251
Baked Breadfruit and Saltfish Stew 186
Baked Cod Cakes 158
Baked Salt Cod Cakes 248
Baked Whole Salt Cod 246
bananas
    Codfish Breakfast 199
    Green Fig and Saltfish Pie 250
    Salt Cod with Bananas 144
Bathed Bread 171

Batter-Fried Salt Cod with Skordalia 230
beans, green
    Shredded Salt Cod Salad 111
    Salt Cod Vens and Bellies 293
beans, lima
    Salt Cod Sounds 287
    Salt Cod Stew 179
beans, white northern
    Salt Cod Salad with Beans 124
Beaten Dried Cod 143
Béchamel Sauce 297
    Red Peppers Stuffed with Salt Cod 131
    Salt Cod in Casserole with Béchamel 239
    Salt Cod Soufflé 236
    Spiritual Cod 244
    Tomatoes Stuffed with Salt Cod 132
beer
    Norwegian Salt Cod over Stew of Grapes 187
    Salt Cod and Onion in Beer Sauce 245
bellies
    Salt Cod Vens and Bellies 293
Black Butter 136
Blended Salt Cod 133
Boiled Salt Cod 194, 196
Bouillabaisse 170
Braised Cod and Potatoes in Tomato Sauce 223
Brandade, Salt Cod 140
Brazilian Cod Cakes 147
Brazilian Fish Stew 183
Bread Soup with Cod 166
Bread Soup with Salt Cod 165
breadfruit
    Baked Breadfruit and Saltfish Stew 186
broccoli
    Salt Cod Salad with Aioli 123
burgers
    Salt Cod Burgers 101

cabbage
    Bread Soup with Cod 166
    Christmas Eve Cod 202
    Cod with Bread Slices in Lafoes Style 246
    Green Broth with Salt Cod 164
    Salt Cod and Cabbage 213
    Salt Cod in Viana Style 256
    Salt Cod over Embers 95
Cabbie-Claw 197
cakes
    Baked Cod Cakes 158
    Baked Salt Cod Cakes 248
    Brazilian Cod Cakes 147
    Cod Cakes 151
    Curried West Indies Saltfish Cakes 155
    Hairy Tatties 147
    Salt Cod Cakes/Croquettes/Fritters 152
    Salt Cod Fish Cakes 146
    Salt Codfish Cakes 153
    Saltfish and Yam Cakes 153
    Stamp and Go 151
capers
    Fried Salt Cod on a Bed of Onions 224
    Salt Cod with Olives and Capers 220
    Sicilian Salt Cod Stew 177
carpaccio
    Salt Cod Carpaccio with Lemon Juice and Olive Oil 111
    Salt Cod Carpaccio with Oven-Roasted Tomatoes and Herbs 108
casseroles
    Casserole of Salt Cod Graciosa 249
    Salt Cod in Casserole with Béchamel 239
Catalan Salt Cod and Sweet Pepper Salad 110
cauliflower
    Salt Cod and Cauliflower Salad 114
    Sweet and Sour Cod Stew 178

cheeks
- Baked Salt Cod Tongues and Cheeks 284
- Fried Salt Cod Cheeks 282

cherries
- Salt Cod with Sour Cherries 135

chickpeas
- Salt Cod, Leek, and Chickpea Soup 163
- Salt Cod Vens and Bellies 293
- Spinach and Chickpeas with Salt Cod Dumplings 190

chowder
- Kale and Salt Cod Chowder 174
- Salt Cod Chowder 172
- Salt Cod Heads Chowder 280
- Traditional Salt Cod Chowder 173

Christmas Eve Cod 202

coconut, coconut milk
- Brazilian Fish Stew 183
- Salt Cod Bahia Style 184
- Salt Cod Sauce and Ducana 212
- Salt Cod Tartlets with Coconut 253
- Salt Cod with Coconut Milk 184
- Salt Cod with Turnip and Mace Purée 218

Cod à Ze do Pipo 243
Cod Cakes 151
Cod Fritters 154
Cod in Wine 134
Cod with Bread Slices in Lafoes Style 246
Codfish Breakfast 199

coriander
- Brazilian Cod Cakes 147
- Brazilian Fish Stew 183
- Bread Soup with Salt Cod 165
- Grilled Salt Cod in Coriander Dressing 98
- Salt Cod Acra 150

croquettes
- Salt Cod Cakes/Croquettes/Fritters 152
- Salt Cod Croquettes 157

cucumber
- Baked Breadfruit and Saltfish Stew 186
- Salt Cod on Onions and Cucumber Slices 113

Salt Cod Parfait 145
Curried Salt Cod and Dumplings 211
Curried West Indies Saltfish Cakes 155

curry powder
- Curried Salt Cod and Dumplings 211
- Curried West Indies Saltfish Cakes 155
- Curry Garlic Mayonnaise 302
- Salt Cod Chowder 172
- Stewed Saltfish 185

Deep-Fried Salt Cod 232
Drawn Butter 300
Dried Salt Cod 200, 201

dumplings
- Curried Salt Cod Dumplings 211
- Salt Cod Dumplings 160
- Salt Cod Sauce and Ducana 212
- Spinach and Chickpeas with Salt Cod Dumplings 190

Egg Sauce 199, 301

eggs
- Salt Cod Scrambled with Eggs and Potatoes 275
- Salt Cod with Eggs 242
- Kippered Salt Cod Benedict 226
- Salt Cod Brandade (Eggs Benedict) 141

fennel
- Bathed Bread 171
- Salt Cod Salad with Aioli 122

figs
- Sweet and Sour Cod Stew 178

Fish and Brewis 272
Fish Mustard 200
Fish Stock 296
Fishermen's Roasted Cod 94
Fried Salt Cod 128, 134, 229
Fried Salt Cod on a Bed of Onions 224

fritters
- Cod Fritters 154

Salt Cod Acra 150
Salt Cod Cakes/Croquettes/Fritters 152
Salt Cod Fritters 148
Salt Cod Fritters with Spinach 129
Stamp and Go 151

Garlic, Onions, and Olive Oil 300
Garlic-Walnut Sauce 182

grapes
- Norwegian Salt Cod over Stew of Grapes 187

grappa
- Fried Salt Cod 229

gratin
- Salt Cod au Gratin 238
- Salt Cod au Gratin with Anchovy Sauce 237
- Salt Cod Gratin 238

Green Broth with Salt Cod 164
Green Fig and Saltfish Pie 250
Green Parsley Oil 301
Grilled Salt Cod 98
Grilled Salt Cod in Coriander Dressing 98
Grilled Salt Cod with Milk and Olive Oil 97
Grilled Salt Cod with Olive Oil and White Wine Vinegar 97
Grilled Salt Cod with Punched Potatoes 99

Hairy Tatties 147

hard bread
- Fish and Brewis 272
- Homemade Hard Bread 274

hash
- Salt Cod Hash 269, 270
- Salt Cod with Red Capsicum 271
- Seamen's Salt Cod Hash 268

heads
- Boiled Salt Cod Heads 280
- Fried Salt Cod Heads 279
- Salt Cod Heads Chowder 280

Herdsmen's Dried Cod Soup 167
Hollandaise Sauce 227
Homemade Hard Bread 274

Hot Avocado with Salt Cod 142

Individual Salt Cod Loaves 264

kale
    Green Broth with Salt Cod 164
    Kale and Salt Cod Chowder 174
Kippered Salt Cod Benedict 226

leeks
    Salt Cod, Leek, and Chickpea Soup 163
    Salt Cod and Leeks 207
    Salt Cod Stew 182
    Salt Cod with Leeks in Lemon Sauce 180
    Salt Cod with Spinach and Leeks 181
Lemon Poppy Seed Scones 227
Lemon Sauce
    Salt Cod with Leeks in Lemon Sauce 180
liver
    Cod-Liver Bannock 289
loaves
    Individual Salt Cod Loaves 264
    Salt Cod Loaf 264
Lyonnaise Salt Cod 204

mace
    Salt Cod with Turnip and Mace Purée 218
Martinmas Cod 92
Mayonnaise 302
    Curry Garlic Mayonnaise 302
    Mustard-Flavoured Mayonnaise 302
    Partridgeberry Mayonnaise 302
    Salad of Salt Cod with Oranges 117
    Salt Cod Salad with Aioli 122
mint
    Kale and Salt Cod Chowder 174
    Salsa Verde 303
    Salt Cod Stew 179
    Salt Cod with Peppers, Black Olives, Mint, and Parsley 126

Mojo Colorado 298
Mojo Verde 298
Molho Branco 298
    Salt Cod with Cream 241
Mustard Sauce 300
    Dried Salt Cod 201

Norwegian Salt Cod over Stew of Grapes 187

okra
    Salt Cod, Okra, and Yam Soup 169
olives
    Orange, Red Onion, Black Olive, and Salt Cod Salad 119
    Salt Cod and Cauliflower Salad 114
    Salt Cod and Vegetable Pudding 263
    Salt Cod Provençale 208
    Salt Cod Salad with Beans 124
    Salt Cod Salad with Olives and Avocado 121
    Salt Cod Scrambled with Eggs and Potatoes 275
    Salt Cod Stew 178, 179, 182
    Salt Cod with Olive Salad 116
    Salt Cod with Olives and Capers 220
    Salt Cod with Peppers, Black Olives, Mint, and Parsley 126
    Salt Cod with White Wine and Olives 209
    Shredded Salt Cod with Tomatoes and Olives 109
    Sicilian Salt Cod Stew 177
    Warm Salt Cod Salad with Oranges 115
omelette
    Salt Cod Vens Omelette 291
onions
    Salt Cod and Onion in Beer Sauce 245
    Fried Salt Cod on a Bed of Onions 224
    Salt Cod, Onions, and Potatoes 240
oranges
    Orange, Red Onion, Black Olive, and Salt Cod Salad 119

    Salad of Salt Cod with Oranges 117
    Warm Salt Cod Salad with Oranges 115
Oven-Roasted Salt Cod 257

Pan-Cooked Salt Cod 176
Pan-Simmered Salt Cod with Fried Polenta 215
Parfait, Salt Cod 145
Partridgeberry Mayonnaise 302
patties
    Salt Cod Burgers 101
    Salt Cod Patties with Garlic Sauce 157
pears
    Sicilian Salt Cod Stew 177
peppers, bell
    Brazilian Fish Stew 183
    Catalan Salt Cod and Sweet Pepper Salad 110
    Red Peppers Stuffed with Salt Cod 131
    Salt Cod Bahia Style 184
    Salt Cod Bordelaise 210
    Salt Cod Club Ranero 217
    Salt Cod with Peppers, Black Olives, Mint, and Parsley 126
    Salt Cod with Red Capsicum 271
    Salt Cod with Red Pepper Sauce 216
    Salt Cod, Red Pepper, and Potato Salad 120
    Saltfish Salad 106
    Saltfish Stew 188
Persillade 207
pies
    Green Fig and Saltfish Pie 250
    Salt Cod Pie 251, 255
    Salt Cod Sounds Pie 286
pine nuts
    Fried Salt Cod on a Bed of Onions 224
    Salt Cod in Tomato Sauce, Roman Style 134
    Sicilian Salt Cod Stew 177
    Sweet and Sour Cod Stew 178
Plank-Grilled Salt Cod on the Barbecue 104
Planked Salt Cod with an Open Fire 102
plantains

Baked Breadfruit and Saltfish Stew 186
Salt Cod Fillets in Plantain Crust with Green Sauce 225
polenta
    Pan-Simmered Salt Cod with Fried Polenta 215
    Whipped Creamy Salt Cod with Soft Polenta 214
prunes
    Sweet and Sour Cod Stew 178
puddings
    Salt Cod Pudding 262
    Salt Cod Puddings 261
    Salt Cod and Vegetable Puddings 263
puffs
    Salt Cod Puffs 156
Punched Potatoes
    Grilled Salt Cod with Punched Potatoes 99

raisins
    Fried Salt Cod on a Bed of Onions 224
    Salt Cod Plaki with Raisins 247
    Salt Cod in Tomato Sauce, Roman Style 134
    Salt Cod Sounds Pie 286
    Sicilian Salt Cod Stew 177
    Sweet and Sour Cod Stew 178
Raw Cod with Onions and Sauce 107
Red Peppers Stuffed with Salt Cod 131
Roasted Scrod on a Wood Fire 93
Roasted/Baked Salt Cod and Potatoes 258
roe
    A Pocketful of Roe 289
    Avocado with Tarama 138
    Boiled Cod Roe 290
    Fried Salt Cod Roe 289
    preserving 288
    Salt Cod Roe Pâté 137
Rounders 195

Salad of Salt Cod with Oranges 117
Salsa Romesco 304
Salsa Verde 303
Salt Cod Plaki with Raisins 247
Salt Cod Acra 150
Salt Cod and Avocado 130
Salt Cod and Cabbage 213
Salt Cod and Cauliflower Salad 114
Salt Cod and Leeks 207
Salt Cod and Onion in Beer Sauce 245
Salt Cod and Potato with Garlic and Herbs 203
Salt Cod and Squid Stew 192
Salt Cod and Tomato Soup 172
Salt Cod and Vegetable Pudding 263
Salt Cod au Gratin with Anchovy Sauce 237
Salt Cod Bahia Style 184
Salt Cod Balls 158
Salt Cod Bordelaise 210
Salt Cod Brandade 140
Salt Cod Burgers 101
Salt Cod Cakes/Croquettes/Fritters 152
Salt Cod Carpaccio with Lemon Juice and Olive Oil 111
Salt Cod Carpaccio with Oven-Roasted Tomatoes and Herbs 108
Salt Cod Chowder 172
Salt Cod Club Ranero 217
Salt Cod Croquettes 157
Salt Cod Dish 196
Salt Cod Dumplings 160
Salt Cod Fillets in Plantain Crust with Green Sauce 225
Salt Cod Fish Cakes 146
Salt Cod Fisherman's Style 223
Salt Cod Fritters 148
Salt Cod Fritters with Spinach 129
Salt Cod Gratin 238
Salt Cod Grilled over Coals 96
Salt Cod Hash 269, 270
Salt Cod in Casserole with Béchamel 239
Salt Cod in Potato Jackets 159
Salt Cod in Tomato Sauce, Roman Style 134
Salt Cod in Viana Style 256

Salt Cod in Vinaigrette 136
Salt Cod Loaf 264
Salt Cod on Onions and Cucumber Slices 113
Salt Cod on Toasted Homemade Bread 269
Salt Cod over Embers 95
Salt Cod Parfait 145
Salt Cod Patties with Garlic Sauce 157
Salt Cod Pie 251, 255
Salt Cod Provençale 208
Salt Cod Puddings 261-263
Salt Cod Puffs 156
Salt Cod Roe Pâté 137
Salt Cod Salad 112
Salt Cod Salad with Aioli 123
Salt Cod Salad with Beans 124
Salt Cod Salad with Olives and Avocado 121
Salt Cod Salad with Small New Potatoes 115
Salt Cod Sauce and Ducana 212
Salt Cod Scrambled with Eggs and Potatoes 275
Salt Cod Slivers 128
Salt Cod Soufflé 235, 236
Salt Cod Stew 178, 179, 182
Salt Cod Tartlet 254
Salt Cod Tartlets with Coconut 253
Salt Cod with Bananas 144
Salt Cod with Black Butter 136
Salt Cod with Coconut Milk 184
Salt Cod with Cream 241
Salt Cod with Eggs 242
Salt Cod with Garlic 127
Salt Cod with Leeks in Lemon Sauce 180
Salt Cod with Olive Salad 116
Salt Cod with Olives and Capers 220
Salt Cod with Onions 127
Salt Cod with Peppers, Black Olives, Mint, and Parsley 126
Salt Cod with Pil Pil Sauce 222
Salt Cod with Red Capsicum 271
Salt Cod with Red Pepper Sauce 216
Salt Cod with Sour Cherries 135
Salt Cod with Spinach 228

Salt Cod with Spinach and Leeks 181
Salt Cod with Turnip and Mace Purée 218
Salt Cod with White Wine and Olives 209
Salt Cod, Leek, and Chickpea Soup 163
Salt Cod, Okra, and Yam Soup 169
Salt Cod, Onions, and Potatoes 240
Salt Cod, Red Pepper, and Potato Salad 120
Salt Codfish Cakes 153
Salt Codfish Pie 251
Salt Cod Baked in the Oven 257
Saltfish and Ackee 276
Saltfish and Yam Cakes 153
Saltfish Balls 155
Saltfish Salad 106
Saltfish Stew 188, 189
sausage
    Kale and Salt Cod Chowder 174
Scones, Lemon Poppy Seed 227
scrod
    Roasted Scrod on a Wood Fire 93
Scrunchions 300
Shredded Raw Cod 107
Shredded Salt Cod Salad 111
Shredded Salt Cod with Tomatoes and Olives 109
Sicilian Salt Cod Stew 177
Skordalia 299
    Batter-Fried Salt Cod with Skordalia 230
    Salt Cod Patties with Garlic Sauce 157
smoked cod
    Kippered Salt Cod Benedict 226
    Salt Cod Fillets in Plantain Crust with Green Sauce 225
    Salt Cod, Leek, and Chickpea Soup 163
snow peas
    Salt Cod Salad with Aioli 123
soufflés
    Salt Cod Soufflé 235, 236
        tips for 234
sounds

Fried Salt Cod Sounds 285
Salt Cod Sounds 287
Salt Cod Sounds Pie 286
Salt Cod Sounds Stew 285
spinach
    Salt Cod Fritters with Spinach 129
    Salt Cod in Potato Jackets 159
    Salt Cod with Spinach 228
    Salt Cod with Spinach and Leeks 181
    Spinach and Chickpeas with Salt Cod Dumplings 190
Spiritual Cod 244
squid
    Salt Cod and Squid Stew 192
Stamp and Go 151
Stewed Saltfish 185
stock
    Fish Stock 296
Sweet and Sour Cod Stew 178

tartlets
    Salt Cod Tartlet 254
    Salt Cod Tartlets with Coconut 253
Tartar Sauce 302
Tomato Sauce
    Codfish Breakfast 199
    Salt Cod in Tomato Sauce, Roman Style 134
    Beer and Tomato Sauce 245
tomatoes
    Braised Cod and Potatoes in Tomato Sauce 223
    Salt Cod and Tomato Soup 172
    Salt Cod Carpaccio with Oven-Roasted Tomatoes and Herbs 108
    Salt Cod in Tomato Sauce, Roman Style 134
    Shredded Salt Cod with Tomatoes and Olives 109
    Tomatoes Stuffed with Salt Cod 132
Tomatoes Stuffed with Salt Cod 132
tongues

Baked Salt Cod Tongues and Cheeks 284
Cod Tongues 282
Fried Salt Cod Tongues 281
Salt Cod Tongue Stew 283
Traditional Salt Cod Chowder 173
turnip
    Salt Cod and Squid Stew 192
    Salt Cod with Red Capsicum 271
    Salt Cod with Turnip and Mace Purée 218

vens
    Salt Cod Vens and Bellies 293
    Salt Cod Vens Omelette 291
vinaigrette
    Salt Cod in Vinaigrette 136
walnuts
    Sweet and Sour Cod Stew 178
    Garlic-Walnut Sauce 182
Warm Salt Cod Salad with Oranges 115
Whipped Creamy Salt Cod with Soft Polenta 214
whole salt cod
    Baked Whole Salt Cod 246
wine
    Salt Cod with White Wine and Olives 209
    Cod in Wine 134

yam
    Salt Cod, Okra, and Yam Soup 169
    Saltfish and Yam Cakes 153
yogurt
    Salt Cod and Potato with Garlic and Herbs 203
yucca
    Saltfish Stew 189

zucchini
    Salt Cod Club Ranero 217
    Salt Cod Stew 182

About the Author

Edward Jones's love for Newfoundland and Labrador's culture and history, and his commitment to its preservation, stems from his parents, Frank and Della Jones. Jones was raised in Foxtrap, their ancestral home, where a strong spirit of community and identity deeply influenced him.

Jones graduated from Memorial University in 1959, taught high school in Norman's Cove and Corner Brook, and earned a PhD from the University of Alberta in 1969. He worked in curriculum development with the Newfoundland and Labrador Department of Education for 27 years, creating high school courses in English, including Canadian literature, heritage, theatre arts, and folklore. He helped edit *Land, Sea & Time* (volumes 1-3), an integrated language arts series about the literary and cultural heritage of Newfoundland and Labrador, released in 2000-2002.

A life-long interest in cooking and experimenting with salt cod was sparked the first time Jones watched his father roast salt cod in the kitchen stove. During 50 years of summer and holiday travel, Jones enjoyed the food in every country he visited, collecting recipes, and ordering a different meal of salt cod at every opportunity. Salt cod dishes from around the world are his favourite choice to serve to family and friends.

Jones knows the central role salt cod holds in the identity of Newfoundland and Labrador and is dedicated to keeping that cultural tradition alive.

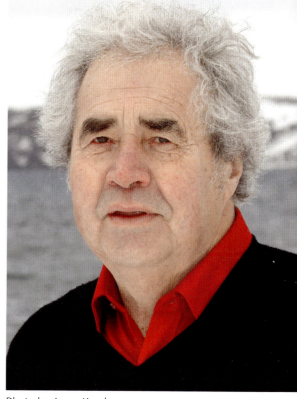

Photo by Jason Kearley